THE
HUDSON
RIVER VALLEY
COOKBOOK

RENSSELAER

Albany•

ALBANY

COLUMBIA

MASSACHUSETTS

CATSKILL
MOUNTAINS

■ OLANA

Woodstock•

Red Hook•

Kingston•

Pine Plains•

DUTCHESS

Stone Ridge•

Hyde Park•

Millbrook•

VANDERBILT MANSION

■ FDR MANSION
■ CULINARY INSTITUTE
OF AMERICA

Ferndale•

ULSTER

•Poughkeepsie

HUDSON RIVER

PENNSYLVANIA

Newburgh•

PUTNAM

CONNECTICUT

•Port Jervis

North Salem•

ORANGE

NEW JERSEY

WESTCHESTER

LONG ISLAND

New
York
City

THE
HUDSON
RIVER VALLEY
COOKBOOK

A Leading American Chef Savors the Region's Bounty

WALDY MALOUF
WITH MOLLY FINN

The Harvard Common Press
Boston, Massachusetts

THE HARVARD COMMON PRESS
535 Albany Street
Boston, Massachusetts 02118

Printed in the United States of America
Printed on acid-free paper

Library of Congress Cataloging-in-Publication Data
Malouf, Waldy.
    The Hudson River Valley cookbook : a leading American chef savors
the region's bounty / Waldy Malouf with Molly Finn.
       p.   cm.
    Includes index.
    ISBN 1-55832-143-8 (pbk. : alk. paper)
    1. Cookery, American.   2. Cookery—Hudson River Valley (N.Y. and
N.J.)   I. Finn, Molly.   II. Title.
TX715.M213   1998
641.5973—dc21   98-29724
                                               CIP

Special bulk-order discounts are available on this and other Harvard Common Press books. Companies and organizations may purchase books for premiums or for resale, or may arrange a custom edition, by contacting the Marketing Director at the address above.

Cover design by Suzanne Noli
Text design by Karen Battles
Set in 11-point Centaur by Pagesetters Inc.

10 9 8 7 6 5 4 3 2 1

*This book is dedicated to Meg, Max, and Merrill,
my wife and children whom, although they may not
believe it, I love more than cooking*

ACKNOWLEDGMENTS

I would like to extend special thanks to:

Elizabeth Carduff for asking me to do this book and to Peggy Tagliarino and Karen Schloss for pushing me to do it.

Angela Miller for introducing me to Molly Finn, without whom there would not be a book.

The owners of the Hudson River Club, especially Peter Higgins, for their support and to Christopher Carey for his encouragement.

My sous chefs Jim Porteus, Michael Smith, Mark Lemoult, Charles Steppe, and John Heuschkel for putting up with so many of my afternoon absences while maintaining the restaurant's high standards.

Pastry chef Martin Howard for generously giving me several recipes.

Calito (Carlos Beach) for his unique food delivery system and his smile.

Carol Gelber for helpful recipe testing.

Elizabeth McMillon for restoring Molly's kitchen after marathon testing sessions.

Dana Madigan and Nick Mautone for sharing their wine expertise.

Alice Thomas and Dalila Mercado for valiantly attempting to keep me on schedule, for covering for me when they couldn't, and for providing their computer skills when mine proved inadequate.

Julia Jordan for keeping me focused.

Elaine and Ed Morrison for providing temporary housing close to the cornfields.

The farmers, growers, winemakers, and cheese makers of the Hudson River Valley whose perseverance and fine products have helped inspire me.

The administrators of New York City's Greenmarkets, the staff of the New York State Department of Agriculture, the Hudson River Foundation, and other organizations that support the Hudson River Valley.

The many Malouf and Finn family members and friends who happily (usually) consumed all our successes and failures.

Waldy Malouf

CONTENTS

RECIPE LIST

SHAD, TROUT, & OTHER FISH

VENISON, PHEASANT, & OTHER GAME

APPLES, BERRIES, & OTHER DESSERTS

VINAIGRETTES, FLAVORED OILS, & OTHER KITCHEN STAPLES

INTRODUCTION

This book is a hymn of praise to the Hudson River Valley, a place we love, a fertile land rich in natural beauty, in tradition, and in its people. We both live in the Hudson Valley, one on the east bank and one on the west. The spirit of the landscape has worked its charm on us and we never fail to take delight in the rolling farmland, the majestic river, or the turn in the road that suddenly reveals layer upon layer of distant mountains, green fading into blue fading into a misty lavender.

In the spring you will find the whole region studded with flowering orchards of apple and pear. In May, search out the first ramps and glory in the abundance of just-picked asparagus and rhubarb. Look for trout fishermen casting their lines in the Esopus Creek; find a shad festival on the banks of the Hudson. Forage for morels at the edge of oak woods when the dogwood blooms. As summer approaches, you will see tender and crisp greens and lettuces on farmstands along with herb plants and baskets of fragrant strawberries. Soon, fields planted with beans, cucumbers, and tomatoes and acres of sweet corn will come into fruit and fill roadside markets with their richness. Magnificent in autumn, the Valley bursts with color and fruitfulness. The fruit trees that flowered in spring are now heavy with apples and pears. In markets, squash, pumpkins, grapes, potatoes, and honey mirror the brilliance of the trees and the mellowness of the autumn sun. And don't neglect the Valley in the winter, with its views of snowy hills through clear cold air and its thick blanket of snow protecting the land while it restores itself, while the farmers restore their tools, while the wine ages before the spring bottling.

Many elements contribute to the character of this extraordinary stretch of earth and water. A magnificent river runs through the Valley, bordered by mountains and gorges, forests and gentle farmland. If you follow the river from its source in a tiny lake in the Adirondacks to the glorious New York harbor you will understand why throughout the mid-nineteenth century America's first school of landscape painters, the Hudson River School, chose to celebrate the valley's dramatic scenery and to capture on canvas its special quality of light. Through all the changes the Hudson Valley has undergone during the more than 350 years since Henry Hudson first explored the river, the region has retained its extraordinary natural beauty. To best appreciate the character of the land, drive through the rolling hills of the Valley on small country roads, passing horse farms, historic mansions of the Roosevelt and Vanderbilt families, the Washington Irving Sleepy Hollow Restoration, and the Culinary Institute of America. These are all on the east bank of the river within 100 miles of New York City, along with farmstands selling fine local produce, apples, and cheese. A variety of game is raised on the east bank, and some of the Valley's newest vineyards welcome visitors.

The Catskill Mountains dominate the west bank of the Hudson; they offer some of the finest hiking, camping, skiing, and trout fishing in the Eastern United States. Many beautiful Dutch stone houses, unique to the region, can be seen in the colonial towns of Kingston, Hurley, and New Paltz. One particular farm on this side of the river supplies nearly all the foie gras grown in the United States, and Ulster County is one of the leading producers of sweet corn in the nation. Other special products are game, free-range chickens, ducks, bread, beer, and black dirt onions. Most of the Valley's older vineyards are on the west bank of the river.

There has been a great awakening of interest in wine and food in America during the last twenty-five years. Knowledgeable people, including a number of chefs working in the region, have recognized that the Hudson Valley is capable of producing food and wine of incomparable variety and quality. These same people have convinced local farmers to expand their range of production in response to the new demands of a public with educated palates, adding new varieties of vegetables, even unfamiliar ones, and gradually creating a new two-way street of supply and demand. All this has led to a wealth of wonderful food. Specialty food stores with arrays of exotic cheeses, spices, sausages, fruits, and vegetables can be found not only in New York City but in villages throughout the Valley. Game, foie gras, cheeses, and wild mushrooms are available by mail order. Delicate baby salad greens, antique apple varieties, fresh herbs, and at least six kinds of potato can be found at ordinary country farmstands, and while they have not yet edged out the Red Delicious and the iceberg, they are making inroads. For an extensive listing of the region's markets and wineries and how to order foods by mail, see the newly updated Sources, pages 301 to 305.

This new paperback edition of *The Hudson River Valley Cookbook* arrives in the midst of surging interest in regional cooking nationwide. Mainstream restaurants and consumers alike now pay much more attention to the quality and origin of the food products they purchase. A greater variety of locally produced fruits and vegetables, as well as game and cheese, is now offered at an increasing number of markets and farms. More and more people are enthusiastically embracing the approach to cooking that Waldy has helped to pioneer: using regional, seasonal food products, harvested and crafted by local farmers, to create intensely flavored, intensely pleasurable dishes. Waldy now puts this philosophy into practice at New York's Rainbow Room.

It is no surprise that a chef who has all these wonderful foods at his doorstep should be both inspired and challenged to develop a fitting showcase for them. The Hudson Valley cuisine presented in this book has been twenty-five years in the making, twenty-five years of selecting, combining, and refining, of searching for the best ingredients and developing recipes that bring out their unique quality. Part of the challenge has been to seek out the best the region has to offer: foie gras, shad and trout, venison and game birds, wild mushrooms, corn, potatoes, apples, and berries are the most abundant of the characteristic foods of the region. When available products haven't met the ever-rising standards of a discriminating and demanding public, local farmers have been encouraged to venture beyond standard varieties and produce greater quantities of an extended range of higher quality fruits and vegetables.

Another challenge has been to retain the essential character of the region's slow-simmered, richly aromatic traditional soups, stews, and braised dishes while incorporating elements of the contemporary taste for lighter fare and exotic seasonings. With the Valley's population becoming ever more diverse, many ingredients from other cooking cultures, such as cilantro, hot peppers, and Japanese greens, are now native products. A glance at the Recipe List immediately preceding this introduction will show that the recipes in this book make use of all the Hudson Valley foods we've mentioned.

The worldwide tradition of bringing the unique gifts of the countryside to the city for all to enjoy has come to the Hudson Valley and to other regions of the country in a major way. City folk have learned to expect and appreciate the finest. In New York City, for one, these markets are recognized as one of the best things to happen to both local farmers and consumers. Farmers come from all over the area to over twenty sites in New York City, bringing fish, bread, plants and flowers, herbs, honey, game, meats, poultry, cheese, wine, and more than four hundred varieties of fruits and vegetables that they have raised or made. They bring not only their products but themselves. They bring the country into the city, and friendly conversation is as great a resource of the greenmarket as the beautiful produce and the experience of the glorious energy in the earth that gives rise to it. It is clear that the greenmarkets and farmstands, the wineries, the specialty stores, the chefs, and a demanding and sophisticated public have become new and powerful natural resources of the Hudson River Valley. We are proud to be part of this company. We hope that you will use this book, explore the Valley, and become part of this company too.

Waldy Malouf and Molly Finn

FOIE GRAS,
SOUPS,
&
OTHER
FIRST COURSES

With the exception of oysters, all the appetizers in this chapter feature Hudson Valley foods. Oysters are included here because they were once harvested by the ton from the Hudson River and were traditional Hudson Valley fare. Today, New Yorkers continue the tradition by eating oysters from other local waters while hoping that the native Hudson River oysters will soon be available again.

Foie gras, a recent regional treasure, is highlighted here in a collection of recipes that demonstrate many different ways of preparing this delicacy. In other first courses, earthy wild mushrooms, walnuts, onions, venison, corn, garlic, apples, crisp fresh greens, and unusual soups provide a good way for you to get acquainted with the distinctive flavors of the Hudson Valley.

Although listed as first courses, these appetizers and soups are all fairly hearty and can be paired with one of the salads to make a complete lunch or late dinner.

 FOIE GRAS

For sheer luxury and sensuality, foie gras is incomparable. It is the food of the gods. A meat almost without substance, tender and delicate, foie gras really does melt in your mouth, and it fills your mouth with flavor as it disappears.

When I was an apprentice, foie gras was a mysterious tinned substance known as "Pâté de Foie Gras" that was kept under lock and key and doled out by the chef in limited quantities. It was used almost exclusively as an ingredient in classic Escoffier cuisine and was served on holidays, particularly Christmas and New Year's. I was introduced to fresh foie gras (literally "fat liver") on

my first trip to France in 1975. I happened to work for a time in real foie gras country, in southwest France. I was surprised to learn that foie gras came from both ducks and geese; in fact, nowadays almost all of it comes from ducks, both in this country and in France. I was even more surprised to see that foie gras was cooked, served, and eaten in many ways. It was sliced and sautéed; it was roasted, or steamed; it was prepared in terrines with different flavorings. Since I didn't have any money, I didn't get to do much more than taste it, just enough to discover that I liked foie gras and thought it was pretty wonderful and deserved its reputation. It wasn't until my return to France five years later that I really fell in love with foie gras; I was very disappointed that it wasn't available to work with anywhere in the U.S. In 1982 the first foie gras was produced here, and I began right away to re-create some of the wonderful ways of eating it I had experienced in France. In the section that follows I pass some of my creations on to you.

And now to raise a delicate question: How is this exquisite substance produced? Do people want to know? Would you like me to demystify the process or do you not want to know anything about it? My own feeling, working backward from the experience of eating foie gras, is that the result justifies the rather benign process by which we acquire foie gras.

In the little village of Ferndale, New York, in the Hudson Valley, the only major commercial foie gras farm in the United States (Hudson Valley Foie Gras and Duck Products) processes 250,000 Moulard ducks every year, raising virtually all the foie gras produced in this country. The ducks, a cross between the Pekin and Muscovy breeds, are raised with a combination of scientific sophistication and loving care that accounts for the extremely high price of foie gras. There's no denying that the ducks are overfed, and there are those who say that this constitutes abuse. But on all of my visits to the farm I was impressed by the humane treatment of the ducks, including the very gentle hand-feeding technique used to fatten the liver. An excellent source for foie gras—perhaps your only source—is a mail-order and wholesale foie gras and game purveyor, D'Artagnan, based in New Jersey (see Sources, page 301).

Foie gras is sold in three grades, A, B, and C. I recommend that you use Grade A for all the recipes in this book. Each Grade A duck foie gras weighs between one and one-and-a-half pounds, is smooth and firm, is pale pinkish tan in color, and has very few veins.

FOIE GRAS TERRINES

When you make terrines, it's important to prepare the foie gras properly, deveining it carefully so you will be able to get solid slices with a good, even color. Chilled foie gras has the texture of chilled butter; it softens as it warms up.

Don't try to prepare the liver when it's cold; it will break up and then have a tendency to fall apart when you slice it.

Take the foie gras out of the refrigerator and unwrap it about two hours before cleaning it. **Deveining the liver** is a somewhat laborious process; work carefully, feeling your way gently with your fingers. Separate the liver into its two lobes. There is a network of veins running down the center of each lobe. Probing gently, locate the largest center vein. Try to loosen it and the veins connected with it. If you are lucky, you will be able to pull them all out together, or lift them out with the point of a knife. If you have to probe further, try to break up the liver as little as possible, and press it together after the veins are removed.

Foie gras melts as it cooks, producing an abundance of yellow fat. This fat is excellent for cooking. Pour it into a jar (scrape it off cold terrines and melt it) and save it to use in mashed potatoes, grain or bean dishes, or to sauté vegetables. The fat will keep for two weeks in the refrigerator.

Foie gras terrines can be flavored or garnished in many ways. Recipes for three different terrines follow.

FOIE GRAS TERRINE
WITH ICE WINE JELLY

Only a couple of vineyards in the Hudson Valley produce ice wine, a strong, rich wine comparable to the fine Sauternes that is the classic accompaniment to foie gras. Ice wine is made from Vidal Blanc or Vignoles grapes that have been left on the vine until January, when they are not only overripe but frozen. The frozen grapes are crushed and the very sweet juice is fermented to make the wine.

A mouthful of this exquisite terrine is a bite of rich meat and a sip of rich wine at the same time. Make this terrine at least four days before serving.

Serves 10 as an appetizer

Equipment: a 5-cup nonreactive loaf pan or ceramic terrine
　　　　　　　a larger pan to use as a water bath

1 duck foie gras
Coarse salt and freshly ground pepper

FOR THE JELLY

½ bottle (12.7 ounces) New York State dessert wine such as Hunt Country Vidal Blanc
　Ice Wine or Brotherhood Winery Late Harvest Eiswein
2 envelopes unflavored gelatin

GARNISH

Lamb's tongue lettuce leaves *(mâche)*
Thin slices of toast for serving

Preheat the oven to 200°F.

Carefully separate and devein the liver as directed on page 3 and salt and pepper it generously on both sides. Line the terrine with plastic wrap, letting at least 10 inches hang over the sides. Place half the liver, smooth side down, in the terrine, lay the other half on top of it, smooth side up, and press the liver firmly into the terrine. Wrap it well in the plastic wrap, being sure all the surfaces are covered.

Line a roasting pan with a double layer of paper towels and place the terrine in the pan. Add boiling water to come halfway up the sides of the terrine and put the roasting pan in the oven. Using an instant-read thermometer, check the temperature of the liver after 45 minutes, and continue to bake until the internal temperature reaches 115°F, 10 or 15 minutes more. Remove the terrine from the water bath, let it cool, and refrigerate it for at least 3 days.

After 3 days, make the jelly. Pour the wine into a small saucepan and sprinkle the gelatin over it. Let it stand for 10 minutes, then heat the wine, stirring until the gelatin is completely melted. Do not bring the wine to the boil.

Remove the foie gras from the terrine and scrape off any membranes and all the fat. Trim the liver so there is ¼ inch of space between it and the long sides of the terrine. Set the liver aside. Wash and dry the terrine, reline it with plastic, and pour in a ½-inch layer of wine jelly. Put the terrine in the refrigerator or freezer until the jelly has set, about ½ hour. Set the foie gras on top of the jelly and pour half the remaining jelly over it. Return it to the refrigerator to set, then pour the rest of the jelly over it. When the jelly is firm, rewrap the terrine in plastic wrap and refrigerate overnight or up to 1 week.

To serve, remove the foie gras from the terrine by pulling up on the plastic. Unwrap the foie gras. Using a thin slicing knife dipped in hot water and dried, slice the foie gras ½ inch thick. Place a slice on each plate, garnish with a small bunch of lamb's tongue lettuce, and serve with toast.

FOIE GRAS TERRINE
WITH PRESERVED SHALLOTS

In this terrine, the tartness of the shallots delightfully offsets the richness of the foie gras. The recipe demonstrates an elegant use for Shallots Preserved in Red Wine from the Kitchen Staples section of this book. Braised Wild Mushrooms, page 199 would also be a wonderful garnish for a foie gras terrine.

Serves 10 as an appetizer

Equipment: a 5-cup nonreactive loaf pan or ceramic terrine
  a larger pan to use as a water bath

1 duck foie gras
Coarse salt and freshly ground pepper
3 tablespoons Shallots Preserved in Red Wine, page 294
Thin slices of toast for serving

Carefully separate and devein the liver as directed on page 3 and salt and pepper it generously on both sides. Before reforming each lobe, spread 1 tablespoon of preserved shallots over the inner surface and close the meat around it. Line the terrine with plastic wrap, letting 10 inches hang over the sides. Spread the remaining shallots over the bottom of the terrine. Lay the large lobe of the liver on top of the shallots, smooth side down, then set the smaller lobe on top of it, smooth side up, and press the liver firmly into the terrine. Wrap it well in the plastic wrap, being sure all the surfaces are covered.

Preheat the oven to 200°F.

Prepare the roasting pan and bake the terrine according to the instructions on page 6. Remove the terrine from the water bath, let it cool, and refrigerate for at least 3 days before serving. The foie gras will keep up to 2 weeks.

Remove the foie gras from the terrine and scrape off any membranes and all the fat. Using a thin slicing knife dipped in hot water and dried, slice the foie gras ¼ inch thick. Place two slices on each plate and serve with toast.

FOIE GRAS TERRINE
WITH SUMMER VEGETABLE RELISH

Hudson Valley vegetables turned into a relish could make this terrine a luxurious element in a summer buffet.

SUMMER
MENU

~ᗣ

Foie Gras
Terrine with
Summer
Vegetable
Relish

Roasted Hot
or Cold
Whole Striped
Bass with
Fennel

Potato Salad
with Five
Peppers

White Peach
and
Raspberry
Cobbler

Serves 10 as an appetizer

Equipment: a 5-cup nonreactive loaf pan or ceramic terrine
            a larger pan to use as a water bath

1 duck foie gras
Coarse salt and freshly ground pepper
1½ cups Summer Vegetable Relish (recipe follows)

Carefully separate and devein the liver as directed on pages 3–4 and salt and pepper it generously on both sides. Line the terrine with plastic wrap, letting 10 inches hang over the sides. Spread ⅓ cup of the vegetable relish on the bottom of the terrine and set half the liver, smooth side down, on top of it. Spread another ⅓ cup of vegetables over the liver, place the remaining half, smooth side up, on top of it and press it firmly into the terrine. Wrap well in the plastic wrap, being sure all the surfaces are covered.

Preheat the oven to 200°F.

Prepare the roasting pan and bake the terrine according to the instructions on page 6. Remove the terrine from the water bath, let it cool, and refrigerate for 3 days.

Remove the foie gras from the terrine and scrape off any membranes and all fat. Using a thin slicing knife dipped in hot water and dried, slice the foie gras ¼ inch thick. Place two slices on each plate and serve with toast. Serve a spoonful of vegetable relish on the side.

SUMMER VEGETABLE RELISH

Every vegetable in this mixture could come right out of your Hudson Valley garden. Summer Vegetable Relish makes a wonderful accompaniment to grilled fish and is delicious on hamburgers.

Makes about 2½ cups

2 tablespoons extra virgin olive oil
1 small onion, diced very fine (about ⅛ inch)
2 cloves garlic, minced with 1 teaspoon coarse salt
1 small sweet red pepper, diced very fine (about ⅛ inch)
6 tablespoons vegetable oil
1 small eggplant, about ¼ pound, diced very fine (about ⅛ inch)
1 zucchini, about ½ pound, diced very fine (about ⅛ inch)
1 medium tomato, peeled, seeded, and diced
Coarse salt and freshly ground pepper
2 tablespoons finely chopped basil

In a saucepan, heat the olive oil, add the onion and garlic, and cook for 3 or 4 minutes, until softened and very lightly browned. Add the red pepper and cook 2 or 3 minutes until softened. Turn off the heat under the saucepan.

Set a strainer over a bowl and put it next to the stove. Heat the vegetable oil in a sauté pan until hot, add the eggplant, and fry over high heat, tossing frequently, for 4 or 5 minutes, until it is well browned. Pour the contents of the pan into the strainer. When the oil has drained into the bowl, return it to the sauté pan and reheat it. Add the eggplant to the onion and garlic in the saucepan. Fry the zucchini over high heat, tossing frequently, until the zucchini is just beginning to turn golden but is still bright green. Pour it into the strainer and drain well. Add the zucchini and the tomato to the saucepan with the eggplant and the onion and garlic, season with salt and pepper, and simmer, covered, over medium-low heat for 2 or 3 minutes. Add the basil and simmer, covered, for another minute.

Serve the relish warm or at room temperature. In addition to the foie gras terrine, use this relish as an hors d'oeuvre, in omelets, and to garnish cold fish or meat.

SALT-CURED FOIE GRAS

Put deliciously tender and meaty slices of this on thinly sliced, lightly toasted bread. Start preparing this four days before you intend to serve it.

Serves 15 as an appetizer
Equipment: a double layer of cheesecloth 4 feet long
a large cylindrical plastic juice pitcher

1 duck foie gras
3 pounds coarse kosher salt
Freshly ground pepper
Thin slices of toast

Carefully separate and devein the liver as directed on page 3. Put the 2 lobes of the liver back together, smooth sides out, season it with salt and freshly ground pepper, and, starting at one end, roll it tightly in cheesecloth, sprinkling the cheesecloth with salt as you go, and forming an even cylinder. Tie one end of the roll with string and twist the other end, compressing the liver into a thick sausage shape. Tie the second end.

You now want to bury the entire roll in salt. This can be done in any nonreactive container; most convenient is a large cylindrical plastic juice pitcher. Put a ½-inch layer of salt in the bottom, stand the roll in the center and pour in salt to surround the roll. Cover the top with salt, then with plastic wrap and a lid, and refrigerate for 3 days. Then take the liver out of the salt, unwrap it, and rewrap it in several layers of plastic wrap. Refrigerate overnight. The foie gras will keep up to one week in the refrigerator.

When you unwrap the foie gras to serve it, it will no longer look raw and it will feel like a solid piece of butter. Using a thin slicing knife dipped in hot water and dried, slice the foie gras ¼ inch thick, place the slices on plates or a platter, and serve with toast.

WARM FOIE GRAS DISHES

Serving foie gras warm is less traditional than using it in terrines, but you may like these sautéed, roasted, and steamed foie gras dishes even better than the cold ones. Although some specialty butchers carry sliced foie gras for sautéing, you will probably find it easier to order a whole foie gras (see Sources, page 301) and to plan the purchase to coincide with a festive occasion when you can serve it to an appreciative group. For a small group, sauté slices of foie gras; for a group of six to eight, roast or steam the foie gras whole and slice it at the table.

If you don't use the whole foie gras right away, you can freeze it for up to two weeks. To freeze, trim the foie gras and wrap it closely and thoroughly in several layers of plastic wrap, then in foil, then in a heavy plastic bag. Defrost it in the refrigerator overnight.

Warm foie gras should be served immediately after it is cooked; accompany it with a glass of fruity white wine such as Amberleaf Vineyards Riesling and give yourself plenty of time to savor it before serving the next course. Plan a main course that can be ready and waiting. Whole Shad Baked in Millbrook Chardonnay (page 61), Poached Trout Filled with Seafood Mousse (page 77), Rabbit Pot Pies (page 106), Chicken and Fresh Morels in Clinton Vineyards Sparkling Seyval Blanc (page 135), or Spiced Loin of Pork with Baked Acorn Squash (page 178) would all be good choices.

SAUTÉED FOIE GRAS
WITH CIDER AND APPLES

If you're not familiar with the flavor and the texture of the silky center of a caramelized slice of foie gras, you're in for a revelation. Familiar or not, you'll appreciate the contrasts between the rich meat, the apples, and the cider. This recipe calls for 4 slices of foie gras. See page 11 for information on ordering and freezing foie gras.

Serves 4 as an appetizer

FOR THE APPLES
2 large Winesap, Northern Spy, or other medium tart apples, unpeeled, sliced ⅓ inch thick
¼ cup brandy
1 cup apple cider

4 slices foie gras, each ½ inch thick
Coarse salt and freshly ground pepper
2 tablespoons brandy
¼ cup cider
1 teaspoon white wine vinegar

Prepare the apples: Cut the seeds and cores from the apple slices, leaving a 1-inch circle in the center of each slice. Put the apples, the brandy, and cider in a sauté pan and boil, uncovered, for 10 minutes, until the apples are tender but not mushy and still hold their shape and the pan juices are reduced to a couple of tablespoonsful. Keep the apples warm and reserve the pan juices.

Cook the foie gras. Heat a sauté pan until very hot. Season the foie gras on both sides with salt and a little freshly ground pepper and lay it in the hot pan. The rapid cooking will render some of the fat out of the foie gras. As soon as the slices have caramelized and browned on the first side, 2 or 3 minutes, turn them and brown the second side, about 2 minutes.

Put the foie gras on 4 warm plates. Pour off all but 2 tablespoons of the fat from the pan and add the brandy, cider, vinegar, and the apple pan juices. Boil the mixture while swirling it around in the pan, reducing it to about 4 tablespoons. The sauce will thicken a little and partially emulsify. Spoon the sauce over the foie gras and garnish each serving with 2 of the reserved apple slices.

SAUTÉED FOIE GRAS WITH CARAMELIZED PEARL ONIONS AND FRESH CURRANTS

Serves 4 as an appetizer

28 pearl onions, peeled
4 slices French-style bread, each ½ inch thick
4 slices foie gras, each ½ inch thick
Coarse salt and freshly ground pepper
1 tablespoon honey
¾ cup Chicken Stock, page 31
1 tablespoon brandy
3 tablespoons white wine vinegar
4 clusters fresh currants

Blanch the onions in boiling salted water for 10 minutes. Drain.

Lightly toast the bread and put a slice in the center of each of 4 plates.

Cook the foie gras. Heat a sauté pan until very hot. Season the foie gras on both sides with salt and a little freshly ground pepper and lay it in the hot pan. The rapid cooking will render some of the fat out of the foie gras. As soon as the slices have caramelized and browned on the first side, 2 or 3 minutes, turn them over and brown the second side, about 2 minutes.

Put the foie gras on top of the pieces of toast on the plates. Pour off all but 2 tablespoons of fat from the pan and add the blanched onions and honey. Sauté the onions over medium heat, tossing and swirling them in the pan almost constantly until they are well caramelized. Arrange the onions around the foie gras. Add the stock, brandy, and vinegar to the sauté pan and boil the mixture until it is slightly thickened and reduced to about 6 tablespoons. Spoon some sauce over each serving and set a cluster of fresh currants on top of the foie gras.

ROASTED FOIE GRAS WITH GRAPES

Serves 6 to 8 as an appetizer

1 duck foie gras
Coarse salt and freshly ground pepper

FOR THE SAUCE
2 tablespoons white wine vinegar
½ cup Clinton Vineyards Late Harvest Riesling or other dessert wine
½ cup Chicken Stock, page 31
36 seedless green grapes off the stem

Crusty bread for serving

Preheat the oven to 400°F.

Carefully separate and devein the liver as directed on page 3. Wrap the small lobe well and freeze it for another use (such as one of the Sautéed Foie Gras recipes above). Salt and pepper the large lobe generously on both sides, put it in a small flameproof roasting pan, and roast it for 20 minutes. Put the foie gras on a warm platter and keep it warm.

Make the sauce in the roasting pan. Pour off all but 4 tablespoons of the foie gras fat. On top of the stove, over medium heat, add the vinegar, the wine, the stock, and the grapes and simmer the sauce until it has emulsified and reduced by about ⅓. Be sure to incorporate all the brown bits from the pan.

Slice the foie gras slightly on the diagonal into 6 equal slices. Put a slice on each plate, spoon some sauce over it, and garnish each serving with 6 grapes. Serve immediately with crusty bread.

STEAMED FOIE GRAS
WITH RHUBARB COMPOTE

Serves 6 to 8 as an appetizer

1 navel orange
1 duck foie gras
Coarse salt and freshly ground pepper
¾ cup good-quality dry white wine
¼ cup brandy
1½ cups thin-sliced rhubarb
2 tablespoons sugar
Fresh chervil sprigs for garnish

Using a vegetable peeler, peel off a 1-inch-wide strip of orange zest and cut it into fine julienne strips. Peel the orange and segment it into a bowl (page 149).

Carefully separate and devein the liver as directed on page 3. Wrap the small lobe well and freeze it for another use (such as one of the Sautéed Foie Gras recipes above). Salt and pepper the large lobe generously on both sides and put it in a steamer basket. Bring the wine and brandy to a boil in the bottom of the steamer. Put the basket into the steamer, cover, and steam the liver for 7 minutes. Without turning off the burner, set the liver aside for a moment and add to the pot the rhubarb, the sugar, most of the orange zest, and any juice that has accumulated in the bowl of orange segments. Replace the liver and cover the steamer. For accurate timing, use an instant-read thermometer. Steam the liver until it has reached an internal temperature of 115° to 120° F, about 5 minutes more. Line a platter with several layers of paper towels and place the steamed foie gras on it.

Warm serving plates.

Cut the foie gras into ½-inch-thick slices. Stir the rhubarb mixture to combine well, put a tablespoon of it on a warmed plate, and set a slice of foie gras on top. Place 2 orange slices on top of the foie gras and garnish with the remaining zest and a sprig of chervil.

ONION-WALNUT MUFFINS

More people ask me for this recipe than for any other. When I was asked to be chef at the Hudson River Club in New York City, I began researching antique cookbooks and menus to find a Hudson Valley cuisine. I never found a Hudson Valley cuisine, but I did find a few old recipes that used local produce and that reflected the background of the region's early settlers, mostly farmers, and a sprinkling of wealthy landowners. One recipe, for an onion-walnut bread, intrigued me because it used two of the major crops of the area a century ago. Although today, walnuts are no longer harvested in significant quantities, onions remain an important Hudson Valley crop. They are grown in the "black dirt" region of Orange County, an area of drained prehistoric wetlands so fertile that vir-

tually any vegetable can be grown there. "Black dirt onions," by far the largest crop of the county and known for their sweetness, were shipped down the river still covered in the rich soil of the region. I liked the idea of finding recipes that were based on local crops but, as is often the case, most of the recipes I found, including this one, turned out to be terrible. After much experimenting and revising I managed to adapt a number of them to modern tastes (see Onion Charlotte with Wild Mushrooms, Apple Charlotte with Sherry Syllabub, Halibut Boiled in Milk and Bread Sauce, and Cedar-Planked Shad). And I transformed the leaden onion-walnut bread into these tender muffins, which we now bake and serve throughout the day at the Hudson River Club.

ONION-WALNUT MUFFINS

Makes 20 muffins

Equipment: muffin tins
                 nonstick spray

1 large onion, or more if needed to make 1 cup puree
½ cup unsalted butter, melted
2 extra-large eggs
6 tablespoons sugar
1½ teaspoons coarse salt
1½ teaspoons baking powder
1½ cups walnut meats, chopped coarse
1½ cups flour

Preheat the oven to 425°F and spray the muffin tins with nonstick spray.

Peel the onion, cut it into quarters, and puree it fine in a food processor. Measure the puree and increase or decrease the amount to make 1 cup.

Beat together the butter, eggs, and sugar and add the onion puree. Stir in the remaining ingredients in the order given and mix the batter thoroughly. Fill the muffin tins almost full. Bake the muffins 20 minutes, or until they are puffed and well browned. Serve warm.

ROASTED OYSTERS WITH LEEKS ON THE HALF SHELL

The Hudson River was once a major source of oysters for the region. In the eighteenth century oysters were consumed by the ton along the river and in New York City as well. Pearl Street in lower Manhattan was named for the oyster shells that were discarded there. The oyster houses of Albany were famous; members of the state's political and business establishments would meet and each consume 100 or more at a sitting. Until the early 1950s, oysters were harvested on the shores of the Hudson all the way up to Albany. In fact, they were overharvested, and by 1953 there were very few left. Shortly thereafter serious pollution of the river began and the remaining oysters were not fit for consumption; New York had to supplement the limited Long Island crop with oysters from New England and the South Atlantic states. A limited number of oysters have recently been commercially harvested from the Hudson as a result of improved breeding practices and years of successful efforts to make the river once again clean and productive.

Serves 4 as an appetizer

3 leeks, white part only
6 tablespoons unsalted butter
¼ cup dry white wine or white vermouth
Coarse salt and freshly ground pepper
¼ cup Chicken Stock, page 31
24 Bluepoint oysters in their shells
Lots of coarse salt
3 tablespoons black peppercorns

Trim the leeks and clean them thoroughly. Slice them vertically into quarters, then cut into ¼-inch pieces. Melt 4 tablespoons of the butter in a heavy-bottomed saucepan, add the leeks and wine, and stew them, covered, over low heat until most of the liquid is absorbed. Season with salt and pepper, add the chicken stock and the remaining 2 tablespoons of butter, bring back to the boil, and turn off the heat.

On an ovenproof platter large enough to hold all the oysters, put a ½-inch layer of coarse salt. Sprinkle the peppercorns evenly over the surface. Open the oysters, discarding the top shells. Loosen the oysters from the bottom shells, being careful not to spill the juices, and lay the shells on the peppercorns.

Preheat the oven to 500°F.

Stir the leek mixture well and put a teaspoon of it on each oyster. Roast just until the edges of the oysters begin to curl, 5 to 8 minutes. Serve the oysters from the platter.

ONION CHARLOTTE
WITH WILD MUSHROOMS

This recipe is a playful interpretation of one of the most popular desserts to be found on American menus of the mid-nineteenth century. Charlottes are rich confections of cake, fruit, and cream and were served at grand public functions and private dinner parties. In this sophisticated version, a miniature savory charlotte is a confection of good bread and a soft, eggy onion custard, with a flavorful mixture of braised mushrooms to serve as a sauce.

Serves 6 as a dinner appetizer or lunch main course

Equipment: six 8-ounce ramekins
            nonstick spray

FOR THE CUSTARD
1 medium onion, chopped
2 tablespoons unsalted butter
4 extra-large eggs
2½ cups heavy cream
¼ teaspoon freshly grated nutmeg
Coarse salt and freshly ground pepper

FOR THE RAMEKINS
15 slices good-quality white bread
½ cup unsalted butter, softened
2 tablespoons chopped parsley

½ recipe Braised Wild Mushrooms, page 199
6 fresh thyme sprigs for garnish

Preheat the oven to 375°F.

To make the custard mixture, sauté the chopped onion in the butter without browning for 4 or 5 minutes, or until it is thoroughly cooked, soft, and translucent. In a bowl, combine the eggs, cream, nutmeg, and salt and pepper.

Transfer the onion to a food processor, puree it, then stir the puree into the egg mixture.

Prepare the ramekins: Trim the crust from the bread and cut each slice crosswise into 4 strips. Spray each ramekin well with nonstick spray. This may sound a little odd, but the spray is actually tasteless and it's the best way to keep the charlottes from sticking. Using a pastry brush, very generously butter the bottom and sides of each ramekin with some of the soft butter, sprinkle each with chopped parsley, and shake out the excess. Stand the strips of bread in each ramekin, pressing them onto the butter. Each ramekin will take 9 strips of bread. The ends of the bread strips will extend about an inch above the tops of the ramekins.

Ladle the custard mixture into the ramekins, filling each one about half full. Line a flameproof roasting pan with a double layer of paper towels and place the ramekins in the pan. Add boiling water to the roasting pan to come halfway up the sides of the ramekins. Bring the water to a boil on top of the stove, put the pan on the bottom shelf of the oven, and bake for 20 to 30 minutes, or until the custard is set around the edges and still quivers very slightly in the middle when the pan is shaken, and the bread is golden brown. Leave the ramekins in the water bath to cool; the heat of the water will cook the custard until it is firm throughout.

While the custard is cooling, prepare the mushrooms and keep them warm.

To assemble the dish, gently turn each charlotte out of the ramekin into your cupped hand and immediately put it on a warm plate. Spoon equal amounts of the mushroom mixture into each charlotte and garnish with sprigs of fresh thyme. Serve immediately.

If you want to prepare this dish several hours in advance, place the charlottes on an ovenproof platter as you remove them from the ramekins. Just before serving time, cover them with foil and reheat for 10 or 15 minutes in a 300°F oven. Serve warm, not hot.

HUDSON VALLEY COUNTRY PÂTÉ

Black trumpet mushrooms and walnuts give this hearty pâté a real Hudson Valley touch. Don't be intimidated by the length of the directions. Pâté is not difficult to make and it's wonderful to have in the refrigerator for an impromptu lunch party, an impressive appetizer, or a satisfying snack. It's good served with Cranberry and Citrus Relish, page 149, or Onion, Orange, and Fennel Relish, page 85. To make the preparation easier, have the right equipment. You will need a meat grinder; a baking pan with a 1½-quart capacity, such as a terrine; a glass or ceramic loaf pan or several smaller baking dishes; a board cut to fit just inside the rim of the baking pan; weights (heavy cans, stones, or bricks work fine). An instant-read thermometer provides the only foolproof way of telling when the pâté is done. The word "terrine" refers to the pan; pâté refers to the meat itself. Cured pork belly (brined pork belly) is available through specialty butchers. You may need to order it in advance.

Equipment: a 1½-quart loaf pan or terrine

Makes approximately 24 ¼-inch slices

2 pounds boneless pork shoulder
1 pound cured pork belly
3 shallots, sliced
2 cloves garlic, sliced
1 cup rendered pork fat or duck fat (do not substitute butter)
½ cup good-quality port wine
½ cup good-quality brandy
2 teaspoons freshly ground pepper
1 teaspoon coarse salt
¾ teaspoon powdered thyme
¾ teaspoon powdered rosemary
¼ teaspoon freshly grated nutmeg
2 bay leaves
¼ pound fresh black trumpet mushrooms or 1 ounce dried, reconstituted in water
  (see page 90)

2 tablespoons rendered pork fat or duck fat

¾ cup walnut meats, chopped coarse

½ pound chicken livers

4 extra-large eggs

GARNISH

1 teaspoon dried thyme

6 bay leaves

2 cloves

Cut the meats into 1-inch cubes. Sauté the shallots and garlic in a little of the rendered pork or duck fat until wilted and let cool. In a bowl, combine the meats, the port, brandy, and shallots and garlic with the pepper, salt, herbs, nutmeg, and bay leaves. Using your hands, mix everything together very thoroughly and refrigerate the mixture, covered tightly, for at least 2 days (but up to 1 week is fine), until the meat has absorbed all the liquid. Remove the bay leaves.

Grinding the meat: Sauté the fresh or reconstituted trumpet mushrooms in a tablespoon or 2 of the pork fat or duck fat for 5 minutes and add them to the meat mixture, distributing them evenly. Using the small gauge blade of a meat grinder, grind the meat mixture. Be sure to grind an even mix of ingredients. Do not force the meat through the grinder; forcing causes the machine to heat up and the meat and fat to separate and break down. The mixture should come out in spaghetti-like strands. If the meat masses together and does not grind evenly, tighten the grinder shield. Clean the blade from time to time if necessary.

When all the meat is ground, add the walnuts. In a food processor, puree the chicken livers with the eggs. Strain the liver mixture and add it to the ground meat mixture. Vigorously mix and knead the pâté mixture with your hands for at least 5 minutes; it will all come together into a mass. From time to time, wet your fingers with cold water and pat the mixture. When your hands do not stick to it, it is ready.

At this point you should taste the mixture for seasoning. Do not taste it raw. Make a small patty and cook it in a small frying pan until it is cooked through and no longer pink. Taste and correct the seasoning.

Put the meat into a 1½-quart loaf pan or terrine. Pat it well to get out all air pockets and mound the meat about ¼ inch above the top of the pan. With your finger, make a groove all around the rim of the pan. Spoon a line of dried thyme down the top of the pâté and decorate with the bay leaves and cloves. Seal the pan well with foil and refrigerate overnight or up to 2 days. Take the terrine out of the refrigerator an hour before baking it.

Preheat the oven to 425°F.

Set the terrine in a roasting pan and pour boiling water to come halfway up the sides of the terrine. Bake the pâté until it begins to come away from the sides of the pan and the internal temperature on an instant-read thermometer is 165°F. This will take about 2 hours and 15 minutes. Use your thermometer to determine cooking time for terrines of any size.

When the pâté reaches an internal temperature of 165° F, take it out of the oven and leave it in the water. Put a board on top of the covered pâté and press down on it to force out the juices. Leaving the board in place, weight the pâté, take it out of the water bath, and let it cool. When it cools to room temperature, refrigerate the weighted pâté.

The next day, remove the weights, the board, and the foil and scrape the surface of the pâté clean of any congealed fat and/or meat juices. Clean the outside of the terrine. Melt the remaining rendered fat and pour it over the pâté to cover the meat by ¼ inch—just enough so that air does not touch the meat. Refrigerate until the fat is solid, then cover the pâté with plastic wrap and with foil. Unopened, the pâté will keep for 4 to 6 weeks in the refrigerator. Once it has been cut, seal well with plastic wrap before putting it back in the refrigerator and use within a week.

To serve, scrape the fat layer off the pâté and turn it out of the terrine. Pass the blunt side of a knife blade over the entire surface of the pâté to remove all fat and congealed juices. Trim a thin slice from one end of the pâté and cut it into ¼-inch slices. See the headnote of this recipe for suggested accompaniments.

VENISON TERRINE

This is the ideal way to use tough cuts and scraps of venison. The flavor is very different from that of Country Pâté, but the procedure is almost identical; cooking time for this terrine is about 15 minutes less and it should be cooked to an internal temperature of only 155°F. Use a meat thermometer for accurate timing. Cured pork belly (brined pork belly) is available through specialty butchers. You may need to order it in advance. Red Wine Jelly, page 114, and Herb Salad with Lemon Vinaigrette, page 55, are especially good with this terrine.

Makes approximately 24 ¼-inch slices

1½ pounds boneless venison
2 pounds cured pork belly
3 shallots, sliced
2 cloves garlic, sliced
¼ cup dry red wine
½ cup good-quality gin
¼ cup good-quality brandy, plus ½ cup for soaking cranberries
5 or 6 crushed juniper berries
1 teaspoon freshly ground pepper
1 teaspoon coarse salt
¾ teaspoon powdered thyme
¾ teaspoon powdered rosemary
¼ teaspoon freshly grated nutmeg
1 bay leaf
½ pound chicken livers
4 extra-large eggs
1 pound thin-sliced bacon
½ pound (1 cup) dried cranberries

GARNISH
1 teaspoon dried thyme
6 bay leaves

Follow the procedure for making the Hudson Valley Country Pâté meat mixture, page 22. To reconstitute the dried cranberries, combine them with the ½ cup brandy in a small pot. Bring to a boil, turn off the heat, cover the pot, and let them steep until they are soft and the brandy is all absorbed, about ½ hour. Chop the cranberries coarse and add them to the meat mixture after it has been ground.

When the pâté mixture is ready, line a 1½-quart terrine with bacon slices, covering the bottom and sides of the pan completely and allowing enough bacon to hang over the edge of the pan to cover the meat mixture completely once it has been added to the pan. Decorate the top of the pâté as described in the Country Pâté recipe and cover the pan tightly with foil. Bake the pâté to an internal temperature of 155°F (approximately 2 hours) according to the directions on page 24.

Directions for weighting, chilling, storing, and serving this pâté are the same as those for Hudson Valley Country Pâté.

CHOPPED FRESH GREEN BEANS WITH CURED DUCK

This dish provides an unusual range of contrasting flavors and textures; the firm crispness of the beans sets off the richness of the cured duck and the tender cracklings.

Serves 8 as an appetizer or salad

2 fresh thyme sprigs
Coarse salt
2 pounds green beans, trimmed and cut in half
2 shallots, minced
2 to 3 tablespoons rendered duck fat
2 pieces Cured Duck with skin, page 141
Freshly ground pepper

Put the thyme sprigs in a large pot of water and bring to a boil. Salt the water, add the beans, and boil them for 5 minutes. Drain the beans and run cold water over them to stop the cooking. Drain well. The beans should still be bright green and a bit crisp.

In a food processor, chop the beans. Do not puree them. They should be rather coarsely chopped and retain their crunchy texture.

Mix the shallots and the duck fat into the beans, season with salt and freshly ground pepper, and let the salad stand for an hour or so.

Remove the skin from the cured duck and reserve it. Slice the duck thin. Cut the skin into thin strips and fry it in a little duck fat until it is very crisp. Drain the skin on a paper towel.

Taste the bean mixture and reseason it to taste with salt, pepper, and a bit more duck fat. Put the beans in a shallow bowl and arrange the sliced duck around the edges. Immediately before serving, sprinkle the crisp skin over all.

Variation

Omit the cured duck and substitute 4 slices bacon, cut into small pieces and fried until crisp and brown. Use bacon fat or olive or vegetable oil to dress the salad.

WHITE BEAN STRUDEL
WITH CURED DUCK

Good for appetizer, lunch, or buffet table, this dish demonstrates the convenience of having on hand homemade staples such as Cured Duck (along with the fat it's packed in) and Tomato Compote, an easily-made version of tomato paste that is infinitely more subtle and flavorful (and can also be frozen so you can always have it on hand).

Makes eight 5-inch-long strudels to serve 8 as a lunch main dish or dinner appetizer

FOR THE FILLING
2 leg and thigh pieces of Cured Duck, page 141
2 cups cooked white beans, page 234
2 tablespoons Tomato Compote, page 293
I teaspoon minced garlic
I tablespoon chopped chervil or parsley
½ teaspoon chopped fresh thyme leaves
2 tablespoons rendered duck fat (from Cured Duck)
½ cup Chicken Stock, page 31, or Roast Duck Stock, page 34
Coarse salt and freshly ground pepper

FOR THE PASTRY
12 sheets phyllo pastry (strudel leaves)
½ cup melted duck fat (from Cured Duck)

GARNISH
Basic Green Salad, page 54

Make the filling: Pull the duck meat off the bones and, using your fingers, shred it coarse. Put all the filling ingredients in a bowl and combine well, using a rubber spatula to partially mash the beans. Season with a little salt and pepper and chill the mixture at least an hour or overnight.

Preheat the oven to 400°F. Grease a baking sheet with duck fat.

Spread 1 sheet of phyllo on the counter and brush it lightly with duck fat. Put a second, then a third sheet on top of the first, brushing each one with duck fat. Cut the pastry in half crosswise. Lay a generous ¼ cup of filling across the pastry, 2 inches from the end. Roll the pastry twice, brush with fat, and turn in one end. Roll over once more and turn in the other end. Brush again with fat and roll up the remaining pastry to make a 5- to 6-inch roll. Place the roll, seam side down, on the baking sheet. Repeat with the remaining ingredients. Brush the tops of the strudels with a little more fat and bake them for 15 minutes, or until they are crisp and brown.

Serve hot. Cut the strudels in half on the diagonal. Put them on plates next to a mound of salad, and drizzle any duck fat remaining on the baking sheet over all.

STOCK

Stock is the single most important element in my cooking. I work amid vats of it; my hand reaches out for it, ladling it with abandon into soups, stews, and sauces. The stock I use is a complex and concentrated brew, an infusion made by slowly simmering bones, vegetables, herbs, and spices until all their flavor has been yielded, their essences transformed into what I think of as the soul of the kitchen. As you follow my recipes you will use stock undiluted in soups; in stews and sauces it will be cooked down to produce a rounded flavor and a silky texture. Reduce it a little more and add a tablespoon or two of it to a vinaigrette; it will emulsify the sauce and add a depth of flavor you can't get any other way.

Since you will need to have plenty of stock on hand when you work from this book, I suggest that you cultivate the stock habit right away. Never let a fish, meat, or poultry bone get away from you. If you're not able to make stock the day you have a fish filleted or a roast boned, put the bones in the freezer until you collect enough for a good pot of stock. Stock cooks for a long time, but it doesn't need any attention—you can even let it barely simmer over very low heat while you're sleeping. I've discovered a good way of storing stock when I make it at home. After it cools, I funnel it into liter-size plastic seltzer bottles and let it stand until all the fat rises to the surface. Then, holding the stock over the sink or a container, I squeeze the plastic bottle and all the fat pours out the top. I'm left with fat-free stock in a convenient freezing container; it even has head room for expansion as it freezes.

There's no substitute for homemade stock. It is a necessity, a primary ingredient in serious cooking. It contributes its rich flavor and subtle texture to everything you use it in, and is well worth the small investment of time it takes to make it. And there's no better use for your freezer: Fill it with good stock and follow my recipes and your success as a cook is insured. This section includes recipes for chicken stock, rich meat stock, roast duck stock, fish stock, and vegetable stock. A recipe for turkey stock is included in the recipe for Roast Turkey with Clinton Vineyards Riesling Gravy, page 146.

THE HUDSON RIVER VALLEY COOKBOOK

CHICKEN STOCK

It used to be easy to buy packages of chicken necks and backs in the supermarket. These bony parts are full of flavor and are the ideal raw material for making this most useful of stocks. Buy some when you see them and freeze them until you're ready to make stock. Otherwise, buy dark meat chicken parts on sale for the second-best way to make first-rate chicken stock.

Makes 1 gallon stock

1 leek, white part and 1 inch green, carefully washed
2 carrots
2 stalks celery
1 turnip
1 onion, peeled
2 cloves garlic, peeled
½ pound mushrooms
2 fresh thyme sprigs or 1 teaspoon dried thyme
2 bay leaves
7 or 8 parsley stems
1 tablespoon black peppercorns
4 pounds chicken backs and necks or thighs and legs, rinsed

Slice all the vegetables and put them, the seasonings, and the chicken parts in your largest stock pot. Cover with 5 quarts (20 cups) cold water and bring to a boil. Simmer, with lid ajar, skimming occasionally, for 4 to 6 hours. Because reduction intensifies the flavor, do not salt the stock until you are ready to use it. Strain the stock and let it cool. Chill it until the fat on top solidifies (or use the easy fat removal system described on page 30). Remove the fat, pour the stock into containers, and refrigerate or freeze it.

RICH MEAT STOCK

You can roast five pounds of chicken necks and backs instead of veal bones to make this richly flavored stock.

Makes 1 gallon stock

5 pounds veal bones, preferably shin, knuckle, or pipe (marrow) bones, cut by the butcher
    into 2-inch pieces
1 leek, white part and 1 inch green, carefully washed
2 carrots
2 stalks celery
1 turnip
1 onion, peeled
2 cloves garlic, peeled
½ pound mushrooms
3 tomatoes
2 fresh thyme sprigs or 1 teaspoon dried thyme
2 bay leaves
7 or 8 parsley stems
1 tablespoon black peppercorns
2 whole cloves
3 cups dry white wine
4 tablespoons tomato paste

FOR THE REDUCTION
½ pound mushrooms, sliced thin
2 shallots, sliced thin
½ cup dry white wine

Preheat the oven to 400°F.

    Lay the bones in a single layer in a roasting pan, and roast for 1 hour.

    While the bones are roasting, slice all the vegetables and put them in your largest stock pot with the seasonings, up to but not including the wine. After 1 hour, add the bones to the stock pot, pour off the fat in the roasting pan, and, over medium heat, deglaze the pan with the white wine. Dissolve the tomato paste in the wine and simmer for 5 minutes, detaching all browned bits stuck to the pan. Using a rubber spatula, scrape the mixture into the stock pot, add 6 quarts (24 cups) cold water, and bring to a boil. With the lid ajar, simmer the stock gently for 6 to 8 hours (3 to 4 for chicken).

Strain the stock into a clean pot and add the ingredients for the reduction. Set the pot on the burner slightly off center so impurities will collect on one side. Simmer the stock over medium heat, skimming frequently, until the stock is reduced to 1 gallon, about 1 to 1½ hours. Strain the stock and let it cool. Chill it until any fat congeals on the surface (or use the easy fat removal system described on page 30). Remove the fat and pour the stock into containers for storing or freezing.

ROAST DUCK STOCK

Use this stock to make any number of wonderful soups and the sauce for Braised Duck with Brandied Prunes, Orange, and Lemon, page 138.

Makes 1 gallon stock

Bones and carcasses from 2 ducks
1 onion, sliced
1 leek, including 1 inch of green, carefully washed and sliced
1 stalk celery, sliced
1 carrot, sliced
1 small turnip, sliced
½ teaspoon dried thyme
2 bay leaves
1 teaspoon black peppercorns
4 cloves garlic, smashed
A handful of parsley stems
3 whole cloves
12 cups Chicken Stock, page 31
2 tablespoons tomato paste

Preheat the oven to 450°F.

Put the duck bones and carcasses in a roasting pan and roast for about 45 minutes, turning once, until they are good and brown. Transfer the bones to a soup pot, add all the remaining ingredients except the tomato paste, and bring to a boil.

Pour off the fat from the roasting pan. Use a little of the stock to deglaze the pan, simmering it over medium heat and dissolving the tomato paste in it. Add the mixture to the soup pot and simmer the stock, with the lid ajar, for 2 to 3 hours. Strain the stock and let it cool. Chill it until the fat congeals (or use the easy fat removal system described on page 30). Remove the fat and pour the stock into containers to store or freeze.

FISH STOCK

Makes 3 quarts stock

4 pounds heads, bones, and collars from flavorful white fish such as striped bass,
  red snapper, or cod
2 tablespoons unsalted butter
5 shallots, sliced
2 stalks celery, sliced
½ pound mushrooms, sliced
1 cup dry white wine
12 parsley stems
1 tablespoon black peppercorns
3 fresh thyme sprigs

Be sure the heads, bones, and collars are clean, fresh (no fishy smell), and free of entrails.
Wash thoroughly under running cold water.

Melt the butter in a soup pot and gently cook the shallots, celery, and mushrooms
without allowing them to brown until they are limp, 6 to 8 minutes. Add the wine and
simmer for 5 minutes to reduce it a bit, then add the fish and seasonings to the pot. Add 14
cups cold water, bring to a boil, and simmer the stock, uncovered, for 45 minutes, stirring
once or twice to redistribute the fish. Strain the stock, let it cool, and pour it into containers
for storing or freezing.

VEGETABLE STOCK

Makes 3 quarts stock

3 tablespoons extra virgin olive oil
2 large onions, peeled and sliced
1 large leek, including 1 inch of green, carefully washed and sliced
2 cloves garlic, peeled and sliced
2 stalks celery
1 bulb celery root, peeled
1 small turnip
2 carrots
2 parsnips
½ pound mushrooms
A small bunch parsley
2 or 3 fresh thyme sprigs
1 bay leaf
1 tablespoon black peppercorns

Heat the olive oil in a stock pot and sauté the onions, leek, and garlic until they are limp and translucent and just turning golden, about 15 minutes. Rough chop the remaining vegetables and add them to the pot along with the seasonings and 4 quarts (16 cups) cold water. Bring to a boil and simmer the stock, uncovered, for 2 to 3 hours, until it is reduced to 3 quarts. Strain the stock, let it cool, pour it into containers, and store or freeze.

POTATO AND SORREL SOUP
WITH RED PEPPER CREAM

This is a soup for spring, especially if you can find some ramps to use with the sorrel. Ramps are pungent wild members of the onion family; they taste like a combination of onions, leeks, scallions, chives, and garlic, and add a distinctively piquant flavor to the already tangy sorrel. This soup is equally good hot or cold and, like almost all soups, improves with age. Make it a day or two in advance of serving.

Serves 10

4 tablespoons unsalted butter
I pound ramps, cleaned and chopped, or 3 leeks, including 2 inches of green,
    carefully cleaned and chopped
2 stalks celery, sliced
2 medium onions, peeled and sliced
2½ pounds baking potatoes, peeled and sliced
6 cups shredded sorrel (about ½ pound)
12 cups Chicken Stock, page 31
I cup heavy cream (use in cold soup only)
Coarse salt and freshly ground pepper
I cup finely chopped sorrel leaves

FOR THE RED PEPPER CREAM
½ cup heavy cream
¼ cup roasted red pepper puree (made from I roasted sweet red pepper, see below)
Coarse salt and freshly ground pepper

Melt the butter in a heavy-bottomed soup pot and cook the ramps, celery, and onions, without browning, until wilted. Add the potatoes and the shredded sorrel and stir well. Add the stock, bring to a boil, and simmer with the lid ajar for I hour. Put the soup through a food mill or sieve and season it with salt and pepper. If you are planning to serve the soup cold, stir in the cup of heavy cream, bring the soup back to the boil, and simmer for 2 or 3 minutes. Stir in the chopped sorrel and reseason the soup. Let the soup cool and refrigerate it, covered, overnight.

Roast the red pepper: Cut the pepper in half from stem to blossom end and remove the stem and seeds. Place the pepper cut side down on a baking sheet and broil it until the skin is completely charred. Put the charred pepper in a paper bag for 10 minutes. Under cold running water, strip all the charred skin from the pepper. Puree the pepper in a food processor.

Make the red pepper cream: In a bowl, whip the cream until it holds soft peaks, fold in ¼ cup of the pepper puree and some salt and pepper, and whip until the cream is stiff.

If you are serving the soup hot, reheat it right before serving and stir in the chopped sorrel.

To serve hot or cold, float a rounded spoonful of pepper cream on each bowl of soup.

THREE CELERY SOUP

You can taste each kind of celery in this unusual and delicious soup.

Serves 8

4 tablespoons unsalted butter
I large onion, sliced
I large bunch celery, sliced, reserving the leaves, chopped, for garnish
2 celery roots, about I pound each, peeled and sliced thin
I level teaspoon celery seed
I bay leaf
10 cups Chicken Stock, page 31
Coarse salt and freshly ground pepper
I cup heavy cream, optional

Melt the butter in a heavy-bottomed soup pot. Over medium-low heat, wilt the onion without browning, then add the celery, the celery root, the celery seed, and the bay leaf. Cook the vegetables without browning for 10 minutes, stirring occasionally. Add the stock, cover the pot, bring to a boil, and simmer the soup, covered, for about 30 minutes. Remove the cover and simmer the soup for another 30 minutes.

Strain the soup into a bowl, remove the bay leaf, and puree the vegetables in a food processor, adding enough of the liquid to make a smooth puree. Return the pureed vegetables and the liquid to the soup pot, stir in the cream, if you are using it, and bring the soup back to the boil. Let the soup cool and refrigerate it, covered, overnight.

Shortly before serving, reheat the soup. Correct the seasoning and serve hot, garnished with chopped celery leaves.

CORN AND CODFISH CHOWDER WITH TOMATO OIL

This hearty soup makes a lovely summer meal. Follow it with a platter of juicy ripe tomatoes, pepper-crusted Coach Farm goat cheese, and crusty bread.

Serves 10 to 12 as a first course, 8 as a main course

4 tablespoons unsalted butter
2 onions, sliced thin
4 large ears fresh corn
2 large baking potatoes, peeled, halved lengthwise, and sliced thin
1½ pounds cod, sliced 1 inch thick, cut into small pieces
About 1 tablespoon coarse salt and some freshly ground pepper
2½ cups Fish Stock, page 35
2½ cups Chicken Stock, page 31
herb sachet: 1 tablespoon black peppercorns
               1 teaspoon dried thyme
               1 bay leaf   Tied together in a
               4 or 5 sprigs parsley   double layer of cheesecloth
               2 cloves garlic, smashed

2½ cups heavy cream

GARNISH
Tomato Oil, page 290
Fresh thyme leaves

Melt the butter in a heavy-bottomed soup pot, add the onions, and sauté gently until the onions are softened but not browned. Cut the kernels from the ears of corn and reserve the cobs. Add the potatoes, half the fish, the corn and corn cobs to the pot, season with some salt and pepper, and stir everything together. Add the stock and the herb sachet and bring the soup to a boil. Turn down the heat and simmer, uncovered, for ½ hour.

Remove the herb sachet and corn cobs from the soup, add the cream, and continue to simmer the soup for another 15 minutes. Cool and refrigerate overnight.

Shortly before serving, reheat the soup. Add the remaining fish and let the soup come back to a simmer. Reseason the soup with salt and pepper and let it simmer for 10 minutes, or until the fish is cooked through. Ladle into warm bowls and garnish each serving with a teaspoon of the tomato oil and a pinch of fresh thyme leaves. Serve immediately.

CHILLED APPLE AND POTATO SOUP

Use tart Hudson Valley apples such as Paula Red, Baldwin, or Macoun to make this unusual variation on the classic leek and potato soup. Be sure to use a food mill, not a processor, to puree the soup; a processor will turn the potatoes gluey. If you don't have a food mill, force the soup through a sieve. This soup can also be served hot. Make the soup at least a day before serving.

Serves 10 to 12

4 tablespoons unsalted butter
5 small leeks, including about 1 inch of the green tops, carefully cleaned and sliced
1 medium onion, sliced
1½ pounds baking potatoes, peeled and sliced
6 Paula Red, Baldwin, or Macoun apples, peeled, cored, and rough chopped
8 cups Chicken Stock, page 31
1 cup heavy cream
1 to 2 tablespoons coarse salt
Freshly ground pepper

GARNISH
1 red-skinned apple
4 tablespoons chopped chives

In a soup pot, melt the butter, add the leeks and onion, and cook over medium heat, without browning, stirring frequently, about 10 minutes. When the vegetables are softened, add the potatoes, apples, and chicken stock. Bring to a boil, lower the heat, and simmer 30 minutes, or until the potatoes are very soft.

Put the soup through a food mill. Add the cream and season with salt and freshly ground pepper. It will take a lot of salt to bring out the flavor of the soup. This is especially important because the soup will be served cold, and cold foods always require extra seasoning.

Chill the soup overnight. Check the seasoning. If the soup is too thick, thin it with a little additional stock. Immediately before serving, cut a red-skinned apple into julienne strips. Garnish each bowl of soup with some of the apple and a sprinkling of chopped chives.

PUMPKIN APPLE SOUP WITH CINNAMON CROUTONS

When you eat a spoonful of this soup, it will remind you of all the flavors of fall. Pumpkins and apples are harvested at the same time and the two flavors complement each other. People expect the soup to be sweet, but it's savory, with a tinge of tart apple. The house smells wonderful when you make a big pot of it on a crisp autumn day. It serves as an excellent main course, and it freezes beautifully.

Oddly enough, canned pumpkin is almost always better than fresh—and certainly a lot easier. The smoky bacon brings the pumpkin and apple flavors together, but the soup is also very good—if less complex—if you leave out the meat.

Serves 10 to 12

2 slices bacon, diced

2 tablespoons butter

4 large tart apples such as Baldwin or Cortland, peeled, cored, and chopped

1 carrot, peeled and chopped

1 medium onion, peeled and chopped

1 stalk celery, peeled and chopped

1 leek, white part only, carefully cleaned and chopped

1 clove garlic, chopped

¼ teaspoon ground cinnamon

A few gratings nutmeg

⅛ teaspoon ground allspice

¼ cup good-quality dry white wine

½ cup apple cider

2 tablespoons good-quality brandy, apple brandy, or Calvados

8 cups Chicken Stock, page 31, or Vegetable Stock, page 36

herb sachet: I tablespoon black peppercorns ⎫
2 bay leaves
½ teaspoon dried thyme   Tied together in a
small bunch parsley   double layer of cheesecloth
4 cloves ⎭

I smoked ham hock
2 cups canned pumpkin puree
Salt and freshly ground pepper to taste

GARNISH
Butter Croutons, page 298
½ teaspoon ground cinnamon
I tablespoon sugar
Chopped parsley

In a heavy-bottomed soup pot, render the bacon over medium heat, add the butter, the apples, and the chopped vegetables and cook, stirring frequently, until the vegetables are lightly cooked, 5 to 10 minutes. Add the cinnamon, nutmeg, and allspice and stir for a minute or 2, allowing the spices to "bloom." Add the wine, cider, and brandy and reduce until almost dry. Pour in the stock, add the herb sachet and ham hock, and stir in the pumpkin puree. Bring to a boil, then lower the heat and simmer gently, with lid ajar, for about I hour, until all the vegetables are soft. Remove the sachet and discard it. Remove the ham hock, take the meat off the bone, and reserve it. Discard the bone. Put the soup through a food mill or sieve into a large bowl. Season the soup with salt and freshly ground pepper and adjust the consistency if necessary with additional stock; the soup should be like a thin porridge.

Chop the reserved ham and add it to the soup. Let the soup cool, cover, and refrigerate it, at least overnight.

Prepare the garnish. Prepare Butter Croutons, tossing with the cinnamon and sugar before you toast the croutons. Reheat the soup, seasoning it with salt and pepper; add a little apple brandy if you wish. Garnish each bowl of soup with cinnamon croutons and chopped parsley.

BUTTERNUT SQUASH CONSOMMÉ WITH GINGER AND SCALLION CUSTARD

Delicate, elegant, vegetarian, this is a little more demanding to make than most soups, and is definitely one for a special occasion. As with all soups, prepare this a day or two ahead, but make the custard an hour before serving.

Serves 6

Equipment: Six 2-ounce or two 6-ounce ramekins
            nonstick spray

3 leeks, white part only
2 stalks celery
1 carrot
1 turnip
1 parsnip
1 small onion
4½ pounds butternut squash

FOR THE CLARIFICATION
6 extra-large eggs
1 clove garlic, peeled
2 fresh sage leaves
A few parsley stems
1 teaspoon fresh thyme leaves
1 clove
1 teaspoon black peppercorns
Coarse salt

FOR THE CUSTARD

3 extra-large egg yolks (separated from above)
1 cup heavy cream
1 tablespoon grated fresh ginger
2 scallions, including green part, chopped
Coarse salt and freshly ground pepper

OPTIONAL GARNISH

4 tablespoons fresh ginger, peeled, sliced thin, cut into fine strips, and fried as shallots,
    page 239

Slice all the vegetables except the butternut squash and set ¼ of them aside to use later in the clarification of the consommé. Put the remaining vegetables in a large heavy-bottomed soup pot.

Cut the unpeeled butternut squash into thick slices without removing the seeds. Add the squash to the soup pot, reserving 3 slices. Add 12 cups water to the pot, cover the pot, and bring the soup to a boil. Simmer the soup over medium-high heat, partially covered, for 2 hours.

While the soup is cooking, peel and seed the reserved squash slices. Cut the squash into fine dice and reserve ½ cup for garnish. Add the remaining diced squash to the reserved clarification vegetables and in a food processor finely chop all the vegetables with the garlic, sage, parsley, and thyme. Put the mixture in a bowl and add the clove and peppercorns.

Separate the eggs, reserving 3 of the yolks for the ginger custard, and add the whites to the chopped vegetable mixture. Combine well, add 1 cup of cold water, and mix thoroughly. Refrigerate the mixture for at least ½ hour.

Strain the soup into a large bowl, pressing hard on the solids with a rubber spatula to extract as much liquid as possible without forcing the solids through the strainer. This will take a little time. You have to coax the liquid out of the vegetables by pressing them against the sides of the strainer and allowing the liquid to run out the middle.

Clarify the soup: Rinse out the heavy-bottomed soup pot, return the soup to it, and bring it back to the boil. Stirring the soup constantly, add the clarification mixture and, as the soup simmers, continue to stir gently, distributing the mixture throughout the broth, for 15 minutes. The clarification mixture will solidify and form a "raft." Put a ladle through the center of the raft to form a hole. Occasionally stirring the soup very gently through the hole, let it simmer for about 1 hour. Set a very fine *chinois* or a strainer lined with a clean, thin dishtowel, several layers of cheesecloth, or a coffee filter over a pot. Carefully ladle the consommé out through the hole in the raft. Let the clarification vegetables rest in the strainer undisturbed until no more liquid drips out. The consommé will be perfectly clear. Season it with a little salt, let cool, and refrigerate overnight. Ten minutes before serving, bring the consommé to a boil, add the diced butternut garnish, and simmer for 5 minutes.

Make the custard: Preheat the oven to 300°F. Spray the bottom and sides of six 2-ounce or two 6-ounce ramekins with nonstick spray. Combine all the custard ingredients except for half of the scallions and divide it among the ramekins. Set the ramekins on a layer of paper towels in a roasting pan and add hot water to come halfway up the sides of the ramekins. Put the pan in the oven and bake until the edges are set and the custards still quiver just a little bit in the center when the pan is shaken, 20 to 25 minutes for the small, 35 to 40 minutes for the larger custards. Remove the pan from the oven and leave the custards in the hot water.

If you are using the fried ginger, prepare it while the custards bake.

To serve, turn the custards out of the ramekins. For individual custards, place one in the center of each of 6 heated shallow soup plates. Cut each of the larger custards into 6 pieces and arrange 2 pieces in each plate. Add the chopped scallions to the soup and ladle it into the plates. Place the optional fried ginger on top of the custard. Serve immediately.

WILD MUSHROOM BROTH

Serve a mug of this rich brew on a cold afternoon or ladle it into a delicate soup bowl and float some chives on top for your most elegant dinner party. The better the stock you use, the better the soup will be. As with all soups, this one will be at its best two or three days after you make it. Read more about wild mushrooms on page 198.

Serves 10

1 ounce dried wild mushrooms such as morels or porcini
2 pounds mixed fresh wild mushrooms such as oyster mushrooms, cauliflower fungus, black
    trumpets, or hen of the woods
herb sachet: 2 bay leaves
               2 large cloves garlic
               1 shallot
               1 teaspoon chopped fresh rosemary   Tied together in a
               2 tablespoons chopped parsley   double layer of cheesecloth
               1 teaspoon black peppercorns
               A pinch of thyme
               2 cloves
½ cup good-quality cream sherry
14 cups Chicken Stock, page 31
Coarse salt and freshly ground pepper

Put the dried mushrooms in a 2-cup measure and fill it with hot water. Clean the fresh mushrooms by brushing off dirt and debris and rinsing them rapidly under cold water. Slice 3 cups of wild mushroom caps and set aside for garnish. Rough chop the remaining fresh mushrooms, both caps and stems, and put them in a soup pot with the seasonings and the sherry. Strain the soaking liquid from the dried mushrooms into the pot. Slice the reconstituted mushroom pieces, reserving nice pieces for the garnish, and add the remainder to the soup pot. Cover the pot, bring to a boil, and steam the mushrooms in the cooking liquid, covered, until they release their juices, about 10 minutes. Uncover the pot, stir the mushrooms, and continue to boil until most of the liquid has evaporated, about 10 minutes more.

Add the stock, bring to a boil, and cook the soup over medium-high heat, uncovered, for 20 minutes. Turn down the heat and simmer gently, uncovered, for another 30 minutes. Strain the soup into a bowl, press the mushrooms lightly to extract all the juice, then discard the mushrooms. Carefully decant the soup back into the pot. Check to see if there's any dirt or grit at the bottom and hold back the last few spoonfuls if necessary. Put all the reserved mushrooms into the pot, bring the soup back to the boil, and simmer for 15 minutes. Season well with salt and pepper and refrigerate, at least overnight.

Reheat the soup and serve as suggested in the headnote.

ROASTED ONION AND GARLIC SOUP WITH GOAT CHEESE CROUTONS

Use any good meat, game, or poultry stock to make this intensely flavored soup. To allow the flavor to develop to the fullest, make the soup two or three days in advance.

Serves 8

1 pound garlic, about 7 large heads
2 pounds onions
¼ cup extra virgin olive oil
Coarse salt and freshly ground pepper
½ cup dry white wine
10 cups Chicken Stock, page 31, or Rich Meat Stock, page 32

FOR THE GOAT CHEESE CROUTONS
3½ ounces fresh goat cheese
1 teaspoon chopped parsley
1 tablespoon shallot minced as fine as possible
½ teaspoon fresh thyme leaves
16 Garlic Croutons, page 297

Preheat the oven to 300°F.

Cut the heads of garlic in half crosswise and boil in lightly salted water for 5 minutes.

Cut the onions into 6 wedges each and lay them in a 9-by-13-inch roasting pan. Scatter the blanched garlic on top, pour the oil over all, and season with salt and pepper. Roast the onions and garlic for 2 hours, until both are very soft.

Put the onions and garlic in a soup pot. Over medium heat, deglaze the roasting pan with the wine and add it to the soup pot. Add the stock, cover the pot, bring to the boil, and simmer the soup for 1 hour. Put the soup through a food mill into a saucepan and return it to the heat. Boil for 15 minutes to reduce it a bit and put it through a strainer, rubbing through the garlic and onions. Refrigerate the soup, at least overnight. Reheat the soup and reseason it with salt and/or pepper.

Make the croutons: Using a rubber spatula, combine the goat cheese, parsley, shallot, and thyme thoroughly and spread the mixture on the garlic croutons. Just before serving, heat the croutons in a 300°F oven until the cheese has just begun to melt.

Ladle the hot soup into warm bowls and float a crouton on each one. Pass the remaining croutons on a plate.

OYSTER STEW WITH LEEKS

The simplest and the best, this nearly traditional oyster stew makes a great prelude to a Thanksgiving or Christmas Eve dinner. Have the oysters shucked to order. Use Bluepoints or another medium-size oyster.

Serves 6

½ cup sliced leeks, white part only
½ cup finely sliced celery (use only the pale, tender inner stalks)
2 tablespoons unsalted butter
½ teaspoon chopped fresh thyme leaves
½ cup good-quality dry white wine
2 cups Chicken Stock, page 31
2 cups heavy cream
1 pint freshly shucked oysters with their liquor (about 36 oysters)

Soften the leeks and celery in the butter, without allowing them to brown, for 6 or 7 minutes. Stir in the thyme leaves, add the wine, and reduce until almost dry. Add the stock, bring to a boil, and simmer for 5 minutes. Add the cream and bring back to the boil. Add the oysters with their liquor, bring to a boil, and simmer the soup for a minute or 2, just until the oysters curl at the edges. Serve immediately.

GREEN SALAD

We've come a long way from iceberg lettuce salads, and Hudson River Valley farmers are constantly expanding the range of salad greens now available to us. Only ten years ago it would have been hard to imagine the variety and the excellent quality of the salad greens and herbs we have now begun to take for granted. Demanding chefs have encouraged farmers to produce finer greens of all kinds and farmers have responded by growing the makings of more flavorful and tender salads. They often use organic methods; greenhouses and hydroponic growing techniques make local produce available year round. The response of an enthusiastic public, willing to try (and pay top dollar for) exotic as well as good-quality familiar produce, has led growers to offer their own mixes of greens (mesclun). Today, in farmstands, greenmarkets, and fine produce stores there are little bins of beautiful green and red salad greens, such as tatsoi, mizuna, mâche, dandelion, oak leaf lettuces, and arugula, encouraging us to develop our own favorite combinations of young, delicate, and mellow; peppery and spicy; sweet, sour, and bitter. An abundance of fresh herbs, including sorrel, chives, dill, green basil, opal basil, chervil, tarragon, and many others can now be readily used not only in cooking but in combination with salad greens or in a salad by themselves (see Herb Salad with Lemon Vinaigrette, page 55).

As for preparation, there are only three things to remember about preparing fresh, crisp, and tender greens for salad: Wash them carefully, dry them thoroughly, and cut or break them into pieces that are easy to manage with a fork. Always wash greens by immersing them in a large quantity (such as a sinkful) of water, swishing them around vigorously and lifting them out of the water, leaving behind any dirt and debris. Spin the greens in a salad spinner or spread them on clean towels and roll them up, pressing gently to dry them thoroughly. This is an important step. Water remaining on the greens will dilute your salad dressing. Cut or break the greens into bite-size pieces and add only enough dressing to coat each leaf without leaving a pool in the plate or bowl.

BASIC GREEN SALAD

A generous handful of greens makes a good-sized serving. Start by tossing the greens with a tablespoon of vinaigrette per handful, adding more to taste.

Serves 4 to 6

½ pound *mesclun* or mixed greens and herbs of your choice, prepared for salad
½ cup Mustard Herb Vinaigrette, page 286

SUGGESTED GARNISHES
½ cup Garlic Roasted Walnuts, page 299
¼ cup grated Coach Farm Aged Grating Stick
2 or 3 buttons warm Hollow Road Sheep's Milk Cheese, cut in half, brushed with olive oil
    and broiled 2 minutes until just melting
½ cup cold Braised Wild Mushrooms, page 199
¼ pound blanched asparagus or green beans, cut into 2-inch pieces
I cup sliced raw mushrooms

Toss the greens with enough vinaigrette to coat each leaf. If you wish, garnish the salad with one of the suggested additions.

HERB SALAD WITH LEMON VINAIGRETTE

A relative newcomer to the Hudson Valley, an exciting array of fresh herbs is grown in greenhouses throughout the region. This is one salad you can make year round, adjusting the ingredients to what is available at the moment. The intense flavor of the herbs in their sprightly vinaigrette provides a surprise to the palate; a small serving brightens the simplest plate of sliced or grilled meat or provides a wonderful foil for a country-style pâté.

Serves 6 to 8 as a salad, 12 or more as a garnish

1 bunch sorrel (about ½ pound)
1 bunch basil
1 bunch opal basil
1 bunch tarragon
1 bunch chervil
1 bunch dill
1 bunch chives

FOR THE LEMON VINAIGRETTE
2 tablespoons white wine vinegar
juice of ½ large lemon
2 shallots, cut into fine julienne
Coarse salt and freshly ground pepper
½ cup extra virgin olive oil

Thoroughly wash and dry all the herbs. As you prepare the herbs, put them in a salad bowl. Trim the stems from the sorrel and cut the leaves in half. Strip off the leaves of the green basil, the opal basil, and the tarragon and discard the stems. Take sprigs of chervil and dill from the main stems and discard the stems. Cut the chives into 3-inch lengths.

Make the vinaigrette: In a bowl, whisk together the vinegar, lemon juice, shallots, and a little salt and pepper. Still whisking, add the olive oil in a thin stream. Pour half the vinaigrette over the herbs in the bowl and toss gently until all the leaves are lightly dressed. Taste the salad and add more vinaigrette to taste.

ARUGULA AND CELERY ROOT SALAD WITH HAZELNUTS AND AGED GOAT CHEESE

At Coach Dairy Goat Farm in Pine Plains, New York, the Cahn family produces very high-quality European-style goat cheeses. A pungent byproduct of the cheesemaking is their very unusual grating stick. You can obtain it by mail order, page 301.

Serves 6

2 bunches arugula
1 small celery root, peeled
3 medium endives, wiped clean
½ cup hazelnuts, rough chopped
1 recipe Mustard Herb Vinaigrette, page 286, made with balsamic vinegar
½ log Coach Farm Aged Grating Stick

Trim the arugula of tough stems, wash and dry the leaves, and cut them into 1-inch strips. Grate the celery root; you should have about 1 cup. Cut the root ends off the endives and separate the leaves.

In a frying pan over medium-high heat, toast the hazelnuts, tossing them constantly, until they are fragrant and slightly browned, 3 or 4 minutes. Set them aside.

Prepare the vinaigrette.

Assemble the salad on a round platter or on individual salad plates. Fan the endive leaves around the edge of the platter and sprinkle them with 4 tablespoons of vinaigrette. Toss the arugula with 2 or 3 tablespoons of vinaigrette and mound it in the center. Strew the grated celery root over the arugula and scatter on the toasted hazelnuts. Sprinkle a little more vinaigrette over the top and grate the goat cheese lightly over all.

ENDIVE, APPLE, AND ROASTED WALNUT SALAD WITH LITTLE RAINBOW BERKSHIRE BLUE CHEESE

This wonderful fall or winter salad takes you on a tour of the Hudson Valley, with its walnuts, apples, and local blue cheese. Even endives are now being grown in the Valley.

Serves 4

½ cup Garlic Roasted Walnuts, page 299
½ cup Mustard Herb Vinaigrette, page 286
4 endives
1 cup mixed baby greens or shredded leaf lettuce
2 small apples, peeled and grated
2 ounces Little Rainbow Berkshire Blue Cheese

Prepare the walnuts and the vinaigrette.

Wipe the endives clean with a damp paper towel and trim the bottoms. Separate one of the endives into leaves and place them pointed side up around the inside of a salad bowl. Mound the greens in the center of the endive leaves. Cut the remaining endives in half vertically, remove the cores, and cut the leaves vertically into ¼-inch shreds. Cover the greens with the shredded endive.

On the coarse side of a grater, grate each apple over the endive. Crumble the cheese over the apples. Crush the walnuts slightly in your hand and scatter them over the salad.

At the table, sprinkle the vinaigrette over the salad, toss, and serve.

SHAD,
TROUT,
&
OTHER
FISH

For centuries before and since Henry Hudson first sailed into the glorious river, the "mighty Hudson" has provided a matchless source of food, a highway for commerce, and a livelihood for generations of people who live in the fertile valley that surrounds it. Until the twentieth century, the river and its tributaries teemed with sturgeon, shad, trout, striped bass, and oysters. Of these, shad and trout are still abundant, bass is steadily returning and breeders are gradually reintroducing oysters.

In this chapter, native fish are combined with a variety of the Valley's seasonal produce; in a few recipes, historical Hudson Valley fish preparations are presented in a new, improved version.

SHAD

Shad is one of the glories of the Hudson River, eagerly awaited and appreciated each spring. The many shad festivals and shad fries held up and down the river are local celebrations complete with blaring country music, "crafts" booths, boat rides, and the smoke from immense drums of glowing wood or charcoal where shad fillets are grilled to a fare-thee-well and taste amazingly good. Roe is fried and eaten in sandwiches; planked shad (see recipe page 64) is traditional fare. Sophisticated diners in New York City eat shad chiefly in restaurants because they don't know how easy it is to prepare at home. Known for its delicious roe, the fish itself has a unique and wonderful flavor. It also has more bones than most fish—769 of them. It's not enough to buy fillets of shad; you have to buy "boned fillets." Only then do you know that the rib bones have been removed. But it is surprisingly easy to make a whole bony shad easy to eat. If a whole shad is cooked slowly, with enough liquid, in a tightly sealed baking pan, it emerges succulent, firm, and, amazingly, without bones. During the long, slow cooking, the bones actually dissolve, something you will probably have to see to believe. Try it. It's undoubtedly the only fish dish you can put up to cook when you leave for work in the morning and serve to guests for an elegant and unusual dinner when you get home.

WHOLE SHAD BAKED IN MILLBROOK CHARDONNAY

For a wonderful spring dinner, serve some simply prepared asparagus and new potatoes with this shad.

Serves 6

A 4- to 5-pound whole shad, cleaned and scaled
1 lemon, cut in 8 wedges
½ bunch parsley
Coarse salt and freshly ground pepper
1 medium onion, sliced
1 stalk celery, sliced
1 carrot, peeled and sliced in rounds
2 bay leaves
3 cups dry white wine such as Millbrook Chardonnay
3 cups Fish Stock, page 35, or Chicken Stock, page 31

Preheat the oven to 275°F.

Rinse the fish well inside and out and wipe it dry with paper towels. Put half the lemon, half the parsley, and some salt and freshly ground pepper in the cavity of the fish.

Spread the sliced vegetables in a flameproof baking dish large enough to hold the fish, and place the fish in the pan. Pour the wine and stock over it and add the bay leaves and the remaining lemon and parsley. Using 2 or 3 layers of heavy-duty aluminum foil, cover the pan completely, tucking the foil tightly around the edges of the pan so no steam can escape. Put the pan over a burner on top of the stove and bring the liquid to a boil. If you see any steam escaping from the pan, tighten the seal, using additional foil if necessary, until no steam escapes.

Place the pan in the oven and let the fish bake for 6 to 7 hours. Using a large spoon, cut the fish into serving pieces. Garnish the fish with some of the vegetables and pour some of the delicious pan juices over each serving.

WHOLE SHAD BAKED IN MILK WITH POTATOES AND BACON

This familiar combination of fish with bacon, potatoes, and milk is reminiscent of a colonial fish chowder.

Serves 6

A 4- to 5-pound whole shad, cleaned and scaled
Coarse salt and freshly ground pepper
1 large onion, sliced
3 large baking potatoes, peeled and sliced thin
2 bay leaves
2 or 3 sprigs fresh thyme or ½ teaspoon dried thyme
5 or 6 slices thick-sliced bacon (enough to wrap the fish completely)
4 cups milk
2 cups Chicken Stock, page 31

Preheat the oven to 275°F.

Rinse the fish well inside and out and dry it with paper towels. Season it with salt and freshly ground pepper.

In a flameproof baking pan large enough to hold the fish, make a bed of the sliced onion and potatoes, the thyme, and the bay leaves. Season with salt and pepper.

Wrap the fish in the bacon slices and lay it on the vegetables. Pour in the milk and stock.

Using 2 or 3 layers of heavy-duty aluminum foil, cover the pan completely, tucking the foil tightly around the edges of the pan so no steam can escape. Put the pan over a burner on top of the stove and bring the liquid to a boil. If you see any steam escaping from the pan, tighten the seal, using additional foil if necessary, until no steam escapes.

Place the pan in the oven and let the fish bake for 6 to 7 hours. Using a large spoon, cut the fish into serving pieces. Include some potatoes and a big spoonful of delicious pan juices with each serving.

BAKED SHAD FILLETS
WITH SORREL SAUCE

The tang of sorrel perfectly complements the rich flavor of shad. You may cook some shad roe in the baking pan along with the shad; it will be done at the same time and it also is very good with the sorrel sauce.

Serves 4

FOR THE SAUCE
¼ pound sorrel
½ cup heavy cream
1 tablespoon chopped chives
Coarse salt and freshly ground pepper

FOR THE FISH
2 boned shad fillets, about ¾ pound each
Coarse salt and freshly ground pepper
2 tablespoons unsalted butter, softened
4 tablespoons heavy cream

Make the sauce: Trim the tough stems from the sorrel and shred the leaves fine, setting aside a little for garnish. Wash the leaves and put them in a saucepan. There will be enough water clinging to the leaves to cook the sorrel. Over medium heat, cook the sorrel for 3 or 4 minutes, stirring constantly, until it is soft and wilted and forms a puree.

In a small saucepan, bring the cream to a boil and let it simmer for 2 or 3 minutes to reduce it slightly. Stir in the sorrel puree and simmer for another minute or two. Strain the sauce, stir in the chives, and season the sauce with some salt and pepper.

Preheat the oven to 450°F.

Season the fish on both sides with salt and pepper. Butter a shallow casserole and lay the fish in it in one layer, skin side down. Dot the fish with butter and spoon on the cream. Bake the fish for 8 minutes, then turn on the broiler and broil it for 4 minutes.

Reheat the sauce and put it in a sauceboat. Serve the fish from the casserole, garnished with some of the reserved finely shredded sorrel, and spoon some sorrel sauce over each serving.

CEDAR-PLANKED SHAD
WITH CHERVIL VINAIGRETTE

Cooking shad on wood planks is an old Hudson River tradition, probably learned from the Indians. Fillets of shad are held to the plank by ribbons of bacon tacked down with nails. The Indians propped the 6-foot plank at an angle downwind from a charcoal or hardwood fire and the shad was gently cooked by indirect heat and flavored with the smoke. In this adaptation, you can plank the shad in your own oven and enjoy the delicate flavor the wood imparts. Serve the shad with Sorrel Mashed Potatoes, page 188.

Serves 4

Equipment: 2 pieces of cedar, 6 inches wide by 14 inches long and
　　　　　　½ inch thick (obtainable at a lumber yard)
　　　　　　12 metal tacks or staples

2 boned shad fillets, ¾ pound each
Coarse salt and freshly ground pepper
6 slices bacon

FOR THE CHERVIL VINAIGRETTE
2 tablespoons dry white wine
2 tablespoons fresh lemon juice
I teaspoon grated fresh ginger
2 tablespoons chopped fresh chervil
I tablespoon extra virgin olive oil

Preheat the oven to 400°F.

Season the fish on both sides with salt and pepper and lay each fillet, skin side down, on one of the planks. Lay 3 slices of bacon across each fillet, trim the ends of the bacon to within ½ inch of the edge of the plank, and attach the ends of the bacon to the plank with tacks or large staples.

Make the vinaigrette: Combine the ingredients in a jar, cover, and shake well.

Place the planks on a baking sheet on the bottom shelf of the oven and bake for 25 minutes. Then place the baking sheet 12 inches from the broiler element and broil for 5 minutes. Present the fish on the planks and pass a bowl of the chervil vinaigrette.

If you want to reuse the planks, scrub them very thoroughly in soapy water, rinse, and dry in the sun.

SHAD ROE

Along with ramps, asparagus, fiddlehead ferns, rhubarb, and sorrel, eating shad roe is considered a rite of spring for many who wait impatiently all year for its short season. Perhaps one of the reasons shad is so treasured is that it's one of the few truly seasonal foods left; if you don't manage to get it between the blooming of the forsythia and the lilacs, you have to wait a whole year. Because local supplies of Hudson River shad were greatly diminished by pollution during the 1960s and '70s, many people growing up during those years never had a chance to cultivate a taste for shad roe. They are missing out on one of the region's great fish dishes. It seems safe to assume that now that shad from the Hudson is once again abundant, its popularity will be restored, especially if an important lesson learned from other fish cookery is applied to shad roe: Don't overcook it. There's no reason for shad roe to be cooked until it is stiff, dry, gray, and grainy. To taste it as it should be, tender and moist with a faintly rosy tinge, pay special attention to cooking times in the recipes that follow. The first is for shad filled with its own seasoned roe. The second is for poached shad roe cleverly combined with three other kinds of eggs—red and black caviars and hard-boiled eggs. The third is a shad roe classic, sautéed and served with bacon, brown butter, and capers.

BONELESS SHAD LAYERED WITH ITS ROE

This easy-to-prepare dish makes the most of both the fish and its delicious roe. Be sure to buy boned shad fillets. Each fillet is cut down the middle to remove the small bones, leaving two flaps that can be opened out. Open the flaps, spread the roe filling over the surface of the fillet, and close the flaps to cover the roe. Serve with boiled new potatoes and Stir-Fried Asparagus and Ramps, page 212.

Serves 4

FOR THE ROE FILLING

1 medium pair shad roe, 7 or 8 ounces
1 tablespoon soft unsalted butter
Coarse salt and freshly ground pepper
½ teaspoon pureed garlic
1 tablespoon chopped chives
1 teaspoon fresh lemon juice

2 boned shad fillets, ¾ pound each
Nonstick spray

FOR THE CRUMB TOPPING

1 cup fresh white bread crumbs
2 tablespoons capers, minced
4 tablespoons unsalted butter, melted
Lemon wedges for garnish

Preheat the oven to 450°F.

Make the filling: Using scissors, carefully split the membrane around the roe and spread the roe open. Using a teaspoon, gently scrape all the eggs away from the membrane and put them in a bowl. Using your forefinger to stir gently, combine the roe with the soft butter and the seasonings.

Season the fish fillets on both sides with salt and freshly ground pepper. Spray the bottom of a shallow baking pan with nonstick spray and lay the fish in the pan, skin side down. Fold open the sides of the fillets and gently spread half of the roe filling in a thin layer over each fillet. Fold the sides of the fish over the filling. Put the bread crumbs in a bowl and combine them with the capers and melted butter. Pat half the mixture over each fish and bake for 20 minutes. Transfer the fish to a warm platter and serve with lemon wedges.

POACHED SHAD ROE WITH CAVIAR SAUCE

This is a very elegant and delicate dish and should be reserved for a romantic evening or for very discerning guests. Serve it with West Park Wine Cellars Chardonnay.

Serves 4 as an appetizer, 2 as a main course

GARNISH
½ cup White Wine and Butter Sauce (recipe follows)
2 teaspoons salmon roe
2 teaspoons osetra caviar
I hard-boiled egg white, chopped fine
I hard-boiled egg yolk, chopped fine
I tablespoon finely chopped chives

I tablespoon unsalted butter
½ cup Fish Stock, page 35, or water
¼ cup good-quality dry white wine
I small shallot, chopped fine
2 medium pairs shad roe, 7 or 8 ounces each

Preheat the oven to 400°F.

Make the butter sauce and have the remaining garnish ingredients ready.

Put the butter, stock or water, wine, and shallot in a 12-inch ovenproof skillet. Add the roe, bring the liquid to a gentle boil, cover, and simmer 2 minutes. Very gently turn the roe over, cover, put the pan in the oven, and cook for another 8 minutes.

Remove the roe from the liquid and cut the pairs apart. Using scissors or your fingers, trim away any unsightly membrane. Place the roe on warm plates.

Gently fold the caviars into the butter sauce and spoon 2 tablespoons of sauce over each half roe. Garnish each serving with a thin line of chopped egg white, chopped yolk, and chopped chives. Serve with boiled new potatoes.

WHITE WINE AND BUTTER SAUCE

This is a basic sauce with many uses. It can be flavored many different ways (see end of recipe) and is a good quick sauce to use on grilled fish and seafood as well as delicately flavored meats.

Makes 1 cup sauce

½ cup good-quality dry white wine
1 tablespoon plus 1 teaspoon white wine vinegar
2 shallots, peeled and sliced thin
2 mushrooms, sliced
1 clove garlic, smashed and peeled
pinch dried thyme
1 bay leaf
1 tablespoon lemon juice
1 cup (½ pound) cold unsalted butter, cut in large dice

Put the wine, 1 tablespoon of the vinegar, shallots, mushrooms, garlic, thyme and bay leaf in a small nonreactive saucepan, bring to a boil and simmer over medium heat until the mixture is nearly dry. The sauce can be made up to this point 4 hours ahead. Finish the sauce as directed below.

About 45 minutes before serving time, finish the sauce. Heat the wine mixture over low heat and stir in the lemon juice and the teaspoon of vinegar. Over very low heat, whisk in the cold butter 1 or 2 pieces at a time. As the butter melts the sauce will become creamy. Keep adding butter until all has been incorporated and continue to whisk the sauce over low heat for 3 or 4 minutes. Don't let it boil. Strain the sauce into a bowl or the top of a double boiler, and keep it warm over hot water, whisking from time to time.

~ Variations ~

RED WINE AND BUTTER SAUCE: Substitute red wine for the white wine and red wine vinegar for the white wine vinegar.

WHITE WINE AND BUTTER SAUCE WITH HERBS: Whisk in 1 tablespoon finely chopped parsley and 1 tablespoon finely chopped chives, dill, chervil, and tarragon just before serving.

CAVIAR SAUCE: Gently fold 2 tablespoons osetra caviar and 1 tablespoon salmon roe into the finished sauce just before serving.

SAUTÉED SHAD ROE
WITH BACON AND CAPERS

Serve this classic with plain boiled potatoes and a big green salad.

Serves 4 as an appetizer, 2 as a main course

4 slices bacon
1 cup flour for dredging the roe
Coarse salt and freshly ground pepper
2 medium pairs shad roe, 7 or 8 ounces each, each pair separated,
    using scissors, and membrane trimmed
3 tablespoons vegetable oil

FOR THE SAUCE
2 tablespoons unsalted butter
Juice of ½ lemon
1 tablespoon finely chopped parsley or mixed fresh herbs
1 teaspoon capers

2 or 4 lemon wedges

Fry the bacon until crisp and set it aside. Season the flour with a little salt and pepper and spread it over a dinner plate. Working with one-half roe at a time and handling it very carefully so as not to break its delicate membrane, dip the roe in the flour to coat it lightly on both sides. Gently shake off excess flour.

Line a platter with paper towels and set it next to the stove. Assemble the sauce ingredients and put them close at hand.

In a 12-inch skillet, heat the oil over medium heat until it is hot and sauté the roe for 5 minutes. Very carefully turn the roe over and sauté for 5 minutes on the second side, until it is crisp and almost cooked through. Put the roe on the lined platter and immediately make the sauce.

In a small clean sauté pan, melt the butter over high heat, shaking it constantly, until the foam subsides and the butter is brown. Remove the pan from the heat and swirl in the lemon juice and the seasonings.

Put the roe on plates and spoon a little sauce over each serving. Garnish each roe with crisp bacon and a wedge of lemon.

TROUT

April Fool's Day marks the official beginning of trout season in the Hudson River Valley. This is highly appropriate because only fools would expect trout to be so foolish as to run in such frigid waters . . . but at least the fishermen get a chance to try out all their gear and begin a season of fishing and camaraderie. By May first it has warmed up a little and streams all over the region are full of fishermen in waders, casting for one of the few indigenous fish. Historically the brown trout was the most prolific here, but today the streams are stocked with rainbow, speckled, and brook trout from the many trout farms all over the Hudson River Valley.

PAN-FRIED TROUT WITH LOVAGE AND PARSLEY SAUCE

Lovage is a perennial herb, handsome enough to grow in your flower border. It's an old-fashioned herb that tastes especially good with trout. It's available all summer and tastes like a combination of celery and parsley. Lovage may be hard to find if you're not near a greenmarket, but ask at your produce market or a nursery.

Serves 4

4 whole 12-ounce trout, cleaned
½ small onion, sliced
2 cups heavy cream
Coarse salt and freshly ground pepper

FOR THE SAUCE
½ cup packed lovage or celery leaves
I cup packed parsley leaves (no stems)
½ cup dry white wine
I small shallot, sliced thin

2 teaspoons fresh lemon juice
4 tablespoons unsalted butter, cut in 4 pieces

2 cups flour for dredging the trout
Vegetable oil for frying

Using sharp scissors, trim the trout of heads, tails, and fins. Put all the trimmings in a saucepan with the sliced onion and a cup of water and simmer for 20 minutes to make a simple fish stock. Strain and reserve for making the sauce. Put the cream in a baking pan and season it with salt and pepper. Lay the trout in the cream, turn to coat all surfaces, and let it marinate for 10 to 15 minutes, turning frequently.

Assemble all the sauce ingredients and set them aside.

Preheat the oven to 200°F.

You will probably have to cook the trout in 2 batches. Put the flour in a shallow pan and season it with salt and pepper. In your largest sauté pan, heat oil to a depth of ¼ inch over medium-high heat. Lay the first 2 trout in the pan of flour and coat them heavily. Turn to coat all surfaces and gently lay them in the hot oil. Turn the heat to medium and sauté the trout until they are well browned on the first side, about 6 to 8 minutes; turn the trout over and cook 4 to 5 minutes on the second side. Place the trout in the oven on a platter. Cook the second batch. You can let the cooked trout rest in the oven up to 10 minutes while you make the sauce.

Set aside a few sprigs of lovage and parsley for garnish. In a small saucepan, bring the wine, shallot, and lemon juice to a boil. Reduce the mixture until almost dry, add the reserved fish stock, and bring it to a boil. Simmer for a moment and add the lovage and parsley. As soon as the mixture boils, pour it into the container of an electric blender, add the butter, and blend until the sauce is green and smooth.

Peel the skin off the top of each trout, fold it in half, and lay it over the tail end of the fish. Spoon a band of sauce across the fish above the skin. Decorate the platter with sprigs of lovage and parsley. Serve the crisp skin with the fish; it's good to eat.

ROASTED TROUT WITH SUMMER VEGETABLES

The trout and summer vegetables make a wonderful combination, but they're also excellent as two separate dishes.

Serves 4

10 tablespoons extra virgin olive oil
2 small Italian eggplants (about ¼ pound each), cut in 6 slices each
Coarse salt and freshly ground pepper
I medium zucchini, cut on the diagonal into 12 slices
I medium yellow summer squash, cut on the diagonal into 12 slices
¾ cup shredded basil leaves
I medium onion, cut in half and each half cut in 6 slices
I large ripe tomato, cut in half and each half cut in 6 slices
4 whole 12-ounce trout, cleaned and boned, with heads removed and fins trimmed
Juice of I lemon
Fresh basil leaves for garnish

Lightly oil a cookie sheet, lay the eggplant slices on it, sprinkle them with salt, and brush a little more olive oil over them. Broil the eggplant 5 minutes on each side and let it cool. Turn the oven down to 450°F.

Combine the zucchini and yellow squash in a bowl and toss with ¼ cup olive oil, the shredded basil, and some salt and pepper. Lengthwise on an oiled 10-by-15-inch jelly-roll pan, arrange the sliced vegetables in sets consisting of I slice each zucchini, yellow squash, tomato, onion, and eggplant laid in an overlapping pattern. You will have enough vegetables to make 3 rows with four 5-slice sets, or 20 slices, per row. Sprinkle any oil and basil remaining in the bowl over the vegetables.

Bake the vegetables for about 30 minutes, until they are tender and the pan juices have evaporated. Using a spatula, lift the sets of vegetables off the pan and arrange them decoratively around the edge of a large platter that will eventually hold the fish. The vegetables may be baked several hours in advance and served at room temperature.

If you have cooked the vegetables in advance, preheat the oven to 400°F. If you have cooked the vegetables immediately before cooking the fish, turn the oven down to 400°F.

Season the cavity of each trout with salt and about a tablespoon of shredded basil. Oil a baking pan and lay the trout in it. Sprinkle the lemon juice and the remaining olive oil over the trout and roast them for 10 minutes. Turn on the broiler and broil the trout, without turning them over, for 5 minutes.

Carefully transfer the trout to the prepared platter. Pour the pan juices over the fish and decorate the platter with the fresh basil leaves.

POACHED TROUT FILLED WITH SEAFOOD MOUSSE

The contrast between the herbaceous green of the mousse and the delicate pale pink flesh of the trout makes this dish almost as appealing to look at as to eat. Preparing this dish takes a bit of time and trouble, but your efforts will be rewarded. In a variation of this recipe, cook the trout a day ahead and serve it cold with Red Pepper Vinaigrette.

Serves 6

FOR THE SEAFOOD MOUSSE
¼ pound boneless, skinless, firm white-fleshed fresh fish such as pike, snapper, or bass
1 ounce scallops
1 egg white
⅓ cup heavy cream
2 teaspoons brandy
Coarse salt and freshly ground white pepper
1 teaspoon chopped fresh tarragon
½ cup chopped chives

1 small onion, sliced very thin
1 small carrot, sliced very thin
1 stalk celery, sliced very thin
1 sprig fresh thyme, chopped fine
Three 16-ounce trout, cleaned and boned, with heads removed and fins trimmed
1 recipe Red Pepper Vinaigrette, page 288, for cold poached trout
1 lemon, sliced
¾ cup Fish Stock, page 35
¼ cup dry white wine
2 tablespoons chopped chives

Make the seafood mousse: Be sure all the ingredients are very cold. Put the fish and scallops in the bowl of a food processor with the egg white and process until very smooth. Then, with the processor running, add the cream in a thin stream until it is absorbed. Add the remaining mousse ingredients and process until everything is thoroughly blended. Chill the mousse, covered, until you are ready to fill the fish. You can prepare the mousse mixture up to 6 hours ahead.

Preheat the oven to 350°F.

Spread the sliced vegetables and thyme in a 9-by-13-inch flameproof roasting pan. Open each fish flat, sprinkle the cavities with salt and pepper, and spread ⅓ of the mousse mixture over each fish. Fold the fish in half, pressing the halves gently together. Using a rubber spatula, clear any excess mousse from the sides of the trout, leaving a clean layer of green showing between the fish halves. Lay the fish over the vegetables, squeeze the lemon slices over them, and lay the lemon slices on top. Pour the stock and wine over the fish. Cover the pan well and bring to a boil on top of the stove. Put the pan in the oven and poach for 30 minutes. Take it out and let the trout rest, covered, for 10 minutes. Remove the lemon slices and peel the skin from the top of the trout.

Cut each trout in half crosswise and arrange on a platter. Scatter the pan vegetables decoratively over the fish. Place the platter in the turned-off oven. Strain the pan juices into a saucepan, bring to a boil, and, stirring from time to time, boil until the juices are reduced by ⅓. Taste and season the sauce. Pour the sauce over the fish and sprinkle with the chopped chives.

SAUTÉED STURGEON WITH MORELS AND SPRING SAGE

Sturgeon were so plentiful in the Hudson fifty years ago that winter fishermen fishing on the ice would stack them up as a barrier against the wind. In 1993, just 24 sturgeon permits were issued to Hudson River fishermen, and only half of them were used. The fish have been reproducing so slowly that state environmental officials felt they had to limit fishing to save the species. It is sad to think that this great food fish may be lost to us. Try to get it while you can; it's delicious paired with the last of spring's morels and the first tender leaves of sage, one of the first perennial herbs to come back each spring. In an issue of *Natural History Magazine* devoted to wild mushrooms, Raymond Sokolov named this dish as one of his favorites.

Buy sturgeon from the fillet. Ask the fishmonger to trim the fillet of all cartilage and bones, then cut it on the diagonal into 3-ounce slices.

Serves 4

6 tablespoons unsalted butter
I large shallot, sliced thin
½ pound fresh morels, stemmed and the caps cut into I-inch slices if they are large
I tablespoon chopped fresh sage leaves plus 4 sprigs sage flowers for garnish
½ cup dry white wine
I cup Chicken Stock, page 31
Coarse salt and freshly ground pepper
Olive oil for the pan
Eight 3-ounce slices sturgeon, each ½ inch thick

In a sauté pan, melt the butter and sauté the shallot over medium heat until it is lightly browned. Add the morels, sage, and wine, simmer for a minute or 2, and add the stock. Bring to a boil, season with salt and pepper, cover the pan, and simmer the mushrooms over medium-high heat for 10 minutes. Uncover the pan and reduce the sauce until it starts to thicken. The mushrooms can be prepared several hours in advance of serving.

Dip a paper towel in olive oil and wipe the surface of a nonstick sauté pan with it. Let the pan get hot over medium-high heat and sauté the fish for 3 minutes on each side. Turn off the heat, turn the fish over, and let it sit in the pan for another 3 minutes.

Place the fish on a warm platter, spoon the mushrooms over and around it, and decorate the platter with the sage flowers.

LOBSTER GRATIN
WITH SUPPAWN

Corn and lobsters have been eaten together in these parts for centuries in boiled or "shore" dinners, although it's usually corn on the cob. This dish demonstrates the incredible versatility of Suppawn (cornmeal mush, see page 208), and takes it to a level of sophistication that neither the American Indians nor the early settlers of this region ever dreamed of. Female lobsters are called for here for their meatier tails and their brightly colored roe (coral). Dividing the preparation of this most unusual dish over two days makes it manageable for a special occasion. The recipe will tell you what you can prepare a day ahead.

Serves 4

½ lemon
Coarse salt
Two 1½-pound female lobsters

FOR THE BROTH
4 tablespoons extra virgin olive oil
3 cloves garlic, chopped
3 shallots, chopped
3 mushrooms, sliced
1 leek, white part only, sliced
1 tomato, sliced
4 or 5 sprigs fresh parsley
1 large sprig fresh tarragon, including stems, chopped
1 teaspoon peppercorns
3 tablespoons tomato paste
⅛ teaspoon cayenne pepper
½ cup good-quality brandy
1 cup good-quality dry white wine
4 cups Chicken Stock, page 31
4 cups Fish Stock, page 35

GARNISH

1 large ripe tomato
1 red pepper, roasted and peeled
1 heaping tablespoon chopped tarragon
2 tablespoons chopped chives

1 recipe Suppawn, page 208, made without cheese but with fresh corn in season
Unsalted butter for gratin dish

Half fill a big pot with water, add the lemon juice and some salt, and bring it to a boil. Put in the lobsters and bring the water back to the boil. Start timing as soon as the water returns to the boil; the lobsters should cook for 12 minutes. Remove them from the pot and let them cool.

Shell the lobsters over a dish to catch the juices. Bend the tail back until it breaks from the body. Using scissors and being careful not to cut the meat, cut the thin shell on the underside of the tail and separate the sides of the shell to remove the tail meat in one piece. Using a mallet, gently crack the claw shells and remove the meat in one piece. Break off and reserve 8 of the legs and set them aside with the tail and claw meat. Using your fingers, remove and reserve all the green tomalley and the red coral from the bodies. Save the shells and the lobster bodies and juices.

Make the broth: Heat the olive oil over medium-high heat in a large, heavy-bottomed soup pot. Add the lobster shells (but not the bodies and juices) and all the broth ingredients up to but not including the tomato paste. Stir and sauté the mixture for 10 minutes. Stir in the tomato paste and the cayenne pepper and continue to cook, stirring frequently, for 10 minutes, until the mixture is as dry as it can be without sticking and burning. Add the brandy, the wine, and the lobster bodies and juices and stir well. Bring to a boil and simmer, uncovered, stirring from time to time, for about 20 minutes, or until the liquid has evaporated almost completely. Add the chicken and fish stocks, stir to combine everything thoroughly, and bring to a boil. Turn down the heat and simmer, uncovered, stirring frequently, for 1½ hours. Strain the broth through a colander into a large bowl or pot. Stir the shells and vegetables vigorously around in the colander and let them drain into the bowl for a few minutes. Discard the solids.

Strain the broth through a fine strainer into a saucepan, tapping the strainer to release all the liquid into the pan without pressing through any of the residue. Measure the broth. If you have more than 4 cups, reduce it to that amount. You can prepare the dish up to this point a day ahead. Let the broth cool and refrigerate it. Wrap the lobster meat, tomalley and coral, and the reserved legs in several layers of plastic wrap and refrigerate.

Next day, prepare the garnish and the suppawn. For the garnish, peel and seed the tomato and cut it into ½-inch dice. Seed the roasted pepper, trim it into a neat rectangle, and cut it into ¼-inch dice. You will need 2 tablespoons of diced pepper. Put the remaining diced pepper into the broth.

Trim the lobster tails into neat cylinders and slice each tail on the diagonal into 6 slices. Set the slices aside with the reserved claws and legs. Chop the trimmings and combine them with the coral and the tomalley.

Make the suppawn according to the directions on page 208, but omit the cheese. When the suppawn is cooked, but before it has set, put it into a mixing bowl and stir in the lobster trimmings, the coral and tomalley, half the chopped tarragon, the chopped chives, and 1 tablespoon of the minced roasted pepper. Mix well. Taste for seasoning and add salt and freshly ground pepper if needed.

Preheat the oven to 300°F. Butter well an 11-inch (5-cup) gratin dish. Spread half the suppawn mixture in the dish. Arrange 3 medallions of lobster in each of the 4 quarters of the dish, spread on the remaining suppawn and bake for 20 minutes. Warm the claw meat and the legs in a little of the broth and arrange 1 claw and 2 legs over each of the 4 sections of the dish. Divide the quarters with crossing rows of diced tomato.

Reheat and season the broth, adding to it any remaining tomato, the diced pepper, and the remaining chopped tarragon. Pour the broth into a small tureen and present the tureen and the gratin together with 4 large heated soup bowls. Place ¼ of the gratin in each bowl and ladle a cup of broth over it.

BLACKFISH WRAPPED IN BACON WITH ONION, ORANGE, AND FENNEL RELISH

During the summer you can find beautiful blackfish at greenmarkets and local fish stores. In other seasons, striped bass or red snapper make good substitutes. Serve with Braised Cabbage, page 101, and Roasted Garlic Mashed Potatoes, page 188.

Serves 4

Four 6-ounce portions blackfish fillet
8 thin bacon slices, at room temperature
Vegetable oil for frying

GARNISH
Onion, Orange, and Fennel Relish (recipe follows)
Fennel Oil, page 291, or extra virgin olive oil
Juice of ½ lemon

Fold and trim the pieces of fish to form compact rectangles about 1½ inches thick. Starting at one end, gently stretch the first slice of bacon around the fish and wrap in overlapping layers to make a tight, unbroken casing. The first slice of bacon will wrap half a portion; repeat with the second slice to complete the casing.

Preheat the oven to 200°F.

Line a baking sheet with several layers of paper towels and set it next to the stove.

In a skillet large enough to hold all the fish, heat ½ inch of vegetable oil over medium-high heat. Let the oil get hot but not smoking. It is hot enough when a little piece of bread sizzles and turns brown almost immediately.

When the oil is hot, place the fish in the pan. The oil should come at least halfway up the sides of the fish. Cook the fish for 5 minutes on the first side. Turn it over and cook for another 4 or 5 minutes. Regulate the heat so the bacon turns brown and crisp without burning and the fish cooks through. Put the fish on the towel-lined pan to drain, then put it on a platter in the warm oven for about 10 minutes.

Place the relish on a platter in 4 mounds and set a piece of fish on each one. Drizzle about a tablespoon of fennel oil over each serving and sprinkle with lemon juice.

ONION, ORANGE, AND FENNEL RELISH

1 sweet red onion
1 bulb fennel, trimmed of leaves and stems
¼ cup white wine vinegar
1 tablespoon extra virgin olive oil
1 teaspoon freshly ground black pepper
1 tablespoon chopped fennel tops or dill
1 navel orange

Slice the onion as thin as possible. Rinse well in cold water and drain. Shave the fennel on a *mandoline* or slice as thin as possible. Put the vegetables in a bowl and mix in the vinegar, the oil, the black pepper, and the fennel tops.

Grate 1 teaspoon of orange rind, zest only, and add to the onion mixture. Slice off the bottom and top ends of the orange. Cut off the peel, the white pith, and the membrane covering the flesh of the orange. Holding the orange in your hand over a bowl, insert a sharp knife between the segments, allowing the flesh of the orange to fall into the bowl, leaving the membrane behind. Rough chop the orange segments and squeeze all the juice from the membrane into the bowl. Using your hands, mix the orange and juice well with the onion and fennel, cover with plastic, and let the relish sit in the refrigerator for at least 4 hours or overnight. The relish will keep, refrigerated, for 1 week.

WORKING WITH A HISTORICAL RECIPE

In 1990 the New York Historical Society opened the Luman Reed Gallery as a home for a splendid collection of Hudson River School paintings that had been in storage for years. Luman Reed, whose estate had donated this collection to the Society, was a wealthy dry-goods merchant who worked in the butter and egg district of downtown Manhattan. He was an early and important patron of the painters of the Hudson River School, especially Asher Durand and Thomas Cole. The gallery was opening just around the time I frequently found myself researching old menus in the Historical Society library, where I found materials from Luman Reed's kitchen, including shopping lists and a menu from a banquet that had been given in his home. I adapted this into a historical menu that evoked the tastes and banqueting customs of the 1830s in New York. The menu was officially made part of the Historical Society collections at the reception held for the opening of the gallery. I wish I could say that I discovered wonderful recipes in these researches. The one from which I adapted the halibut recipe that follows consisted of the stark instruction to combine stale bread or crackers, milk, and fish and boil for 2 hours. I hope you like my adaptation.

HALIBUT BOILED IN MILK AND BREAD SAUCE

Serve with Steamed Ozettes, page 186.

Serves 4

1 small onion
1 carrot
2 stalks celery
1 small Kirby cucumber
4 large mushroom caps
4 tablespoons softened unsalted butter
1 cup fresh bread crumbs (loosely packed)
Four 6-ounce, 1½-inch-thick slices halibut from boneless fillet, not steaks
Coarse salt and freshly ground pepper
2 cups milk
1 cup Fish Stock, page 35
2 tablespoons chopped parsley

Bring a large pot of water to a boil.

While the water is heating, prepare the vegetables: Peel the onion and slice it thin. Peel the carrot, cut it in half lengthwise, and cut it on the diagonal into thin slices. Thinly slice the celery. Peel the cucumber, cut it in half lengthwise, seed it, and slice it thin on the diagonal. Slice the mushroom caps thin. Put the vegetables in a sieve and lower it into the boiling water to blanch for 3 minutes. Drain.

Using half the butter, thickly butter a 12-inch sauté pan. Mix the blanched vegetables with half the bread crumbs and line the bottom of the pan. Season the fish with salt and freshly ground pepper and lay it on the vegetables. Add the milk and stock and sprinkle on the remaining bread crumbs. Dot the fish with the remaining butter. Bring the liquid to a boil, turn down the heat, cover the pan, and simmer for 6 minutes. Turn off the heat and let the fish rest, covered, for 4 minutes. Put the fish on a platter. Stir together the vegetables and the sauce and spoon over the fish. Sprinkle on the chopped parsley and serve immediately.

ROASTED HOT OR COLD WHOLE STRIPED BASS WITH FENNEL

Striped bass, one of the great fish of the Hudson, has re-emerged from the disgrace of PCB pollution and is once more safe to eat. Its availability is a reflection of the encouraging restoration of the Hudson as a waterway that not only looks magnificent but is a mighty source of food for the entire region. Attempts to farm this splendid fish have been unsuccessful, producing a two-pound specimen with little flavor or texture, no rival for the uniquely flavorful, firm wild striped bass, which can weigh up to 70 pounds. In 1991 the season for harvesting this seasonal fish was extended, and it is now legal for commercial fishermen to catch ten-pound and over striped bass by line only (no nets) from September 15 through January 15. Celebrate the reappearance of this great fish by cooking a whole ten-pounder. Serve it hot with Braised Fennel and a creamy sauce. Or serve the bass at room temperature with Spicy Fennel Slaw and Tomato Vinaigrette.

Serves 8

A 10-pound line-caught striped bass, about 5½ pounds after cleaning, with head and tail
    removed and reserved to make stock
Coarse salt and freshly ground pepper
4 shallots, sliced
4 cloves garlic, sliced
¾ cup finely sliced fennel tops (stalks with a few leaves)
1 small onion, sliced
1 stalk celery, sliced
2 carrots, peeled and sliced thin
3 tablespoons extra virgin olive oil
1 cup good-quality dry white wine
2 cups Fish Stock (made with bass trimmings), page 35

FOR THE HOT SAUCE
½ cup Fish Stock, page 35
4 tablespoons arrowroot
½ cup heavy cream

I tablespoon chopped fennel tops or fresh dill
Lemon juice

FOR THE COLD FISH
I recipe Tomato Vinaigrette, page 289

GARNISHES
For hot fish: a double recipe of Braised Fennel, page 218
For cold fish: Spicy Fennel and Cabbage Slaw, page 219
          lemon slices

If you are serving the fish hot, make the Braised Fennel first and reheat it when you take the fish out of the oven. Preheat the oven to 425°F.

Rub the fish inside and out with salt and freshly ground pepper. Put the shallots, garlic, and fennel in the cavity and tie string around the fish in 3 places. Put the onion, celery, and carrots in a roasting pan, lay the fish on top, and pour the oil over all.

Bake the fish for 15 minutes. Add the wine and stock and continue to cook for 45 minutes more, until the internal temperature of the fish is 165°F. Let the fish rest in the pan for 15 minutes.

If you are serving the fish hot, transfer it to a platter and cover it loosely with foil to keep it warm. Make the sauce: Strain the pan juices into a saucepan and reserve the vegetables. Rinse out the baking pan with the fish stock and add it to the juices. Bring to a boil and simmer over very low heat for 10 minutes. Combine the arrowroot with 2 tablespoons of water, stir well, and add it to the pot. Whisk constantly as the sauce thickens. Over medium-low heat, stir in the cream and let the sauce simmer for 5 minutes, skimming off any foam. Just before serving, add the chopped fennel tops and taste for seasoning, adding salt, pepper, and lemon juice to taste.

Surround the fish with braised fennel. Arrange the reserved onion, celery, and carrot on top of the fish and garnish with a few branches of fennel leaves. Peel the skin from the top side of the fish as you serve it. Serve the sauce in a sauceboat.

If you are serving the fish cold, transfer the fish to a platter and peel off the skin while it is still warm. Cover loosely and allow the fish to come to room temperature, 3 to 4 hours. Strain the pan juices into a container and reserve for another use. Make the tomato vinaigrette and the fennel slaw. Garnish the platter with branches of fennel leaves and arrange lemon slices down the top of the fish.

STRIPED BASS POACHED IN MUSHROOM BROTH WITH CARROT VINAIGRETTE

This light meal in a bowl is delicate and hearty at the same time. Serve with plenty of good bread.

Serves 4

1 recipe Roasted Root Vegetables, page 228
1 recipe Carrot Vinaigrette, page 287
4 dried mushrooms, such as *porcini* or morels
1½ cups Fish Stock, page 35, heated to a boil
4 fresh mushrooms, sliced
2 tablespoons extra virgin olive oil
Four 6-ounce portions striped bass, 1½ inches thick
Coarse salt and freshly ground pepper
4 sprigs fresh chervil

Have ready the Roasted Root Vegetables and the Carrot Vinaigrette.

Reconstitute the dried mushrooms: Using your fingers, break the dried mushrooms into pieces, put them in a small saucepan, and pour the boiling fish stock over them. Set them aside to soak for 30 minutes. Drain the reconstituted mushrooms, reserving the liquid. Put the reserved mushroom liquid and the reconstituted mushrooms into a small saucepan, add the fresh mushrooms, and simmer over low heat for 20 minutes. Strain the mushroom liquid and set it and the mushrooms aside.

Preheat the oven to 450°F.

Pour 1 tablespoon of the olive oil into an ovenproof skillet or baking dish just large enough to hold the fish. Season the fish with salt and freshly ground pepper and put it in the pan. Add 1 cup of the mushroom broth, cover the pan, and bring to a boil. Put the pan in the oven and poach for 7 minutes. Turn the oven off and leave the fish in it for another 3 minutes.

In a large sauté pan, heat the remaining tablespoon of olive oil. Add the roasted vegetables and the reserved mushrooms and sauté over high heat just until the vegetables begin to caramelize. Add the remaining broth and simmer for 3 or 4 minutes.

Put the poached fish on a dish and return it to the oven. Add the fish cooking liquid to the simmering vegetables and season with salt and pepper.

Ladle the vegetables and the mushroom broth into 4 large warmed soup bowls and set a piece of fish in each bowl. Spoon 1 tablespoon of the carrot vinaigrette over each piece of fish and garnish with a sprig of chervil.

VENISON, PHEASANT, & OTHER GAME

In the course of an autumn afternoon's drive along Hudson Valley country roads it is not at all unusual to see deer, rabbits, and pheasant in the meadows, woods, and roadsides. The terrain of the Hudson Valley, its mountains, woods, and streams, makes it a natural habitat of game animals and birds. Deer, rabbits, partridge, quail, wild ducks, and turkeys, along with the humble squirrel and woodchuck, have always been hunted and eaten here. Though most of the game is indigenous, varieties such as pheasant, introduced to the region by early settlers, thrive in this setting. Today deer are so abundant in the Valley that much time and ingenuity are spent keeping them from eating people's vegetables and exotic shrubbery. Hunters shooting deer in the wild are lucky when they get one of these well-fed deer.

Although many people still hunt, very little of the game eaten nowadays is truly wild. In fact, only farm-raised game can be sold legally and even hunt clubs stock their territory with farm-bred birds. Because game is now readily available through the many game farms in the region, people are cooking and eating it for the first time. Today's game does not have the characteristically gamy taste that made many people timid about eating it. Although there are some who bemoan the loss of the strong, "high" flavor of aged game, the milder-tasting and more tender game available now has a wider appeal. One of the pleasures of eating game is its compatibility with great wines. Try serving game with one of the Hudson Valley's Burgundy-style reds such as Cascade Mountain Vineyards Private Reserve or a Bordeaux-style wine such as Cuvee des Vignerons from Benmarl Vineyards.

Through the sources listed on page 301 you can easily order game ranging from a 10-ounce saddle of rabbit to a 10-pound saddle of venison. The recipes in this section will give you an overview of game preparation. With 5 recipes for venison, you'll have a chance to use those mystery gift packages from well-intentioned hunters. Each game bird is cooked by a different method and served with its own special garnish. The chapter ends with the most unusual venison recipe you're ever likely to see.

COOKING GAME

Once you master the art of game cookery, you'll become the envy of many hunters and their families, and you'll probably become the recipient of gifts from those who know how to shoot game but not how to make it palatable. I have found that the trials encountered in preparing game (such as proper butchering, aging, and trimming) are well worth enduring for the pleasures of eating it. Game provides unusual flavors and textures along with the health benefits of eating low-fat "natural" meat with no added hormones or preservatives. Game is a natural to pair with bold, full-bodied wines; intense game stocks enhance soups and sauces. Most of all, the satisfaction is great when you can enjoy every aspect of the process, from shooting, butchering, and aging to cooking, serving, and eating the food you hunt.

General advice when cooking game: Cook most game birds medium to medium-rare. Hoofed game loin cuts should be cooked rare to medium-rare, whereas shoulders and legs, except for top rounds, should be braised or stewed. Reserve the top rounds for roasts or steaks.

MALLARD DUCK BREASTS WITH WILD RICE CUSTARD

Mallard ducks are found only in the wild and are available only during their season, October through February. If you don't shoot them yourself, you can order them through a specialty butcher or by mail order (see Sources, page 301). Mallards are smaller and much less fatty than domesticated varieties. The breasts of these ducks are denser, meatier, and more gamy than the ducks we are accustomed to and they have almost no fat layer. They lend themselves to being roasted and served rare to medium-rare as they are below. Serve the duck breasts with Wild Rice Custard.

Serves 6

3 mallard ducks

TO FILL THE CAVITIES
½ lemon, cut into 3 pieces
½ orange, cut into 3 pieces
3 bay leaves
I teaspoon dried thyme
I clove garlic, chopped
I small shallot, chopped
I tablespoon olive oil
Coarse salt and freshly ground pepper

FOR THE SAUCE
⅔ cup Hudson Valley Concord grape juice
⅔ cup good-quality port wine
6 tablespoons good-quality red wine vinegar
3 cups Chicken Stock, page 31

Wild Rice Custard (recipe follows)

GARNISH

6 small clusters Concord grapes
6 large sprigs fresh chervil

Preheat the oven to 400°F.

Remove the legs and thighs from the ducks and reserve for another use (see Cured Duck, page 141). Fill the cavity of each duck with ⅓ of the ingredients listed and tie the opening closed with string. Rub the ducks all over with the olive oil and season them with salt and pepper. Set them on a rack in a flameproof roasting pan and roast for 35 minutes. Let the ducks rest for 15 minutes.

While the ducks are roasting, start the sauce: Combine the grape juice, the port, and the vinegar in a 3-quart saucepan. Bring to a boil and reduce by half.

After they have rested, carve the ducks. Remove each duck breast in one piece, leaving all the bones attached to the carcass. The meat will be rare. Put the breasts, skin side up, on a broiler-proof platter and set them aside to reheat later. Reserve the carcasses.

Pour off any fat from the roasting pan and add the stock. Place the roasting pan over high heat, deglaze the pan, and pour the stock into the saucepan with the grape juice mixture. Add the reserved duck carcasses and cook over medium-high heat, turning frequently, for 20 minutes. Strain the sauce into another saucepan and simmer until it is reduced to 2 cups. The dish can be prepared up to this point 4 hours in advance.

While the sauce is simmering, prepare the Wild Rice Custards. You can prepare the custards 1 hour in advance; if you do so, remove them from the water bath and set them on a baking sheet. Twenty minutes before serving, reheat them in a preheated 275°F oven.

At serving time, broil the duck breasts, skin side up, just until they are warmed through, about 5 minutes. Invert the rice custards onto a warm serving platter and lean 1 breast on each custard. Spoon a little sauce over each breast and serve the remaining sauce in a sauceboat. Garnish the platter with Concord grapes and chervil.

WILD RICE CUSTARD

Serves 6

Equipment: Six 5-ounce ramekins
            nonstick spray

½ cup wild rice

1 tablespoon unsalted butter

2 tablespoons minced shallot

1 teaspoon minced garlic

2 tablespoons cream sherry

½ cup Chicken Stock, page 31

Coarse salt and freshly ground pepper

FOR THE CUSTARD

¾ cup heavy cream

½ cup Chicken Stock, page 31

4 extra-large eggs

1 tablespoon chopped parsley or chervil or chives or a mixture of all 3

Boil the wild rice in 2 quarts of salted boiling water until each kernel has burst open, about an hour. Drain the rice.

Melt the butter in a saucepan and cook the shallot and garlic for a minute or 2, until softened. Add the rice, the sherry, and the stock, stir well, and season with a little salt and pepper. Cover the pot and simmer over medium heat for about 15 minutes, or until the rice has absorbed most of the liquid.

Preheat the oven to 325°F.

Make the custard: Whisk together the cream, stock, and eggs, season with salt and pepper, and add the chopped herbs. Spray the bottoms and sides of six 5-ounce ramekins with nonstick spray and divide the rice mixture among them. Pour the egg mixture over the rice. Line a roasting pan with a double layer of paper towels and place the ramekins in the pan. Add boiling water to come halfway up the sides of the ramekins, put the pan in the oven, and bake 20 to 25 minutes, until the custard is set around the edges and the center barely quivers when the ramekins are shaken. Remove from the oven before the custard is completely set; its own heat will finish cooking it until it is firm throughout. If you leave the ramekins in the water bath, the custard will stay warm for ½ hour.

PARTRIDGE WITH TOMATO OIL, BASIL, AND YOGURT

Partridge are the mildest of game birds. In the Hudson Valley two kinds of partridge, Hungarian and Chukar, are available both commercially and through hunt clubs and can be used interchangeably. Unlike most game birds, which are hunted in the autumn, partridge is available in the late summer when it can be paired with tomatoes and basil in a light sauce. This preparation lends itself well to chicken, too. It needs no accompaniment beyond a simple pasta.

Serves 4

6 large basil leaves with stems
4 partridges
Coarse salt and freshly ground pepper
Flour for dredging the partridge
Tomato Oil, page 290
I shallot, chopped
I teaspoon chopped garlic
½ cup dry white wine
1½ cups Chicken Stock, page 31
Two 6-ounce containers Coach Farm Goat's Milk Yogurt or other full-fat yogurt
I ripe tomato, peeled, seeded, and diced fine
Basil leaves for garnish

Remove the basil leaves from the stems. Reserve the stems for the sauce, shred the leaves fine and set them aside.

Have the partridges cut into 4 pieces each, backbones, breastbones, and wings removed. Dry the partridge pieces with paper towels, season with salt and pepper, and dredge them in flour, shaking off the excess.

In a sauté pan, heat ¼ cup of the tomato oil over medium heat and gently sauté the partridge pieces, skin side down, until golden, 3 or 4 minutes. Keeping the heat at medium so as not to burn the tomato oil, turn the partridge pieces and brown the second side. Remove the breasts after 2 minutes and continue cooking the leg pieces for 4 or 5 minutes more. Remove the legs and add the shallot and garlic to the pan. Sauté until softened, 2 or 3 minutes. Add the wine and basil stems and reduce the mixture until almost dry. Add the stock and bring to a boil, stirring to incorporate any browned bits sticking to the pan. Let the stock reduce to a syrup, turn off the heat, and stir in the yogurt. Stirring constantly, let the yogurt melt into the sauce. Return all the partridge pieces to the pan and turn the heat to medium. As soon as the sauce begins to simmer, turn the heat as low as possible and cover the pan. (The partridges can be prepared up to this point 4 hours ahead and set aside in the pan. Bring slowly back to heat at a very gentle simmer.) Very gently steep the partridge pieces for 15 minutes. The sauce should never bubble; it shouldn't even move. If you remove the lid, you will see it gently steaming.

Remove the partridge pieces to a serving dish. Strain the sauce over the partridge, strew the diced tomato and the shredded basil over all, and drizzle 2 teaspoons of tomato oil over the dish. Garnish the platter with whole basil leaves.

WILD-SHOT PHEASANT
WITH BRAISED CABBAGE AND
FOIE GRAS MASHED POTATOES

Traditionally, game has been the food of the rich and the poor. Most people in between have neither the opportunity nor the need to collect food from the wild. The pheasant is a good example. Hunt guide Carl Ekblom told guests at a bird shoot hosted by Sandi Eberhart and Ed Schoenmaker at Millbrook Venison Farm in Dutchess County that the bird we know as pheasant is commonly eaten as chicken in China and is called by hunters here "Chinese chicken." European royalty had these birds imported, attracted by their gorgeous plumage and by the fact that they fly and can therefore be hunted. Thus they became the food of the aristocracy. At the other end of the economic spectrum, poachers probably made pheasant a food of the poor. A sizable group of hunters has brought game of all kinds into much wider use and it is increasingly available through hunt clubs, at specialty butcher shops, and by mail order, page 301. Order male pheasants; they're meatier.

Choosing and handling your pheasant will have a dramatic effect on the success of this dish. The pheasant available in the United States varies tremendously, ranging from bland farm-raised and frozen birds to wild, well-aged, flavorful birds that have been hung, feathers and viscera intact, for six to eight weeks. It is almost impossible to purchase native birds that have been handled properly; you have to hunt them yourself. But in fall and early winter aged pheasant is imported from Scotland and is available commercially in the United States by mail order or from specialty butchers. It's important to remember this whenever you cook or eat wild-shot birds: Watch for bird shot. Try to take it out before serving, but remind diners to beware. Serve with Foie Gras Mashed Potatoes. A Riesling from Cascade Mountain Vineyards in Amenia, NY, is the wine of choice with this dish.

Serves 6

FOR THE CABBAGE
1 head cabbage
2 slices bacon
2 tablespoons unsalted butter
2 bay leaves

3 carrots, peeled and sliced into 18 pieces
3 turnips, peeled and shaped into 18 pieces
3 cups Chicken Stock, page 31
Coarse salt and freshly ground pepper

FOR THE PHEASANT
2 male pheasants, about 2½ pounds each
2 shallots, smashed
4 cloves garlic, smashed
4 bay leaves
½ teaspoon dried thyme
4 slices bacon

FOR THE SAUCE
¼ cup chopped shallots
2 cloves garlic, chopped
4 mushrooms, sliced
1 cup Cascade Mountain Riesling
3 tablespoons tomato paste
4 cups Chicken Stock, page 31

1 recipe Foie Gras Mashed Potatoes, page 188
Unsalted butter at room temperature

Cut the cabbage into 6 wedges and steam until tender, 10 to 15 minutes. Let it drain on towels for at least an hour or overnight—the drier the better.

Preheat the oven to 375°F.

Prepare the pheasants: Put a shallot, 2 cloves of garlic, 2 bay leaves, and some thyme in the cavity of each bird. Truss the birds and put them on a rack in a roasting pan. Lay the bacon slices on the breasts and tie them in place. Roast the birds for 45 minutes. Take them out of the oven and let them rest for 20 minutes, propped against the side of the roasting pan, with the juices draining into the pan.

Braise the cabbage: Render the bacon in a shallow flameproof casserole just large enough to hold the vegetables, remove it from the pan, and set it aside. Brown the cabbage wedges well on both sides in the bacon fat, adding butter as needed. When the cabbage is browned, add the carrots, turnips, bay leaves, and chicken stock, return the bacon to the pan, and bring to a boil. Cover the casserole and bake it in the oven for 1 hour. Set aside.

Make the sauce: Remove the birds from the roasting pan and set aside. Remove and discard the bacon slices. Over medium heat, add the chopped shallots, garlic, and mushrooms to the roasting pan and sauté for 4 or 5 minutes. Add the wine and the tomato paste and cook the mixture, stirring constantly and being sure to scrape in all the browned bits from the pan. Transfer the mixture to a soup pot and continue to cook it over low heat for about 10 minutes or until it has the consistency of marmalade.

Remove the legs and thighs from the pheasants. The meat will be very rare. Separate the leg from the thigh by cutting through the joint. Using a very sharp knife, bone the thighs. Cut down the length of the thigh bone on each side, and, staying as close to the bone as possible, slice off the thigh meat and reserve it. Add the legs and the thigh bones to the sauce. Bone the breasts and set the meat aside. Break up the pheasant carcasses and add them and the stock to the soup pot. Stir well, bring to a boil, and cook over medium-high heat, stirring frequently, until the sauce is reduced and slightly thickened, about 20 minutes. Strain the sauce into a 2-quart saucepan and reserve. The dish can be prepared to this point several hours in advance.

Prepare the Foie Gras Mashed Potatoes.

Half an hour before serving time, preheat the oven to 350°F and place the cabbage in it to reheat. Put the pheasant thighs and breasts on a broiler pan, season them with salt and freshly ground pepper, and spread a little butter over them. When the cabbage is hot, remove it from the oven and turn on the broiler. Bring the sauce to a boil and keep it simmering. Place the pheasant under the broiler, with the thighs directly under the heat and the breasts off to the side, and broil until the meat is hot and completely cooked, 5 minutes at the most. Slice the pheasant breasts on the diagonal into ½-inch slices and cut the thighs in half.

Place the cabbage wedges in the center of a large heated platter and arrange the sliced meat around it. Garnish the platter with the cooked carrots and turnips. Spoon some sauce over the pheasant and pass the rest in a sauceboat. Serve the mashed potatoes from a casserole.

BONELESS QUAIL FILLED WITH FOIE GRAS AND BLACK TRUMPET MUSHROOMS

Black trumpet mushrooms (also called horn of plenty), with their pungent flavor and mysterious appearance, could well be called the truffles of the Hudson Valley. Like true black truffles, their flavor complements that of the foie gras used in the stuffing here. Cook six quail even if you don't intend to serve six people; it's excellent sliced and served cold (that is, at room temperature).

Serves 6

FOR THE FILLING
1 pound boned chicken breast, all skin and sinews removed
1 egg white
2 tablespoons brandy
1 cup heavy cream
2 teaspoons coarse salt and freshly ground pepper
Freshly grated nutmeg
6 ounces foie gras, cut in ¾-inch dice
1 pound Braised Wild Mushrooms, page 199, using black trumpet mushrooms only
½ pound spinach, blanched, chopped, and squeezed as dry as possible
1 teaspoon chopped fresh thyme

6 boneless quail, available from specialty butchers, wings removed
6 slices bacon
2½ cups Rich Meat Stock, page 32

Make the filling: Put the chicken, the egg white, and the brandy in the bowl of a food processor and process until smooth. With the processor running, add the cream in a thin stream, then the salt and pepper and a few gratings of nutmeg, and process until all is well combined. Scrape the mixture into a bowl and, using a rubber spatula, gently mix in the remaining filling ingredients, reserving half the braised mushrooms for the sauce.

Preheat the oven to 425°F.

Using a pastry bag with a ¾- to 1-inch opening, squeeze the filling mixture into the cavities of the quail, restoring their whole, plump shape. Lay the quail on their backs and cross their legs to close in the stuffing. Starting at the head end, wrap a piece of bacon around the sides of the quail and back to the head end to cover both openings. The quail will look as if they are lying in a bed of bacon. Tie the bacon in place with string, wrap a little piece of foil around the quails' legs to keep them from burning, and place the quail on a rack in a roasting pan, alternating filling-side up and filling-side down.

Roast the quail for 40 minutes. Turn off the oven, remove the quail to a platter, and let them rest in the turned-off oven while you make the sauce. Pour off the fat from the roasting pan, leaving any pan juice behind. Add the reserved braised mushrooms and the meat stock to the pan, stir well, and transfer to a saucepan. Reduce to 1½ cups.

Using a very sharp slicing knife, carefully cut each quail in half lengthwise down the center and arrange the halves on the platter. Spoon half the sauce on and around the quail and serve the rest in a sauceboat.

RABBIT POT PIES

Rabbit is hunted in the Hudson Valley pretty much all year round, except for a brief period in the winter during hibernation, and is a traditional Hudson Valley food. Wild rabbit is good, but so is farmed rabbit—tender and mild, not gamy, but with a real flavor of its own. Stewed or braised, it enriches sauces and it makes an excellent stock. It's too bad rabbit is not as popular in this country as it is in Europe and Asia, but because it is lower in fat and cholesterol than chicken, Americans are finally rediscovering it.

Pot pies, a means of dressing up leftovers with a pastry top, are traditional fare, but have always been made with birds, usually chicken. This is an untraditional pot pie, calling for puff pastry, seasonal vegetables, and rabbit, and is made with an intense wine-based sauce instead of the usual rather bland cream sauce. Stewed game birds make a good alternative to rabbit for the filling, and the autumn vegetables could easily be replaced by asparagus, peas, and/or morels in the spring. Feel free to use frozen puff pastry, but be sure to buy pastry made with all butter. One whole rabbit will give you enough meat for six pot pies. If you are buying rabbit already cut up, choose the leg and thigh pieces for this dish. Since the braised rabbit filling improves with age, start preparing this dish at least a day before you plan to serve it.

Makes 6 individual pot pies

Equipment: six 2½-cup casseroles

1 recipe Braised Wild Mushrooms, page 199 (save the trimmings)
½ cup vegetable oil
6 rabbit legs and thighs
Coarse salt and freshly ground pepper
Flour to dredge the rabbit
3 tablespoons unsalted butter
1 medium onion, sliced
1 shallot, sliced
3 cloves garlic, sliced
3 tablespoons flour
3 tablespoons tomato paste

2 tablespoons chopped fresh tarragon

1 large carrot, sliced

1 stalk celery, sliced

1 sprig fresh thyme

1 cup good-quality dry white wine

¼ cup good-quality brandy

5 cups rabbit or Chicken Stock, page 31

FOR THE GARNISH

½ cup sliced carrot

½ cup tiny green beans, cut in half

1 pound frozen all-butter puff pastry, thawed

1 egg, beaten with a little salt and 1 tablespoon water

Prepare the Braised Wild Mushrooms.

Preheat the oven to 350°F.

Heat the oil in a large skillet. Season the rabbit with salt and pepper, dredge it lightly in flour, and brown it over medium-high heat on all sides. Remove and drain the rabbit and discard the oil. Melt the butter in the hot skillet, add the onion, shallot, and garlic and cook over medium heat until lightly browned, 4 or 5 minutes. Sprinkle on the 3 tablespoons of flour, stir well, and continue cooking over low heat for another 4 or 5 minutes, stirring almost constantly, until the mixture is golden brown. Add the tomato paste, the mushroom trimmings, the tarragon, carrot, celery, thyme, wine, and brandy. Turn the heat up, whisk well, and cook over medium heat until the wine is almost evaporated and the mixture resembles marmalade, 7 or 8 minutes. Add the stock, raise the heat, and stir the mixture thoroughly as you bring it to a boil. Put the rabbit in an ovenproof casserole big enough to hold it in a single layer and pour the sauce and vegetables over it. Cover the casserole and bake for 45 minutes. Set the lid askew and continue to cook for another 45 minutes.

When the rabbit is done, remove the pieces from the casserole and let them cool a bit. Strain the sauce from the casserole over the braised mushrooms, bring to a boil, and reduce over medium-high heat for 10 to 15 minutes, skimming any fat or foam from the surface.

Meanwhile, remove the rabbit meat from the bones, keeping the pieces as large as possible, and put it in a bowl. Pour the sauce and mushrooms over it, cover, and refrigerate overnight.

At least 2 hours before serving (but up to 6 hours is fine), take the rabbit out of the refrigerator. Blanch the carrots and green beans in some boiling salted water and drain. Divide the braised rabbit and mushrooms among six 2½-cup casseroles. Garnish each casserole with some of the blanched carrots and green beans, leaving at least 1½ inches of headroom in each casserole; when the filling gets hot, the warm air above it will cause the crust to rise into a dome.

Preheat the oven to 400°F.

Roll out the puff pastry ⅛ inch thick on a floured surface and cut it into rounds 1 inch larger in diameter than the tops of the casseroles. Brush each round thoroughly with egg wash. Place the pastry rounds, *egg side down,* on top of the casserole and press the overlapping pastry firmly around the edge, making sure the pastry adheres to the casseroles. Trim the edges neatly. Put the casseroles on a baking sheet and bake until the pastry is golden brown and the tops are well puffed, about 30 minutes.

RABBIT SADDLES WITH MUSTARD AND SAGE SAUCE

This simple and quick recipe deserves to be the centerpiece of a very special dinner. Serve with any simple green vegetable or a sautéed green such as Broccoli Rabe with Shallots, page 224.

Serves 6

FOR THE MARINADE
1 tablespoon Pommery-style mustard with seeds
1 tablespoon Dijon mustard
1 tablespoon chopped fresh sage
3 tablespoons extra virgin olive oil
1 teaspoon chopped garlic
Freshly ground pepper

3 saddles of rabbit, available through specialty butchers or by mail
2 medium onions, ends removed and onions cut into 3 thick slices each
1 tablespoon extra virgin olive oil
12 fresh sage leaves
Coarse salt

FOR THE SAUCE
¼ cup dry white wine
1 tablespoon Dijon mustard
1 teaspoon Pommery-style mustard with seeds
½ cup heavy cream
½ cup rabbit or Chicken Stock, page 31, if needed

Combine the marinade ingredients and coat all the surfaces of the rabbit meat, rubbing it in well. Fold the flaps under to make neat packages. Put the rabbit in a bowl, cover with plastic wrap, and refrigerate at least 4 hours or overnight.

Preheat the oven to 400°F.

You will use 2 thick onion slices as a rack for each of the saddles of rabbit. Oil a roasting pan and lay the onion slices in 2 rows down the center of the pan. Put a sage leaf on each slice and lay each saddle, flap sides down, across 2 onion slices. Roast the rabbit for 30 minutes. Remove the meat to a platter, place the sage leaves on the meat, and garnish the platter with the onion slices. Turn off the oven and return the platter to the warm oven for 30 minutes.

While the rabbit is resting, make the sauce: Over high heat, deglaze the roasting pan with the wine, scraping up all the brown bits from the pan. Pour the wine into a small saucepan, whisk in the mustards, and reduce the mixture over medium heat until it has the consistency of cream. Add the cream and bring the sauce to a boil, whisking constantly. If the sauce is too thick, thin it with a tablespoon or so of chicken stock.

Each saddle is 6 inches long and 4 inches wide with a bone (the spine) down the center lengthwise. On each side of the bone is a fillet that is to be sliced.

Carving the saddles: Using a long, sharp slicing knife or electric carving knife held parallel to the spine bone, cut long slices, each ¼ inch thick. Start slicing each fillet from the outside edge of the roast, working toward the center bone.

Place the slices on the platter, leaning them on the onion slices. Spoon a little sauce over the meat and serve the rest in a sauceboat. Garnish with the remaining 6 sage leaves.

VENISON-APPLE CHILI WITH RED WINE AND NEW YORK STATE CHEDDAR

This is a good way to use cuts of venison that are very flavorful but too tough to cook in other ways. Enough for at least fifteen people, this is a large batch of chili, and you could cut the recipe in half. Since this chili freezes so well, though, it's a good idea to cook the whole amount. The flavor improves with age, so make the chili three or four days in advance. Suggested accompaniments: fried Suppawn, page 208, or boiled rice.

Serves 15 generously

½ cup vegetable oil
5 pounds venison stew meat, cut into small dice or ground coarse
5 large onions, peeled and cut into ¼-inch dice
½ cup ground cumin
2 or 3 tablespoons good-quality chili powder
Coarse salt
1 tablespoon freshly ground black pepper
3 or 4 small jalapeño peppers, seeded and chopped fine
6 firm, tart cooking apples such as Cortland, Macoun, or Winesap, peeled and cut into
    ½-inch dice
½ cup chopped fresh garlic (2 medium heads or about 40 cloves)
Two 6-ounce cans tomato paste
Three 16-ounce cans crushed tomatoes
2 cups dry red wine
4 cups Chicken Stock, page 31

GARNISH
New York State cheddar cheese, grated
Chopped scallions

Heat the oil in a 5- or 6-quart pot or Dutch oven and brown the venison in batches over medium-high heat. Remove the meat from the pot and lightly brown the onions for 15 minutes or so. Pour off as much fat as possible, stir in the spices, peppers, apples, and garlic and brown for 10 minutes. Return the meat to the pot and add the tomato paste, crushed tomatoes, wine, and stock. Stir well, bring to a boil, and simmer, uncovered, for 2 hours. Adjust the seasoning. Cover the chili, let it cool, and refrigerate overnight.

Reheat the chili gently on top of the stove or in a preheated 300°F oven and garnish with grated cheese and scallions.

GRILLED VENISON RIB CHOPS WITH WATERCRESS RELISH AND RED WINE JELLY

When venison is being butchered, the rack (here used as chops) and the saddle (see page 115) should be separated out and given special treatment. If you're a hunter, or the lucky recipient of winter gifts from one, save these choice cuts for special occasions.

Any time you cook loin parts of venison, whether it be saddle or ribs, this very lean meat should be cooked no more than rare or medium-rare, or it becomes dry and chewy. The rack can be frozen whole and roasted whole, or it can be cut into chops and frozen in portions to make a welcome change from steaks and hamburgers on the summer grill. For this simple recipe, all the preparation is done in advance. Warm Potato Salad with Bacon and Shallots (page 196) is a good accompaniment.

Serves 6

12 venison rib or loin chops, 1 inch thick each

FOR THE MARINADE
1½ cups dry red wine
1 clove garlic, sliced
2 shallots, sliced
1 tablespoon freshly ground black pepper
1 tablespoon chopped juniper berries

FOR THE RELISH
2 bunches fresh watercress, washed, trimmed of thick stems, and rough-chopped to yield
    2 cups
4 large ripe tomatoes, peeled, seeded, and diced
¾ cup chopped fresh mint
Coarse salt and freshly ground pepper
Juice of ½ lemon
½ cup extra virgin olive oil

FOR THE JELLY
2 cups dry red wine such as Brotherhood Winery Cabernet Sauvignon
1 tablespoon chopped shallot
1½ teaspoons coarsely ground black pepper
1 clove garlic, split
One 12-ounce jar red currant jelly

Everything, except grilling the chops, should be done a day in advance: Put the chops in a nonreactive baking pan. Combine the marinade ingredients and pour over them. Cover and refrigerate overnight.

Combine the relish ingredients, cover, and refrigerate overnight.

Make the jelly: In a small saucepan, bring the wine to a boil. Stir in the shallots, pepper, and garlic and boil to reduce the wine. It will take at least ½ hour to reduce the wine to approximately 2 tablespoons of very concentrated, peppery syrup. Watch it carefully toward the end and be sure not to let it burn. Remove the garlic and stir in the currant jelly. Over low heat, cook the mixture, whisking from time to time, just until the jelly is completely melted. Pour the jelly into a jar. Refrigerate overnight.

At serving time, remove the chops from the marinade and grill them on a fairly hot grill for about 3 minutes per side, until rare or medium-rare. Serve immediately, 2 chops per person, with a teaspoon of jelly on top and a large spoon of relish on the side. Pass the remaining relish and jelly.

ROAST SADDLE OF VENISON WITH WILD HUCKLEBERRIES

This grand dish is the centerpiece of a very elegant autumn dinner party. A whole saddle is an unusual roast and it contains the most succulent meat. It is usually cut into chops or medallions for more versatile use, but there's a grandeur to taking the best part of the animal, roasting it all at once and presenting it at a gala dinner. The saddle consists of the two loins and the two fillets of the venison, the most tender of all the muscles. This saddle is sauced with huckleberries, sweet-tart little nuggets of flavor that can still be found in the wild but can also be ordered, flash-frozen, year round (see page 301). Serve the saddle with three vegetable purees: Chestnut Puree, page 216, Celery Root Puree, page 215, and Butternut Squash and Sweet Potato Puree, page 232, or as part of the menu given here.

Serves 10

A saddle of venison, trimmed and tied

FOR THE MARINADE
1 bottle dry red wine
1 small onion, sliced
4 shallots, sliced
2 cloves garlic, sliced
2 bay leaves
1 teaspoon dried thyme
1 tablespoon crushed juniper berries
1 tablespoon black peppercorns

Vegetable oil to rub the meat
Coarse salt and freshly ground pepper
1 medium onion, chopped
1 stalk celery, chopped
1 carrot, peeled and chopped
4 cloves garlic, chopped

FALL MENU

Wild Mushroom Broth

Roast Saddle of Venison with Wild Huckleberries

Brussels Sprouts with Chestnuts

Celery Root Puree

Warm Apple Sacks with Clabbered Cream

5 or 6 parsley stems, chopped
1 tablespoon crushed juniper berries

FOR THE SAUCE
2 tablespoons unsalted butter
1½ pints huckleberries
2 tablespoons flour
2 cups apple cider
2 tablespoons red wine vinegar
4 cups Rich Meat Stock, page 32
Chopped parsley

Ask the butcher to trim off the side flaps of the saddle, remove the kidneys, and tie the roast snugly 3 or 4 times.

In a large nonreactive bowl, combine all the marinade ingredients. Add the venison, cover, and marinate in the refrigerator for at least 48 hours, turning twice.

Take the venison out of the refrigerator at least 2 hours before cooking to allow it to come to room temperature.

Preheat the oven to 450°F.

Remove the venison from the marinade and pat it dry with paper towels. Discard the marinade. Rub the meat all over with a little vegetable oil and season it with salt and freshly ground pepper. Put the venison in a roasting pan and roast for 20 minutes. Combine the onion, celery, carrot, garlic, parsley, and juniper berries and add them to the pan, spreading them in an even layer and pushing some under the meat. Turn the oven down to 400°F and roast the meat for another 40 minutes. Remove it from the oven and put the meat on a platter on top of the stove while you make the sauce.

Add the butter and 1 pint of the huckleberries to the vegetables in the roasting pan and cook and stir them over medium heat on top of the stove until they are soft, adding a little more butter if they are dry. When the vegetables are soft, sprinkle them with the flour, stir well, and cook for 2 or 3 minutes. Add the cider and deglaze the pan. Scrape the mixture into a saucepan and cook over medium-high heat, stirring frequently, until it is reduced to a thick marmalade. Stir in the vinegar and cook for 2 or 3 minutes; add the stock, stir well, bring the mixture to a boil, and cook until the liquid is reduced by half, about 20 to 30 minutes.

Strain the sauce into a clean saucepan; press out all the liquid, but do not push any solids through. Bring the sauce to a boil, skim off any fat or scum, and taste and season the sauce.

Carving: Follow the directions for carving a saddle of rabbit, page 110. When the whole loin has been carved, turn the roast upside down and, using your carving knife, scoop out the whole fillets. Slice them into 1-inch-thick medallions.

Put the slices on a platter. Spoon a little sauce over the meat and sprinkle the platter with the reserved ½ pint huckleberries and a little chopped parsley. Serve with the 3 vegetable purees listed in the headnote or as part of the menu on the preceding page.

VENISON STEW WITH CHESTNUTS AND CRANBERRIES

Warm up a cold November day by serving this stew over soft Suppawn, page 208.

Serves 8 to 10

2 bottles full-bodied dry red wine such as Millbrook Cabernet Sauvignon
I cup vegetable oil
4 pounds venison stew meat, preferably shoulder, neck, or shank
4 tablespoons unsalted butter
I large onion, peeled and cut in chunks
2 stalks celery, cut in chunks
I leek, white part only, carefully cleaned and cut in chunks
I large turnip, peeled and cut in chunks
I large carrot, peeled and cut in chunks
I pound mushrooms, quartered
4 tablespoons flour
herb sachet: ½ head garlic, unpeeled and cut crosswise ⎫
               I tablespoon juniper berries   ⎪
               6 whole cloves   ⎬ Tied together in a
               2 tablespoons black peppercorns   ⎪ double layer of cheesecloth
               ½ teaspoon dried thyme   ⎪
               4 bay leaves   ⎪
               4 or 5 sprigs parsley   ⎭

2 tablespoons tomato paste
3 tablespoons currant jelly
12 cups Chicken Stock, page 31, or veal stock
Coarse salt and freshly ground pepper

Soft Suppawn, page 208

GARNISH

4 tablespoons unsalted butter

1½ pounds mushrooms, caps only, quartered

1½ cups peeled cooked chestnuts, page 152

1½ cups cranberries

Chopped parsley for garnish

In a nonreactive saucepan boil the wine until it is reduced to 1½ cups.

In your largest skillet or braising pan, heat the oil over medium-high heat and thoroughly brown the meat in batches. Do not crowd the meat in the pan or it will not brown properly. As each batch is browned, remove it to a colander with a slotted spoon and let it drain thoroughly. Discard the oil that drains from the meat, put the meat into a serving casserole, and set it aside.

Preheat the oven to 325°F.

In a large Dutch oven or braising pan, melt the butter, add the vegetables, and toss them over medium-high heat until they are just beginning to brown, about 4 or 5 minutes. Sprinkle on the flour, stir to combine well, and cook for 3 or 4 minutes, stirring frequently. Add the herb sachet, pour in the reduced wine, and stir in the tomato paste and the currant jelly. Mix to combine well and add the stock. Bring to a boil, stirring, and add the mixture to the meat in the casserole. Cover the casserole and bake the stew until the meat is tender, about 2 hours.

When the meat is done, remove it from the pot, separating it from the vegetables, and set it aside. Strain the sauce into a 3-quart saucepan. Press hard on the vegetables and the herb sachet to extract the flavorful liquid from them, and discard the solids. Bring the sauce to a boil, turn the heat to medium, and let it simmer, skimming it from time to time. This simmering will help to clarify the sauce and reduce it to 5 or 6 cups. Taste the sauce. Add salt to taste and plenty of freshly ground pepper, which gives the sauce a distinctive fragrance. Return the meat to the casserole, pour the sauce over it, and refrigerate overnight.

Three hours before serving, take the casserole out of the refrigerator. An hour and a half before serving, put the casserole in the oven and turn it to 300°F. Let the stew reheat while you prepare the garnish.

Make the suppawn.

Prepare the garnish: Melt the butter in a sauté pan and sauté the mushrooms for 3 or 4 minutes. Toss in the chestnuts and continue to cook for 5 minutes. Toss in the cranberries and turn off the heat. Put the garnish on top of the hot stew.

Serve the stew in large warm soup bowls. Put a large spoon of soft suppawn in each bowl and ladle some stew over it. Be sure to include a portion of the garnish on each serving and sprinkle with chopped parsley.

CURING MEAT AND POULTRY

This book contains three examples of home-cured meat and poultry: Salt-Cured Foie Gras, page 10, Venison Prosciutto, next recipe, and Cured Duck, page 141.

Salting, pickling, spicing, and drying are among the most common ways people had to preserve food in the millenia before the refrigerator was invented. Most of those cured foods were abandoned the minute there was another way to keep food fresh and safe to eat. But a few cured foods were so good that they are still appealing, and even today we cure certain foods for their flavor and convenience even though we could keep them fresh in the refrigerator.

The main curing agent for food is salt, which creates an environment in which bacteria can't live or grow. Packing food in dry coarse salt is called a "dry cure"; submerging it in brine (salt dissolved in water) is called "corning," or a "wet cure." Today, spices and flavoring agents are added to the cure to enhance the flavor of the finished meat. Sometimes cured foods are ready to eat without any further processing (see Salt-Cured Foie Gras). Some foods, such as corned beef, that have been soaked in brine, are then cooked; some go through a drying and aging process (see Venison Prosciutto). Some foods are cooked after curing (see Cured Duck).

HOME-CURED VENISON PROSCIUTTO

If you are lucky enough to receive a leg of venison as a gift, or if you have ever tasted this delicious preparation and can't wait to have it again, be assured that it is possible to cure a leg of venison in an ordinary household without undue effort or inconvenience. If you have back stairs, an unused hallway, or a garage, the only thing you need is a sense of adventure and a bucket large enough to soak a leg of venison. Prosciutto made from venison is uniquely delicious and it's likely you'll never get a chance to taste it unless you make it yourself. Serve the prosciutto with New York State pears, peeled and sliced, or with melon or a salad of baby greens. Put it in a sandwich on good bread with unsalted butter. As the Italians do with their own famous prosciutto, you can use this to flavor a vegetable soup, a pot of beans, or a pasta sauce. A leg of venison will yield about three pounds of trimmed prosciutto. The venison must be cured and hung during cool weather. Avoid the hot summer months. The curing process takes five weeks.

A leg of venison

FOR THE BRINE
3 gallons water
2 pounds kosher salt
1 pound (2⅓ cups) sugar
2 carrots, sliced
2 large onions, sliced
6 cloves garlic, sliced
2 teaspoons dried thyme
6 bay leaves
8 whole cloves
2 tablespoons juniper berries, slightly crushed
4 tablespoons black peppercorns

SEASONING AFTER SOAKING
Lots of freshly ground pepper
¼ cup juniper berries, crushed and chopped

Have the venison leg butchered as follows: Remove hip and thigh bones; trim off shank bone up to the point where the meat starts; trim the meat neatly.

Soaking the venison: Boil the brine ingredients together for ½ hour. Cool completely. The brine must cool to room temperature or cooler. Do not use it if it is warmer than 70°F. Put the venison leg in a bucket or large stock pot and pour the cold brine over it. Weight the meat so it is all below the surface of the brine (a wine bottle filled with water and securely corked makes a good weight) and cover well with plastic wrap and a lid. Make a note of the date you set the venison to marinate and the date you will hang it to dry. Marinate the venison for 2 weeks in a cool place, such as a barn, garage, or fire escape, checking from time to time to make sure the meat remains immersed in the brine.

Hanging the venison: Drain the meat and discard the marinade. Wash the meat in cold water, letting water run over it for 5 minutes. Then soak it in cold water for 30 minutes and drain. Repeat the process. If you are afraid the meat will be too salty, soak it one more time.

Lay 3 feet of butcher's string along a counter. Then, down the length of the string, lay a whole unrolled package of cheesecloth. Place the venison at one end of the cheesecloth and season it with half the pepper and juniper berries, rubbing the seasonings in well. Roll the seasoned side of the meat over onto the cheesecloth and season the second side, rubbing the seasoning in well. Wrap the whole leg tightly in several thicknesses of cheesecloth and tie tightly with string at 2-inch intervals down the whole length of the leg. Twist the cheesecloth around the top and bottom and tie it securely closed. Securely tie a long piece of strong string around the bone end of the venison and hang it in a cool, airy place for 21 days. Remember that the venison will shrink as it dries, so be sure the string is securely attached. Make a note of the date you hung the venison to dry and the date you can unwrap it.

Unwrap the venison. It will need considerable trimming before it looks appealing. Trim off all mold, dried ends and edges, membranes, and gristle. Break the meat into 3 pieces where it divides naturally. Using a very sharp carving knife, an electric knife or a slicer, slice the meat across the grain, not lengthwise, as thin as possible. You will get larger slices if you cut at a slight angle. Slice only as needed. Wrap the prosciutto tightly in plastic wrap and refrigerate. It will keep for up to 4 weeks.

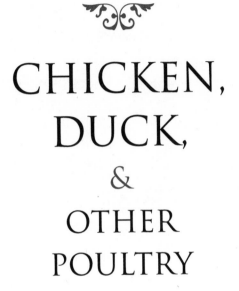

CHICKEN,
DUCK,
&
OTHER
POULTRY

Going as far back as we have records of what people like to eat, grilled, roasted, or spit-roasted birds of all kinds have been favored by every ethnic strain that settled the Hudson Valley. By now these different strains have all blended into a modern example of American regional cooking at its best—a melting pot of poultry recipes.

In recent years, poultry farms producing delicious free-range, organically fed chickens have sprung up throughout the Hudson Valley. Now restaurants and the general public can easily find chickens that have been raised without chemicals and hormones, providing a readily available, more flavorful alternative to commercially mass-produced chickens. The chicken recipes included here range from the most homey to the most sophisticated. You'll also find in this chapter three very unusual recipes for duck as well as a roast goose dinner that can be almost completely prepared a day in advance. Recipes for a grand holiday turkey dinner include a winy gravy, a most unusual cranberry relish, and four wonderful stuffings that can also be used for chicken or goose.

BRAISED CHICKEN WITH TARRAGON AND TOMATO

Best made with a juicy free-range chicken in August or September, when Hudson Valley farmstands are overflowing with rich, ripe tomatoes. Serve this chicken with soft Suppawn, page 208, or Corn Bread and Fisher's Island Oyster Stuffing, page 153.

Serves 4

8 pieces of chicken, breasts, thighs, or legs
Coarse salt and freshly ground pepper
Flour for dredging
¼ cup vegetable oil
2 tablespoons unsalted butter, plus 4 tablespoons very cold unsalted butter,
    cut in small chunks
I shallot, chopped
I clove garlic, chopped
2 tablespoons chopped fresh tarragon leaves and stems
½ cup dry white wine
2 tablespoons tarragon vinegar
3 large ripe tomatoes, rough chopped
I cup Chicken Stock, page 31

GARNISH
I teaspoon chopped fresh tarragon
I small tomato, peeled, seeded, and diced
Tarragon sprigs

Wipe the chicken dry with paper towels and season it with salt and pepper.

Dredge the chicken in flour, shaking off the excess. In an ovenproof sauté pan, heat the oil, add the chicken, skin side down, and brown it over moderate heat for 7 or 8 minutes, until it is crisp and golden. Turn the chicken over and continue to cook for another 3 or 4 minutes. If your sauté pan is not big enough to comfortably accommodate all the chicken, brown it in 2 batches. Remove the chicken from the pan and set it aside. Let the fat continue to cook until the solids stick to the pan without burning and the fat is clear. Discard the fat and let the pan cool for a few minutes.

Preheat the oven to 375°F.

Melt the 2 tablespoons butter in the pan, add the shallot and garlic, and cook gently, stirring, until they are lightly browned. Add the chopped tarragon, the wine, and the vinegar and bring to a simmer, stirring to incorporate all the browned bits. Reduce the liquid by half and add the tomatoes and stock. Bring the liquid to a boil and return the chicken to the pan, skin side up.

Put the chicken in the oven and bake, uncovered, for 10 minutes. Then remove the breast pieces, keep them warm, and cook the dark meat 5 minutes longer. Remove the chicken to a serving casserole and keep it warm in the turned-off oven. Pass the sauce through a food mill or press it through a strainer, leaving only tomato skins and seeds behind.

Bring the sauce to a boil and reduce it until you have about 1½ cups and the sauce is beginning to thicken and is a little shiny. Turn the heat to low, season the sauce with salt and pepper, and whisk in the 4 tablespoons cold butter 1 tablespoon at a time, whisking each tablespoon until incorporated before adding the next.

Pour the sauce over the chicken, sprinkle with chopped tarragon, and garnish with the diced tomato and the tarragon sprigs.

CHICKEN PAILLARDS WITH HERB VINAIGRETTE

A paillard is a piece of meat, fish, or poultry that has been pounded between two pieces of wax paper into a very thin sheet. Veal, beef, venison, swordfish, and chicken all make good paillards. Quick, easy, and delicious, paillards cook in 2 minutes on a griddle or grill. Have the rest of the meal ready and on the table when you start to cook them. Any of the potato salads in this book would be an excellent accompaniment, along with a steamed green vegetable.

Serves 4

Four 6-to 8-ounce whole boneless chicken breasts
½ cup chopped fresh herbs: a mixture of basil, thyme, rosemary, chives, and tarragon
   (¼ cup for the vinaigrette and ¼ cup for the chicken)

FOR THE CHICKEN
Coarse salt and freshly ground pepper
¼ cup chopped herbs (see above)
2 tablespoons minced shallot

FOR THE HERB VINAIGRETTE
1 tablespoon white wine
1 tablespoon white wine vinegar
1 teaspoon lemon juice
4 tablespoons extra virgin olive oil
Coarse salt and freshly ground pepper
¼ cup chopped fresh herbs (see above)

Have the butcher prepare the paillards: Tell him to cut the chicken breasts in half lengthwise and remove the tenderloin from each. Put each breast piece between two pieces of wax paper and pound ¼ inch thick. Leave the chicken on the wax paper. Reserve the tenderloins for another use.

Prepare the chicken: Season the exposed side of each chicken breast with salt and freshly ground pepper and pat some chopped herbs and shallots onto each piece. Let the chicken sit for 15 minutes or so.

Make the vinaigrette: Put all the ingredients in a jar and shake vigorously.

Set a platter next to the stove. Set the vinaigrette nearby. Heat a griddle hot. Dip a paper towel in olive oil and wipe the surface of the griddle with it. Place as many pieces of chicken as will fit, herb side down, on the griddle and press down firmly on the wax paper to be sure the whole surface of the chicken is touching the griddle. Immediately peel off the wax paper. The chicken will begin turning white around the edges and within a minute the entire surface will be almost white, with just a little pink showing. Using a spatula, carefully but quickly detach the chicken from the pan and flip it. After 15 seconds, put the chicken, herb side up, on the platter. Immediately cook the remaining chicken, put it on the platter, and drizzle the vinaigrette over all.

ROAST CHICKEN WITH MAPLE AND WALNUT GLAZE

This recipe, which highlights Hudson Valley products, is a good showcase for a locally grown, free-range chicken. In early spring, buckets attached to thousands of maple trees collect sap and syrup is boiled in hundreds of sugar houses as steam drifts out into the cold, clear air. In this chicken dish, maple syrup is combined with walnuts to create an unusual and festive sweet-and-sour chicken. Serve it with Suppawn with Tomato and Mushrooms, page 208, or any of the potato dishes on pages 185–186, and perhaps some braised greens.

Serves 3 or 4

A 3-pound chicken
2 tablespoons olive oil
Salt and freshly ground pepper
5 shallots, sliced thin
3 cloves garlic, sliced thin
3 sprigs fresh thyme

FOR THE GLAZE
½ cup walnut meats, chopped fine but not ground
⅓ cup maple syrup
1 tablespoon red wine vinegar

FOR THE SAUCE
1 cup Chicken Stock, page 31
1 tablespoon unsalted butter
1 tablespoon flour
2 tablespoons red wine vinegar

Preheat the oven to 400°F.

Rub the chicken all over with 1 tablespoon of the olive oil, season it inside and out with salt and pepper, and put about ¼ of the shallots, garlic, and thyme in the cavity. Truss the chicken, put it in a roasting pan, and roast for 15 minutes. Add the remaining shallots, garlic, and thyme to the pan, set the chicken on top, and roast for 15 minutes more. Turn the oven down to 300°F and pour off any fat that has accumulated in the roasting pan.

Make the glaze: In a small bowl, combine the walnuts, maple syrup, and vinegar. Spoon half the glaze over the chicken.

Add the stock to the roasting pan and return the chicken to the oven. After 20 minutes, baste with the remaining glaze and continue to roast the chicken for 25 minutes more. Turn the oven off, remove the chicken to a platter, and return it to the oven while you make the sauce.

In a small saucepan, melt the butter, whisk in the flour, and cook, whisking frequently, over low heat for a minute or 2, until the mixture is tinged with color. Strain the pan juices into the pan and stir the sauce over medium-low heat until it is smooth and slightly thickened. Let it simmer gently for 5 minutes, stirring frequently. Season the sauce with salt and pepper and stir in the vinegar.

Carve the chicken and serve the sauce in a sauceboat on the side.

HOME-STYLE ROAST CHICKEN WITH GARLIC AND FINGERLING POTATOES

As you might guess from the name, fingerlings are small potatoes approximately the size and shape of a thick finger. They are grown in the Hudson Valley and are available in both yellow and white varieties. Look for them in country markets, farmstands, and fancy produce stores.

This recipe calls for one three-pound chicken, enough for three generous servings. With the addition of a first course, a salad, and a dessert, a chicken this size will easily serve four, unless the group includes a teenager. For more people, or if you want to have leftovers, double this recipe and cook two three-pound chickens. While the chicken is roasting, you can use the chicken giblets (without the liver) to make the cup of chicken stock you need for the sauce.

Serves 3

A 3-pound chicken
2 tablespoons olive oil
Coarse salt and freshly ground pepper
1 shallot, sliced
1 large head garlic plus 4 additional cloves garlic
2 bay leaves
Four 3-inch sprigs fresh rosemary plus 1 tablespoon rosemary leaves
1 medium onion, sliced
12 fingerling potatoes, scrubbed
1 cup hot Chicken Stock, page 31

Preheat the oven to 400°F.

Rub the chicken all over with 1 tablespoon of the olive oil and season it inside and out with salt and pepper. Put the shallot, the 4 cloves of garlic, smashed, the bay leaves, and 2 sprigs of the rosemary in the cavity of the chicken and truss it. Push the remaining 2 sprigs of rosemary between the skin and meat over each breast. Spread the onion slices in the middle of a roasting pan and set the chicken on top. Separate the head of garlic into cloves, trim off the toughest skin, and slit each clove at the sprout end. In a bowl, combine the garlic, the potatoes, and the rosemary leaves, sprinkle generously with salt and pepper, toss with the remaining tablespoon of olive oil, and arrange the vegetables around the chicken.

Roast the chicken for 30 minutes, add the hot stock, and return the chicken to the oven. Roast for 30 minutes more and remove from the oven. Using a slotted spoon, lift the vegetables out of the roasting pan and arrange them on a platter. Set the chicken on top and return the whole platter to the turned-off oven for at least 20 minutes.

Pour the pan juices into a glass bowl or pitcher and let the fat rise to the surface. Remove the fat, season the juices with salt and pepper, and reheat. Carve the chicken, setting the pieces back on the platter, and pour the pan juices over all.

CHICKEN AND FRESH MORELS IN CLINTON VINEYARDS SPARKLING SEYVAL BLANC

Ben and Phyllis Feder, the proprietors of Clinton Vineyards in Clinton Corners, New York, make a wonderful sparkling Seyval Blanc, using the traditional method for making champagne. They love to have visitors and you can buy the wine on the spot. Simple blanched asparagus is an ideal accompaniment for this dish.

Serves 4

8 pieces of chicken, breasts with rib bones removed, thighs, or legs
Coarse salt and freshly ground pepper
Flour for dredging
¼ cup vegetable oil
2 tablespoons unsalted butter
2 cups fresh morel caps
¾ cup Clinton Vineyards Sparkling Seyval Blanc
¾ cup Chicken Stock, page 31
1 cup heavy cream

GARNISH
¼ cup Herb Oil, page 290, made with chives only
2 tablespoons chopped chives

Preheat the oven to 425°F.

Wipe the chicken dry with paper towels and season it with salt and pepper.

Dredge the chicken in flour, shaking off the excess. In an ovenproof sauté pan, heat the oil, add the chicken, skin side down, and brown it over moderate heat for 7 or 8 minutes, until it is crisp and golden. Turn the chicken over and continue to cook for another 3 or 4 minutes. If your sauté pan is not big enough to comfortably accommodate all the chicken, brown it in 2 batches. Remove the chicken from the pan and set it aside. Let the fat continue to cook until the solids stick to the pan without burning and the fat is clear. Discard the fat and let the pan cool for a few minutes.

In the same pan, melt the butter, add the morels, and sauté them for 10 minutes. Add ½ cup of the wine, reduce it by half, and add half the chicken stock. Reduce the mixture until it has the consistency of marmalade. Add the remaining stock and the cream and stir well. Return the chicken to the pan, put the pan in the oven, and bake, uncovered, for 10 minutes. Remove the breasts from the pan and keep warm. Bake the dark meat pieces for 5 minutes more.

Arrange the chicken and morels on a warm platter. To finish the sauce, bring it to a boil and whisk in the remaining wine; the wine will make the cream bubble and thicken a bit. Boil for a minute and strain the sauce over the chicken. Drizzle with the chive oil and sprinkle chopped chives over all. Serve immediately.

GRILLED BREAST OF CHICKEN WITH FORAGED DANDELION GREENS

It's fun to collect food from the wild, and foraged foods often bring flavors you won't find in their cultivated counterparts. Foraged dandelion greens are very easy to obtain. Just go into a park or your front yard and pick the newest and smallest dandelions. Remove all flower buds, wash the greens, and, *voilà*, foraged dandelion greens. Many foods can be foraged in this part of the country; your garden, yard, or woods can yield wild greens, wild berries, herbs, and nuts. With experience, your eyes learn to pick these out of the mass of other growing things. But please do not eat any wild mushrooms you forage yourself: Mistakes can lead to disaster.

Serves 4 as a main course

4 whole skinless, boneless chicken breasts
Mustard Herb Vinaigrette, page 286
4 cups dandelion greens, trimmed, washed, and cut in half
½ recipe Warm Potato Salad with Bacon and Shallots, page 196
2 hard-boiled eggs, chopped coarse

Trim the chicken well, put it in a shallow bowl, and pour half the mustard vinaigrette over it, reserving the remainder. Rub the vinaigrette well into all surfaces of the chicken and let it marinate for 2 hours.

Grill the chicken breasts for 3 minutes per side over hot coals or under a preheated broiler. Remove to a platter and let the chicken rest for 5 minutes. Slice each chicken breast on the diagonal ¼ inch thick, keeping the breast intact.

Dress the dandelion greens with ¼ cup of the vinaigrette and spread them over 4 salad plates. Sprinkle the eggs over the greens. Put ¼ of the potato salad in the center of each plate and lay a whole sliced breast on top of the potatoes, hiding the potatoes. Sprinkle a tablespoon of vinaigrette over each chicken breast.

BRAISED DUCK WITH BRANDIED PRUNES, ORANGE, AND LEMON

Anybody who's ever eaten a good stew knows how rich, complex, and round the flavor of slow-cooked meats can be. And anyone who's cooked a stew knows how simple the procedure is. This uncommonly good braised duck is made essentially the same way as any other stew: You brown the meat, add seasonings, and cook it slowly in its own stock. As with any stew, you should make it a day or two ahead; it tastes better after its flavors have had a chance to marry and you have the convenience of advance preparation. Serve the duck with something simple such as boiled potatoes or rice or Suppawn with Bacon, page 208.

Serves 8

Two 4½- to 5-pound Long Island (Pekin) ducks
Coarse salt and freshly ground pepper
¾ cup vegetable oil
3 tablespoons unsalted butter
3 cloves garlic, sliced
3 shallots, sliced
1 sprig fresh thyme
1 small sprig fresh rosemary
2 tablespoons flour
1 tablespoon tomato paste
4 cups Roast Duck Stock, page 34
1 clove garlic, cut in half
1 cup fresh orange juice
3 tablespoons fresh lemon juice
1 cup good-quality brandy
24 pitted prunes
1 navel orange, halved and cut into ¼-inch slices
1 lemon, cut in ¼-inch slices and seeded
2 tablespoons red wine vinegar

Have the butcher bone each duck into 2 breasts and 2 leg and thigh sections. Ask for the bones to make Duck Stock, page 34, and the fat to save for Cured Duck, page 141.

Browning the duck: The main reason for browning the duck is to render out as much fat as possible. Browning it in oil enables you to keep the temperature high enough to render out the fat without burning the skin. Keep the oil hot but not smoking; the duck will not absorb the oil. In a large skillet, heat the oil over medium-high heat and put in the duck breasts, skin side down. Brown them very thoroughly; it will take at least 10 minutes to render out most of the fat under the skin. Brown the second side for 5 minutes, then brown the leg pieces about 8 minutes on the skin side, 5 minutes on the other side. Drain the duck on paper towels and discard the fat, leaving the brown bits in the pan.

Melt the butter in the hot pan and add the sliced garlic, shallots, and thyme and rosemary sprigs. Brown them lightly over low heat, sprinkle on the flour, stir well, and continue to cook over low heat, stirring, for another couple of minutes. Add the tomato paste and cook for another minute or 2. Add the stock, stir well, and bring to a boil. Let the sauce simmer, uncovered, for 30 minutes.

Rub the inside of an earthenware casserole with the cut side of the remaining clove of garlic and put the duck in the casserole, skin side up.

Preheat the oven to 350°F.

Put the orange juice, the lemon juice, the brandy, and the prunes in a nonreactive saucepan and bring to a boil. Reduce the heat and let the mixture simmer for 20 minutes. Add the sliced orange and lemon and bring the mixture back to a boil. With a slotted spoon, remove the prunes and orange and lemon slices from the pan and arrange them on top of the duck in the casserole. Let the liquid from the fruit continue to boil until it is reduced to ½ cup. Be careful not to let it burn. Add the vinegar; strong vinegar fumes will rise from the pot. Simmer for 5 minutes. Turn off the heat, strain the stock into the fruit sauce, and bring to a boil. Taste and season with salt and pepper if necessary. Pour the sauce over the duck, cover the casserole, and braise in the oven for 1½ hours, until the duck is very tender. Remove the casserole from the oven, let cool, and refrigerate overnight.

Three hours before serving, remove the duck from the refrigerator and with a spoon remove any fat that has congealed on the surface. An hour and a half before serving, put the covered casserole in the oven, turn it to 300°F, and reheat the duck. Serve the duck from the casserole.

CURED DUCK

The hardest part of moving this wonderful preparation to the Hudson Valley is learning to call duck confit *"cured duck,"* but everything about this preparation of duck preserved in its own fat makes it a natural for this region. Ducks are plentiful and good here; there is a long tradition of curing and preserving food; hearty dishes such as this are especially welcome where winters are cold; sophisticated cooks and consumers appreciate it and are willing to order it in restaurants or prepare it themselves.

I first came to know and love duck confit in southwestern France in the mid-1970s, when I spent a few days working in the restaurant of André Daguin. Total immersion in the characteristic preparations of the region began the minute I walked in the back door of the restaurant and caught intoxicating whiffs of goose fat, confit, foie gras, and cassoulet, which is perhaps the world's most famous and delicious pot of baked beans. These spe-cialties made such a profound impression that I returned several years later with my wife, Meg, on our honeymoon, which Daguin's generous attentions quickly turned into a luxurious series of foie gras picnics.

Only a kind fate could have set me down in the Hudson Valley a few years later with the specific assignment to develop a cuisine based on regional products. The area not only produces plenty of ducks, both wild and domesticated; it is also by far the largest producer of foie gras in the United States. I developed my recipe for cured duck and the foie gras recipes on pages 3–15 in the years following my trips to France. Though I have not managed to find a way to transplant cassoulet to the Hudson Valley, if you mix the filling for *White Bean Strudel*, page 28, with some bean stock, page 234, you'll come pretty close.

CURED DUCK

This duck is preserved in a dry cure mixture of salt, spices, and herbs, then cooked and sealed in its own fat. There are several recipes in this book starring cured duck: Grilled Cured Duck, page 143, White Bean Strudel with Cured Duck, page 28, Chopped Fresh Green Beans with Cured Duck, page 27. You can also slice it thin and serve it with green salad or potato salad. Using the carcasses of the ducks you cure and using the recipe on page 34, you can make a pot of Duck Stock to use in Roasted Onion and Garlic Soup with Goat Cheese Croutons, page 50, and Braised Duck with Brandied Prunes, Orange, and Lemon, page 138.

The two ducks called for in this recipe will yield between two and a half and three cups of rendered fat. If this is not enough to completely cover the ducks as they cook, supplement the duck fat with lard.

Two 4½- to 5-pound ducks

THE DRY CURE
1 head garlic, unpeeled
4 shallots
1 large bunch parsley
4 bay leaves
2 teaspoons chopped fresh thyme
4 or 5 tablespoons coarse salt
1 heaping teaspoon freshly ground pepper

Additional rendered duck fat or lard, if needed

Have the butcher cut the ducks into 4 pieces each: 2 leg and thigh pieces and 2 breast pieces, wing tips removed and the duck boned except for the wing bones. Ask the butcher to reserve and give to you the duck carcasses and all the bones, fat, and skin.

At home, trim the duck into neat pieces. Have ready a heavy-bottomed 3-quart saucepan for rendering the fat. Cut the skin into strips and the fat into 1-by-1-inch chunks and put it all in the saucepan. Add about an inch of cold water, cover the pot, and bring the water to a boil. Turn down the heat, uncover the pot, and gently cook until the fat has melted and the pieces of skin are crisp and brown. Turn off the heat and let the brown bits settle a bit, then strain the rendered fat into jars. Turn the pieces of crisp skin onto paper towels to drain, sprinkle with salt, and enjoy a delicious cook's treat. You will have about 3 cups of rendered fat. Refrigerate it.

Put the duck in the dry cure: Finely chop together the garlic, shallots, parsley, bay leaves, and thyme. Lay the meat on a dry surface and sprinkle it with a good layer of coarse salt and plenty of freshly ground pepper. The salt is part of the cure, so don't be stingy. Use about 1½ teaspoons of salt per piece, sprinkling it on both sides. Beginning with the garlic and shallot mixture, layer the duck pieces and the seasoning mixture in a wide, shallow, nonreactive bowl or baking pan, making sure all the duck comes in contact with the seasoning. End with a layer of the seasoning mixture. Cover the dish well with plastic wrap, pressing it closely around the duck, and put it in the refrigerator for 48 hours.

In a saucepan, slowly melt the duck fat. Take the duck out and scrape off the seasoning mixture, then wipe it clean with paper towels. Lay the duck in a sauté pan or Dutch oven large enough to hold it all and pour the fat over it. It must be covered completely by fat; the 3 cups you rendered from the ducks may not be enough. Melt enough additional rendered duck fat or lard to cover the pieces of duck completely.

Cook the duck in the fat, uncovered, *as slowly as possible,* with the fat barely simmering. The slower the cooking, the more tender and succulent the meat will be. It will take 2 to 2½ hours to cook. The duck is done when you can easily pull out a pin bone from the leg, the breast is very tender, and there is no juice when you pierce the breast with a fork. Let the duck cool in the fat.

Transfer the duck to a container just big enough to hold it and pour the fat over it. It must be completely covered with fat. Cover the container and store in the refrigerator. Wait a week before using the duck. With the seal unbroken, it will keep up to 3 months and aging only improves the flavor. Once you've broken the seal, use the duck within 2 to 3 weeks.

GRILLED CURED DUCK

This is a good and easy way to serve Cured Duck. That recipe yields enough to serve 8 people as a main course, but you may prefer to save some to use with crisp green beans, page 27, or in a strudel with white beans, page 28.

For 4 servings

Remove 4 pieces of duck from the container, rub off as much fat as possible, and allow the duck to come to room temperature. Fifteen minutes before serving, place the duck under the broiler 6 to 8 inches from the element and cook until it is heated through and the skin has become a little crisp. Serve with Sautéed Watercress, page 227, Sautéed Spinach with Garlic, page 225, or Herb Salad with Lemon Vinaigrette, page 55.

GRILLED MOULARD DUCK BREAST WITH PICKLED WATERMELON RIND

For the most elegant cookout possible, try these rich and extremely flavorful duck fillets. Moulard ducks are bred to produce foie gras. Hudson Valley Duck Products sells the duck breasts in vacuum-sealed packages, two breasts per package (see Sources, page 301). To cook this duck properly, you will need a grill with a lid. Serve with any of the potato salads in this book.

Serves 6

4 whole boned Moulard duck breasts (2 packages), split

FOR THE DRY MARINADE
Coarse salt
Lots of freshly ground pepper
4 tablespoons fresh ginger, peeled and shredded or grated
3 shallots, minced

GARNISH
Pickled Watermelon Rind (recipe follows)

Rub the duck all over with salt and lots of freshly ground black pepper. Combine the ginger and shallots and spread the mixture on the meat side of the duck breasts. Sandwich the breasts together, meat sides touching. Marinate at least 4 hours or overnight, covered, in the refrigerator.

Place the duck, skin side down, on a preheated grill set 5 or 6 inches above the coals. Cover the grill and let the duck cook for 8 or 9 minutes. Uncover the grill; the flames will be raging around the duck. Put the duck on a platter until the flames die down, then return it to the grill for another 2 or 3 minutes. Turn the duck and grill it for another 10 minutes. Remove it from the grill and let it rest for 10 minutes before serving. The duck will be medium-rare to medium.

Slice the duck on the diagonal into ¼-inch slices, arrange it on a platter, and serve with a bowl of the watermelon rind.

PICKLED WATERMELON RIND

Pickled watermelon rind harks back to my youth in Florida, where we never had a picnic or backyard barbecue without Jeannette Malouf's famous pickles. A transplanted Yankee, my mother adapted only a few Southern recipes. This is her best. I am not sure that it has a legitimate place in the Hudson Valley, *but it tastes good anywhere and we do grow watermelon here. Since watermelon is a perennial favorite, I don't think you will object to the excursion southward. Of course I couldn't leave my mother's recipe alone; I added ginger, which works very well with grilled duck.*

PICKLED WATERMELON RIND

The pink flesh of the watermelon makes a wonderful fruit salad or sorbet.

1 tablespoon kosher salt
4 cups watermelon rind, all pink flesh and green skin removed, cut into 2-by-½-inch strips

FOR THE SYRUP
1 quart apple cider vinegar
8 cups sugar
2 teaspoons whole cloves
2 cinnamon sticks

½ cup thinly sliced peeled fresh ginger

In a bowl big enough to hold the watermelon rind, dissolve the salt in 1 quart of water. Add the rind and soak overnight in the refrigerator.

Next day, drain the rind and boil it in fresh water to cover, just until it is translucent, about 10 minutes. Drain. Put several jars and lids through the dishwasher, including the dry cycle, and let them remain in the dishwasher until you are ready to use them.

Make the syrup. In a nonreactive saucepan, combine the vinegar, sugar, cloves, and cinnamon, bring to a boil, and simmer for 10 minutes, stirring occasionally, until the sugar is dissolved. Strain the syrup into another saucepan, add the rind and the ginger, bring to a boil, and simmer for 15 minutes. Using a slotted spoon, put the rind and ginger in the warm jars, fill with syrup, and cover loosely with the lids. Let the pickle cool, tighten the lids, and store in the refrigerator where it will keep for 2 months.

ROAST TURKEY WITH CLINTON VINEYARDS RIESLING GRAVY

Why are 95 percent of all turkeys sold in this country sold at Thanksgiving? The reason must be that although turkey is available year round and is always a favorite, it is at its best when combined with the fruits and vegetables that are still available locally during the holiday season that extends from Thanksgiving through New Year's Day. This is a wonderful time of year, when the last fruits of the season are being harvested. Farmstands are overflowing with ten varieties of apples, with pumpkins and squashes piled on the ground or tumbled together in huge wooden bins, great frilly bluegreen bunches of kale and boxes of shiny chestnuts. The chill in the air makes our thoughts turn to hearty foods cooking in warm fragrant kitchens. As November arrives, start planning the first of the holiday season's family gatherings.

Use the turkey in the recipe that follows as the centerpiece of a grand meal of the season. Choose one or two of the four stuffing recipes to accompany it. Here is a list of some of the recipes in this book that can contribute to a festive holiday dinner; look in the index for page numbers. Pumpkin Apple Soup, Cranberry and Citrus Relish, Baked Acorn Squash, Roasted Root Vegetables, Swiss Chard with Golden Onions, Brussels Sprouts with Chestnuts, Mushroom and Onion Gratins, Braised Wild Mushrooms, Baby Turnips and Carrots Caramelized in Buckwheat Honey, Butternut Squash and Sweet Potato Puree, Poached Pears with Tear of the Clouds Sabayon, Apple Pie with a Cheddar Crust, or Indian Pudding with Butterscotch Sauce.

You need a little game plan to help preparations go smoothly. Do the marketing three days ahead. Two days ahead, make the stock and cranberry relish, season the turkey, and cut up and dry out the bread for the stuffing. Get as much done as possible the day before the feast. Since you have already made so many preparations you should have time to work on the vegetables and the desserts and maybe even get the table set. On the day itself you can cook the turkey and stuffing and enjoy the celebration along with everyone else.

The Hudson Valley region Riesling you use in the gravy is the perfect wine to drink throughout the meal.

Serves 10

A 12-pound turkey

FOR THE TURKEY STOCK

2 turkey wings or drumsticks or 1 of each, purchased separately

1 onion, sliced

1 stalk celery, sliced

1 carrot, sliced

2 cloves garlic, sliced

Coarse salt and freshly ground pepper

4 cups Chicken Stock, page 31

FOR THE TURKEY

2 onions, peeled

2 stalks celery

2 carrots, peeled

4 cloves garlic, peeled

2 shallots, peeled

8 large sage leaves

3 large sprigs fresh thyme or 1 teaspoon dried thyme

2 bay leaves

5 tablespoons unsalted butter, softened

Coarse salt and freshly ground pepper

4 to 5 cups turkey stock

3 tablespoons flour

½ cup Clinton Vineyards Riesling

GARNISHES

Small bunches of grapes

Fresh sage leaves

Cranberry and Citrus Relish (recipe follows)

Make the turkey stock a day or 2 in advance: Preheat the oven to 400°F. Cut the 2 end pieces off each wing of the turkey and put them and the additional turkey wings or drumsticks in a roasting pan. Roast until the skin is well browned, 45 minutes to 1 hour. Put the turkey pieces in a soup pot. Remove the giblets from the cavity of the turkey and add the neck, gizzard, and heart to the soup pot. Set the liver aside. Add the sliced vegetables, a teaspoon of salt, and several grinds of pepper to the pot. Add the chicken stock and enough cold water to cover the meat and vegetables, bring to a boil, and simmer the stock over medium-low heat, partially covered, for 2 to 3 hours, until the meat is falling from the bones and the turkey gizzard is very tender. Poach the turkey liver in the stock for 6 or 7 minutes, remove it and refrigerate it. Strain the stock, reserving the giblets, and refrigerate it. You should have 5 to 6 cups of stock. Put the cooked giblets with the liver in the refrigerator.

Slice the remaining onions, celery, carrots, and garlic and chop the shallots and the sage. Put half these vegetables in the cavity of the turkey along with the thyme and the bay leaves. Put the remaining vegetables in a plastic bag and refrigerate. Partially truss the turkey by tying the legs together and wrapping the string around the tail to close the opening. Place the turkey on a platter and refrigerate it, uncovered, until you are ready to proceed with the recipe.

About 5 hours before serving time, remove the turkey from the refrigerator. Rub it all over with about 2 tablespoons of the softened butter and season it with salt and freshly ground pepper. Spread the reserved sliced vegetables over the bottom of a roasting pan and lay the turkey on top. Add a cup of stock to the pan.

About 4 hours before serving time, preheat the oven to 400°F. Put the turkey in the oven and roast for 1½ hours. Check to see if the turkey is browning evenly, and turn the pan if necessary. Fold a 30-inch piece of aluminum foil in half crosswise, then fold it loosely again and set it loosely over the turkey breast. Turn the oven temperature down to 325°F and put the stuffing in the oven. If the turkey is well browned, leave the foil tent on the breast for the remainder of the roasting time. If not, remove it for the last ½ hour of cooking. Roast the turkey for another 1½ hours, or until the internal temperature of the thigh is 165°F and the juices run clear yellow with no tinge of pink. Turn off the oven. Transfer the turkey to a platter, return it to the oven, and leave it (and the stuffing) in for another hour.

While the turkey is roasting, take the stock out of the refrigerator, remove the congealed fat from the top and heat the stock. Use a little stock to moisten the vegetables in the roasting pan if they are browning too fast or too much. While the turkey is resting, strain the roasting pan juices into the stock, reserving the vegetables. Use a little of the stock to thoroughly deglaze the roasting pan and return the liquid to the stock pot. Keep it simmering over very low heat. Cut the giblets, including the liver, into very fine dice.

Melt the remaining 2 or 3 tablespoons of butter in a sauté pan and add the vegetables from the roasting pan. Stir to combine, then sprinkle on the flour. Cook the mixture over medium heat, stirring frequently, until it is very thick and brown. Add the wine, stir to blend thoroughly, and cook, stirring frequently, until the wine is mostly evaporated and the mixture is very thick. Watch it carefully to see that it does not burn.

Add the remaining stock (about 3 cups) to the sauté pan. Stir the gravy to blend well and let it simmer for 10 minutes. Strain the gravy into a saucepan and simmer it gently for another 20 minutes or so, skimming as necessary. Add the chopped giblets to the gravy, and simmer 5 minutes more. Taste and reseason the gravy and put it in a sauceboat.

Present the turkey, garnished with bunches of grapes and fresh sage leaves, before carving. Serve the cranberry relish, the stuffing, and the other side dishes separately.

CRANBERRY AND CITRUS RELISH

In addition to its obvious affinity with turkey, this relish can also be served as a garnish with sliced cold meats and pâtés and terrines, or even as a topping for vanilla ice cream.

Makes 4 cups

1 navel orange
1 lemon
1 lime
½ cup shelled pecans
3 cups fresh cranberries
½ cup Grand Marnier or other orange-flavored liqueur
1 cup sugar

Using a zester or a vegetable peeler, remove the zest (colored part only—no white) from the orange, lemon, and lime and cut it into thin 1½-inch-long julienne strips. Set the peel next to the stove.

Slice off the bottom and top ends of the fruit and cut off the white pith and membrane. Holding the orange in your hand over a bowl, insert a sharp knife between the segments, cutting the flesh of the fruit from the membrane. Allow the flesh of the orange to fall into the bowl and squeeze out any juice remaining in the membrane. Discard the membrane. Repeat the process with the lemon and lime, removing all seeds as you proceed. Set the bowl of fruit next to the stove. Rough chop the nuts and place them next to the stove. Wash the cranberries and have them and the Grand Marnier at hand.

Caramelize the sugar: Put the sugar in a heavy-bottomed 2-quart saucepan and, stirring with a wooden spoon, melt it over medium heat. Let it continue to cook until it is completely dissolved and has become a clear amber syrup. This will take 3 to 4 minutes. Be careful not to let the sugar get too dark. As soon as it is ready, quickly add the nuts and roast them in the caramel for a minute or 2, until the nuts darken a bit and the sugar foams. Add the zest and stir constantly for 30 seconds. Immediately add the fruit with its juices, stir well, and cook another 30 seconds. Add the cranberries and let the mixture cook, stirring from time to time, until it has a jamlike consistency and most of the cranberries are broken, 11 or 12 minutes. Turn off the heat and stir in the Grand Marnier. Let the relish cool and refrigerate it, covered. Serve at room temperature.

The relish will keep for 1 week in the refrigerator.

STUFFINGS FOR CHICKEN AND TURKEY

Moist, delicate, almost like a savory bread pudding, these stuffings are simultaneously rich and light. You can make excellent stuffing by using the bags of bread for stuffing that are sold in supermarkets. But be sure to buy *unseasoned* stuffing. Both white bread and corn bread are available unseasoned. If you want to prepare the bread from scratch, it's best to cut up the fresh bread a day or two in advance, spread it out on baking sheets, and let it dry thoroughly before preparing the stuffing mixture.

Since all four of the stuffings that follow are baked in a pan, not inside the turkey, they can be prepared a day ahead and refrigerated, covered, until you put the turkey in the oven. Follow the baking directions in each recipe.

CRANBERRY AND CHESTNUT STUFFING

A testament to the season, chestnuts lend texture, cranberries their tart flavor to this stuffing.

1½ pounds chestnuts, to yield 1½ cups chestnut meats
6 tablespoons unsalted butter
1 cup chopped celery
1 cup chopped onion
2 cloves garlic, chopped
2 shallots, chopped
½ cup brandy
3 cups Chicken Stock, page 31
One 15-ounce package unseasoned bread for stuffing or 1 pound stale white bread,
    cut in ¼-inch cubes
¼ cup chopped parsley
1 tablespoon chopped thyme leaves

1 cup cranberries, chopped coarse
3 extra-large eggs
1 cup heavy cream
Coarse salt and freshly ground pepper

Preheat the oven to 400°F.

Roast and shell the chestnuts. Cut an X on the flat side of the shell of each chestnut. Put the nuts in a single layer in a roasting pan and roast for 45 minutes. Take the nuts out of the oven and, as soon as you can handle them, peel them. Keep the pan covered while you work: If the chestnuts cool, the bitter skin will adhere to the chestnut meat and the chestnuts will be very difficult to peel. Rough chop the chestnuts.

Generously butter a shallow 3-quart serving casserole or a 9-by-13-inch baking pan.

Melt 4 tablespoons of the butter in a large sauté pan and cook the celery, onion, garlic, and shallots over medium heat until wilted. Add the chestnuts and cook for 5 minutes more to brown the nuts a little. Add the brandy and 1 cup of the stock and cook until the liquid has almost evaporated.

Put the bread in a very large bowl. Add the parsley, the thyme, the cranberries, and the chestnut mixture. Break in the eggs and add the cream and the remaining 3 cups stock. Using your hands, combine everything thoroughly. Season liberally with salt and freshly ground pepper. Spread the stuffing mixture evenly in the buttered casserole, dot with the remaining butter, and cover with foil. You can prepare the stuffing up to this point a day in advance. If you do so, remove it from the refrigerator 4 hours before serving time.

If you want to cook the stuffing separately, preheat the oven to 350°F. Put the stuffing in the oven and bake for 45 minutes. Remove the foil and bake about 20 minutes more, until the stuffing is firm and a light crust has formed.

If you are cooking the stuffing with the turkey, remove the foil, put it, uncovered, in the oven when you turn the temperature down to 325°F and leave it in the oven until the turkey is carved.

CORN BREAD AND FISHER'S ISLAND OYSTER STUFFING

This stuffing has a year-round appeal and is especially good with Braised Chicken with Tarragon and Tomato, page 127.

6 tablespoons unsalted butter
1 cup chopped onion
1 cup chopped celery
3 cloves garlic, chopped
2 shallots, chopped
2 tablespoons chopped tarragon
1 cup good-quality dry white wine
1 pound package unseasoned cornbread stuffing mix or 1 pound cornbread,
    crumbled and allowed to dry for 1 or 2 hours
Coarse salt and freshly ground pepper
36 freshly shucked Fisher's Island oysters with their liquor or 18 large oysters,
    cut in half
3 extra-large eggs
½ cup heavy cream
1 cup Chicken Stock, page 31

In a large sauté pan, melt 4 tablespoons of the butter and cook the onion, celery, garlic, and shallots until they are wilted. Add the tarragon and cook another minute. Add the wine, turn the heat to high, and cook, stirring frequently, until the wine has almost completely evaporated.

Generously butter a shallow 3-quart serving casserole or a 9-by-13-inch baking pan.

Put the corn bread in a large bowl and season with a little salt and plenty of freshly ground pepper. Add the oysters, the eggs, cream, and stock, and mix well with your hands, breaking up the corn bread so it absorbs as much liquid as possible. Add the vegetable mixture and combine well. Season with more salt and pepper. Spread the stuffing mixture evenly in the buttered casserole, dot with the remaining butter, and cover with foil. You can prepare the stuffing up to this point a day in advance. If you do so, remove it from the refrigerator 4 hours before serving time.

If you want to cook the stuffing separately, preheat the oven to 350°F. Put the stuffing in the oven and bake for 45 minutes. Remove the foil and bake about 20 minutes more, until the stuffing is firm and a light crust has formed.

If you are cooking the stuffing with the turkey, remove the foil, put it, uncovered, in the oven when you turn the temperature down to 325°F and leave it in the oven until the turkey is carved.

WILD MUSHROOM STUFFING

The earthy mushroom flavor goes well with a plain roast chicken. Use spring or fall mushrooms in season.

1 recipe Braised Wild Mushrooms, page 199, but omit the final 2 tablespoons of butter
6 tablespoons unsalted butter
1 cup chopped onion
1 cup chopped celery
2 cloves garlic, chopped
2 shallots, chopped
3 cups Chicken Stock, page 31
One 15-ounce package unseasoned bread for stuffing or 1 pound stale bread,
    cut into ¼-inch cubes
2 teaspoons chopped thyme
¼ cup chopped parsley
3 extra-large eggs
1 cup heavy cream
Coarse salt and freshly ground pepper

Melt 4 tablespoons of the butter in a large sauté pan and cook the onion, celery, garlic, and shallots until they are wilted. Add the mushrooms and 1 cup of stock, stir well, and cook the mixture until the liquid has almost all evaporated.

Generously butter a shallow 3-quart serving casserole or a 9-by-13-inch baking pan.

Put the bread in a large bowl. Add the thyme, the parsley, and the mushroom mixture. Break in the eggs and add the cream and the remaining stock. Using your hands, combine everything thoroughly. Season the mixture with some salt and freshly ground pepper. Spread the stuffing mixture evenly in the buttered casserole, dot with the remaining butter, and cover with foil. You can prepare the stuffing up to this point a day in advance. If you do so, remove it from the refrigerator 4 hours before serving time.

If you want to cook the stuffing alone, preheat the oven to 350°F. Put the stuffing in the oven and bake for 45 minutes. Remove the foil and bake about 20 minutes more, until the stuffing is firm and a light crust has formed.

If you are cooking the stuffing with the turkey, remove the foil, put it, uncovered, in the oven when you turn the temperature down to 325°F and leave it in the oven until the turkey is carved.

SAUSAGE, APPLE, AND PINE NUT STUFFING

A variation on a traditional sausage stuffing, the fruit and pine nuts contribute another level of flavor. This stuffing, served with a salad, would make an excellent lunch.

1 pound bulk breakfast sausage meat
1 cup chopped onion
2 cloves garlic, chopped
2 shallots, chopped
1 cup pine nuts
2 large tart apples such as Baldwin or Ida Red, peeled and cored
1 cup chopped celery
4 tablespoons unsalted butter plus additional for pan and dotting top
1 tablespoon chopped thyme
5 large sage leaves, chopped
½ cup dry white wine
½ cup apple cider
One 15-ounce package unseasoned bread for stuffing or 1 pound stale bread,
      cut into ¼-inch cubes
3 extra-large eggs
1 cup heavy cream
2 cups Chicken Stock, page 31
Coarse salt and freshly ground pepper
2 tablespoons chopped parsley

Put the sausage meat with a little water in a large sauté pan and over high heat mash it until all lumps are broken up. Cook the sausage until it changes color and the water has evaporated. If the sausage is fatty, pour off all but 2 tablespoons of fat from the pan. Stir in the onion, garlic, shallots, and pine nuts and cook over medium-high heat. Cut the apples into ¼-inch dice and add them and the celery to the pan. Add the butter and half the chopped thyme and sage and continue to cook, stirring frequently. After 3 or 4 minutes, when the apples and celery have begun to soften, add the wine and cider and stir well. Raise the heat and boil until the liquid is almost gone.

Generously butter a shallow 3-quart serving casserole or a 9-by-13-inch baking pan.

In a large bowl combine the bread with the sausage mixture. Break in the eggs and add the cream and the remaining stock. Combine thoroughly, using your hands. Season the mixture with salt and freshly ground pepper, add the remaining chopped thyme and sage, and the parsley, and mix to combine everything well. Spread the stuffing mixture evenly in the buttered casserole, dot with butter, and cover with foil. You can prepare the stuffing up to this point a day in advance. If you do so, remove it from the refrigerator 4 hours before serving time.

If you want to cook the stuffing separately, preheat the oven to 350°F. Put the stuffing in the oven and bake for 45 minutes. Remove the foil and bake about 20 minutes more, until the stuffing is firm and a light crust has formed.

If you are cooking the stuffing with the turkey, remove the foil, put it, uncovered, in the oven when you turn the temperature down to 325°F and leave it in the oven until the turkey is carved.

ROAST GOOSE WITH SPICED PEARS AND WILD RICE AND SOUR CHERRY SALAD

Roast goose, with its crisp skin and succulent meat, conjures up images of happy feasting in a warm house while the winter rages outside. It may be a surprise to learn that it can also be a convenient meal; cooking your goose a day ahead and reheating it considerably reduces last-minute scramble. In order to give the goose a chance to age a little, improving its flavor and texture, buy it two days in advance (three days if you plan to cook it a day ahead), season it as directed below, and let it sit, uncovered, in the refrigerator until 2 hours before roasting time. The pears are cooked in Brotherhood Winery Pinot Noir, a good choice for drinking with the goose.

Serves 6

1 goose
1 tablespoon extra virgin olive oil
Coarse salt and freshly ground pepper
½ orange (save remaining half for garnish)
½ lemon (save remaining half for garnish)
1 shallot, peeled
2 cloves garlic, smashed
2 bay leaves
3 or 4 sprigs fresh thyme

FOR THE PEARS
6 New York State Bosc pears
One 3-inch stick cinnamon
3 or 4 cloves
1 tablespoon freshly ground black pepper
1 to 2 bottles Brotherhood Winery Pinot Noir (enough to cover the pears)
½ orange
½ lemon

1 recipe Wild Rice and Sour Cherry Salad (recipe follows)

FOR THE SAUCE
1½ cups pear cooking liquid
½ cup good-quality red wine vinegar
4 cups Chicken Stock, page 31
2 tablespoons flour
1 tablespoon tomato paste
½ lemon

GARNISHES
1 orange, cut into thin half-moon slices
1 lemon, cut into thin half-moon slices
Sprigs of fresh thyme in bunches

Cut off the first 2 joints of the wings of the goose and cut off all visible fat. Cut the neck into 1-inch pieces. Reserve the gizzard, covered, in the refrigerator. Rub the goose all over with the olive oil and season it inside and out with salt and pepper. Put the ½ orange and lemon, the shallot, garlic, bay leaves, and thyme in the cavity of the goose and truss it. Set the goose on a rack in a roasting pan and lay the wing and neck bones around it. Refrigerate, uncovered, for 2 days.

Preheat the oven to 400°F.

Take the goose out of the refrigerator 2 hours before cooking (5 hours before serving) to allow it to come to room temperature. Roast the goose for 1 hour.

While the goose is roasting, cook the pears. Peel them carefully to retain the shape, leaving the stems on. Cut a thin slice from the bottom of each pear so it can stand upright; stand the pears in a saucepan just big enough to hold them and deep enough so they will be completely covered with wine. Add the cinnamon, cloves, pepper, wine, and sugar and squeeze the orange and lemon into the pan, adding the rind to the liquid. Bring to a boil, cover, and cook gently until the pears are just tender, 30 to 40 minutes. Let them cool in the wine.

While the goose is roasting, prepare the wild rice salad.

After an hour, take the goose out of the oven. Remove the bones from the pan and put them in a saucepan. Cover the drumsticks with foil to keep them from drying out, turn the oven down to 350°F, and return the goose to the oven to roast for 1 hour more. Then turn the oven off and leave the goose in the oven for an additional hour without opening the oven door.

Start the sauce. Remove the pears from the cooking liquid and set them aside. Add the gizzard and 1½ cups of the pear cooking liquid to the bones in the saucepan, bring to a boil, and reduce to a syrup. Add the vinegar and again reduce the liquid to a few tablespoons of syrup. Add the stock, bring to a boil, and simmer for 15 minutes.

When the goose has rested in the turned-off oven for an hour, remove it on the rack to a carving board, tilting it to allow the juices in the cavity to run into the pan. Over low heat, cook the juices and goose fat in the roasting pan until the fat is clarified and all solids have sunk to the bottom of the pan. Pour off all but 2 tablespoons of the fat, stir in the flour, and cook for 2 or 3 minutes. Stir in the tomato paste and strain the pear juice/stock mixture into the pan. Mix well and transfer it all to a saucepan. Add the lemon and reduce the sauce to 2 cups, about 20 minutes.

If you have cooked the goose a day ahead, remove it from the refrigerator 5 hours before serving. Preheat the oven to 300°F and reheat the goose for 45 minutes to 1 hour. Serve immediately.

A whole roasted goose is a handsome sight; you may wish to present it whole before carving. To carve, cut off the drumsticks and place them at opposite ends of a platter. Carve the thigh and breast meat and arrange it on the platter. Garnish the platter with the pears, the lemon and orange slices, and bunches of fresh thyme and spoon a little sauce over the goose. Serve the remaining sauce in a sauceboat and pass a bowl of wild rice salad.

WILD RICE AND SOUR CHERRY SALAD

Fresh Hudson Valley sour cherries are available at farmstands and greenmarkets during the first three weeks of July. Dried sour cherries can be bought at specialty grocery stores.

Serves 6 to 8

8 ounces wild rice
¼ cup fresh or dried sour cherries
½ cup good-quality brandy
1 large carrot, grated fine
¾ cup sliced almonds, toasted

2 shallots, minced

1 large apple, peeled and grated

3 tablespoons balsamic vinegar

3 tablespoons olive oil

Coarse salt and freshly ground pepper

Boil the wild rice in plenty of salted water until tender, about 1 hour. Drain.

Combine the cherries and brandy in a small saucepan, bring to a boil, turn off the heat, and let them steep for ½ hour. Drain.

While warm, toss the rice with the remaining ingredients. Let the salad rest for 1 hour or so, reseason, then serve at room temperature.

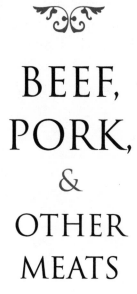

BEEF,
PORK,
&
OTHER
MEATS

Although there are still many farms where animals are raised, the Hudson Valley is not a big producer of beef or veal. But on farms throughout the region pork, lamb, and goat are increasingly being raised for sale in local markets. This meat is of high quality and much of it is being raised on organic feed without the use of hormones or other chemicals.

In this chapter, very contemporary recipes for roasts, stews, and grilled steak combine meats with garlic, onions, potatoes, cabbage, apples, squash, horseradish, and lettuce from local farms to evoke the old-fashioned character of farm food of a hundred years ago.

BRAISED BEEF WITH BLACK PEPPER, SHALLOTS, AND GARLIC

As with most soups, stews, and braised dishes, you can make this at least a day before serving it. You'll need an additional two days to marinate the meat, so start your preparations at least four days in advance. Cabernet Sauvignon from Baldwin Vineyards in Pine Bush, New York, on the Shawangunk Wine Trail, one of the boldest Cabernets in the region, is a good wine to cook the beef in and to drink with the meal.

Serves 8

3 pounds boneless beef shank, well trimmed of fat and sinew

FOR THE MARINADE
3 shallots, sliced
3 cloves garlic, sliced
1½ cups dry red wine, or enough to cover the meat

2 tablespoons freshly ground pepper
Coarse salt
1½ cups vegetable oil for browning the meat
2 tablespoons unsalted butter
36 small shallots, peeled
36 cloves garlic, peeled
2 tablespoons flour
2 cups dry red wine such as Baldwin Vineyards Cabernet Sauvignon
6 cups Rich Meat Stock, page 32, reduced to 3 cups
2 tablespoons chopped parsley

Cut the meat into large pieces, about 2 by 2 inches, put it into a bowl just large enough to hold it, and mix in the shallots and garlic. Add just enough red wine to cover the meat. Cover the meat with plastic wrap and marinate it in the refrigerator for 48 hours.

Preheat the oven to 325°F.

Take the meat out of the marinade and blot it dry on paper towels. Discard the marinade.

Spread the freshly ground pepper on the meat and pat it into all the surfaces. Sprinkle the meat with salt. Heat 1 cup of the oil in a large sauté pan and, over high heat, brown the meat well on all sides. In order not to crowd the meat, you will probably have to brown it in 3 batches. When you have one batch left to brown, discard the oil, wash and dry the pan, and add the remaining ½ cup of oil to the pan. Heat it and brown the remaining meat. Drain the browned meat on paper towels and put it in a serving casserole. Pour off the oil and add the butter to the hot pan. Add the whole shallots and garlic and brown them gently in the butter for 6 or 7 minutes. Remove them from the pan and spread them over the meat.

Stir the flour into the butter in the sauté pan and cook the *roux* until it is lightly browned, 2 or 3 minutes. Add the wine and whisk well. Cook the mixture over medium-high heat, stirring frequently, until the wine is almost cooked away. Be careful not to burn the mixture. Add the reduced stock, stir well, and simmer 3 or 4 minutes. Pour the sauce over the meat, loosely cover the casserole with foil, and put it in the oven. After about 1 hour, uncover the casserole and continue to cook the meat for 1 hour and 15 minutes more. Let the casserole cool. Cover and refrigerate overnight.

Three hours before serving, remove the casserole from the refrigerator to let it come to room temperature. With a spoon, remove any fat that has congealed on the surface. An hour and a half before serving, put the casserole in the oven, turn the temperature to 300°F and reheat.

Sprinkle the dish with chopped parsley and serve with Horseradish Mashed Potatoes, page 187.

ROASTED PRIME RIB OF BEEF WITH CARAMELIZED ONIONS

This is a classic rib roast, a wonderful focal point for a holiday menu. To be sure this feast is as good as you want it to be, you need to know not only how to cook the roast, but exactly what to order from the butcher. In this country, all cuts of meat are standardized by the U. S. Department of Agriculture. When an oven-ready rib roast is called by butchers a "109 rib" or "prime rib," the word prime identifies the cut, not the grade of the meat. Thus, you could order a choice prime rib or a prime prime rib. Either one is excellent; the prime prime rib will be very expensive. If you ask for a 109 rib, the bones will be cut properly, the deckle (a protective layer of fat covering the eye of the rib) will be lifted off, the shoulder bone removed, the chine bones properly trimmed, and the fat will be trimmed to a certain percentage. Ask for four ribs from a 109 rib; be sure it is cut from the loin end, not from the shoulder or chuck end. Remind the butcher to loosen the deckle for you. To be sure of getting what you want, order the meat a week in advance. If the butcher insists on selling you the whole rib, have the remaining three ribs cut into three chops and freeze them for future use. Each rib makes a wonderful broiled steak for two. So remember: order, one to two weeks in advance, half (four ribs) of a 109 oven-ready rib, loin end only. The butcher will be impressed that you did your homework! This recipe does not include a sauce or a *jus*—the meat doesn't require one as the onions provide a rich complementary flavor. If you wish, serve prepared horseradish on the side.

Serves 12

A 4-rib roast of beef, cut from loin end (see above)
Coarse salt and freshly ground pepper
24 medium onions, peeled
1 bunch fresh thyme, for roast and garnish

Preheat the oven to 400°F.

Fold back the deckle and season the top of the roast heavily with salt and pepper. Put the deckle back in place, put the roast, bone side down, in a roasting pan and roast 1½ hours.

While the meat is cooking, cut a thin slice off the bottom of each onion so it will stand securely without falling apart. Using a skewer, pierce through each onion in 3 or 4 places and

WINTER
MENU

Endive, Apple,
and Roasted
Walnut Salad
with Little
Rainbow
Berkshire
Blue Cheese

Roasted
Prime Rib of
Beef with
Carmelized
Onions

Horseradish
Mashed
Potatoes

Sautéed
Watercress

Brown Sugar
and Chestnut
Pudding

insert stems of thyme through the holes. After 1½ hours, skim off half the fat in the roasting pan, add the onions, and turn the oven down to 300°F. Turn the onions over after 30 minutes and continue to roast for another 30 minutes. Then turn the onions again, turn the oven off, and leave the roast in the oven for another hour without opening the oven door. Remove the roast to a carving board and set the onions on paper towels to drain. The roast will be medium rare.

Carving hint: Before the roast goes to the table, remove the deckle and the chine bones (small bones perpendicular to the rib bones) and trim off the piece of solid fat that runs the entire width of the roast between the eye and the end of the rib bones. Carve slices the thickness you prefer and put them on a platter. Garnish with the caramelized onions and sprigs of fresh thyme.

BOILED BEEF SHANK SALAD WITH POTATOES AND HORSERADISH

This salad turns a boiled dinner into something light and summery. You'll have to cook the meat at least a day in advance.

Serves 6 as a main course

FOR THE BEEF
2½ pounds boneless beef shank, well trimmed of fat and sinew
1 large carrot, sliced
1 stalk celery, sliced
2 cloves garlic, smashed
1 medium onion, sliced
2 bay leaves
2 pinches dried thyme
1 teaspoon black peppercorns
1 teaspoon salt

FOR THE SALAD
18 small boiling potatoes, such as Yukon Gold or fingerlings
1 bunch radishes
2 heads Bibb lettuce
¾ cup Mustard Herb Vinaigrette, page 286
2 tablespoons prepared horseradish
Coarse salt and freshly ground pepper

GARNISH
¾ cup sour cream
2 tablespoons prepared horseradish
1 piece fresh horseradish, peeled

Prepare the beef: Put the meat in a heavy soup pot or Dutch oven and cover by 2 inches with cold water. Add the remaining ingredients for the beef, bring to a boil, turn down the heat, and simmer, partially covered, until the meat is tender, 2 to 2½ hours. Let the meat cool in the broth and chill it in the broth overnight. Remove it from the refrigerator 2 hours before serving. Remove any congealed fat and reserve the broth for another use.

Boil the potatoes 20 to 30 minutes, until they are tender, and drain them. When they are cool enough to handle, peel them and cut them into ¼-inch slices. Carefully separate the leaves of the lettuces, wash them, and dry them thoroughly. Trim the radishes and slice them ⅛ inch thick. Prepare the vinaigrette and stir the 2 tablespoons prepared horseradish into it. Combine the sour cream and prepared horseradish for the garnish. Trim the meat and cut it into neat slices, each about ⅜ inch thick.

Arrange the salad on a large round or oval platter as follows: Fan the lettuce leaves in concentric arcs over ⅔ of the platter, starting with the largest leaves and ending with the smallest. Leaving a wide border of lettuce, scatter potato and radish slices in several layers over the lettuce. Arrange the slices of beef on the bottom third of the platter. Sprinkle everything with coarse salt and freshly ground pepper and spoon the vinaigrette evenly over the entire salad. Then grate a generous snowfall of fresh horseradish over all. Don't omit this step—it's the secret ingredient that makes all the difference.

Serve the salad at the table on individual plates and pass the horseradish sauce in a bowl.

SLICED BUFFALO STEAK WITH GRILLED ONIONS AND GARLIC

For a cookout that's off the beaten track, grill buffalo steaks. Buffalo meat is lean, sweet, juicy, and much lower in fat than beef. Though you probably can't get it in your local supermarket, some butcher shops carry it or can get it for you, and it's easy to order (see page 301). Although they aren't quite as unusual as buffalo, 18-ounce beef sirloin steaks are also delicious. Follow the same cooking instructions.

Serves 4

FOR THE MARINADE
1 cup dry red wine
2 tablespoons olive oil
2 cloves garlic, sliced
2 bay leaves
1 tablespoon green peppercorns, drained and crushed
1 tablespoon green peppercorn juice

Two 18-ounce boneless sirloin buffalo steaks, 2 to 2½ inches thick
Grilled Onions and Garlic, page 235

GARNISH
1 tablespoon whole green peppercorns, drained
1 teaspoon coarse salt

Combine the marinade ingredients and marinate the steak, covered, in the refrigerator for 4 hours or overnight. Blanch the onions and garlic.

Take the meat out of the refrigerator 1 hour before cooking and let it come to room temperature. These thick steaks must be cooked over very hot coals and turned several times while cooking. When turning meat, always use tongs rather than a fork to avoid piercing the meat and releasing the juices.

Remove the meat from the marinade, reserving the marinade. On a hot but not flaming grill, place the steaks 4 to 5 inches from the coals. Baste with the marinade every time you turn the meat, making sure some of the green peppercorns adhere to the surface. After 5 minutes, turn the steaks over and let them cook another 5 minutes before turning them again. Total cooking time for very rare meat is about 15 minutes. Cook it another 4 or 5 minutes, turning several times, for medium-rare meat. Let the meat rest for 10 or 15 minutes before slicing. While the meat is resting, grill the onions and garlic.

Slice the steak ¼ inch thick, put it on a platter, and arrange the grilled onions and garlic around the meat. Sprinkle the meat with the green peppercorns and a little salt.

BRAISED VEAL SHANKS WITH CITRUS AND SAGE

In this interesting spinoff from *osso buco*, the familiar flavors of veal and vegetables are set off by an unusual combination of citrus fruits. The gelatinous quality of the veal binds the meat and fruit juices into an almost syrupy, wonderfully complex sauce. The fresh sage, floral and aromatic, adds a final dimension to a satisfying dish. This dish can be prepared from two to five days ahead.

Serves 12

Twelve 1½-inch slices veal shank (4 shanks), bone in, 12 to 14 ounces each
   (also sold as *osso buco*)
Coarse salt and freshly ground pepper
1 cup vegetable oil
1 cup unsalted butter
2 carrots, peeled and chopped
2 large onions, chopped
2 leeks, white parts only, carefully cleaned and chopped
2 stalks celery, chopped
2 medium turnips, peeled and chopped
4 tablespoons fresh sage, chopped
1 cup flour
6 tablespoons tomato paste
1½ cups dry white wine
4 cups fresh orange juice, plus extra for finishing sauce
10 cups Rich Meat Stock, page 32, or just enough to cover the meat
herb sachet: Stems of fresh sage
              2 tablespoons black peppercorns
              3 bay leaves
              3 cloves garlic, split   tied together in a
              1 teaspoon dried thyme   double layer of cheesecloth
              4 or 5 sprigs parsley

GARNISH
8 large leaves fresh sage
4 oranges
2 lemons

Preheat the oven to 300°F.

Season the veal with salt and pepper. Heat the oil in a heavy Dutch oven and brown the meat very thoroughly over high heat, 10 minutes on each side. Remove the meat from the pot and pour off and discard the oil.

Melt the butter in the same pot. Add all the chopped vegetables and the sage and sauté them for 10 minutes, stirring frequently. Sprinkle the flour over the vegetables, stir well, and cook, stirring for another 2 or 3 minutes. Add the tomato paste and wine and bring to a boil, stirring frequently to deglaze the pan. Reduce the mixture until almost dry. Add the orange juice and stock, stir well, add the herb sachet, and return the meat to the pan. Bring to a boil, cover the pot, and braise in the oven for 1½ to 2 hours, or until the meat is almost falling from the bones.

When the meat is done, remove it from the pan, trim off any fat, place the meat in a serving casserole, and cover. Strain the liquid from the Dutch oven into a saucepan. Reduce the liquid, skimming frequently, until the sauce is syrupy and clarified, but not too intense. Season with salt and pepper and adjust the flavor and consistency with some fresh orange juice. Strain the sauce over the meat, cover the dish again, and let the casserole cool. Refrigerate at least overnight, or up to 4 or 5 days.

Three hours before serving, remove the casserole from the refrigerator to allow it to come to room temperature. With a spoon, remove any fat that has congealed on the surface. An hour and a half before serving, put the covered casserole in the oven and turn it to 300°F.

While the meat is reheating, cut the sage into fine julienne and prepare the citrus garnish. Using a vegetable peeler, peel the zest from one orange and one lemon and cut the zest into very thin strips. Blanch the zest in a little boiling water for a couple of minutes, drain, and reserve. Over a bowl, segment all of the oranges and lemons.

Garnish each piece of meat with alternating orange and lemon segments and decoratively sprinkle the zest and fresh sage. Serve the veal from the casserole.

ROAST FRESH HAM WITH RED CABBAGE AND APPLES

This fresh pork roast will serve a large gathering of people who appreciate hearty food. Don't worry if the group includes the most jaded epicures; they always turn out to love delicious simple fare. Start cooking the ham at least six hours before you plan to serve it. Serve the ham with Cascade Mountain Seyval Blanc.

Serves 12

A whole fresh ham (not cured, not smoked), about 12 to 15 pounds

FOR THE ROASTING PAN
1 large onion
1 stalk celery
2 carrots
4 cloves garlic
2 shallots
3 large sprigs fresh thyme
2 bay leaves

FOR THE CABBAGE
2 large onions, sliced
3 medium Mutsu or Cortland apples, peeled, cored, and cut into 12 wedges each
Coarse salt and freshly ground pepper
1 cup good-quality dry white wine
1 cup Chicken Stock, page 31
5 pounds red cabbage

FOR THE SAUCE
1 cup apple cider
1 cup good-quality dry white wine
1 cup Chicken Stock, page 31
2 tablespoons good-quality red wine vinegar

GARNISH

1 large red-skinned apple

Don't remove the rind of the ham, which is crisp and delicious when roasted. If you can, have the butcher score the rind in a 1½-inch crisscross pattern. You can do it yourself; use a sharp serrated knife because the rind is quite tough.

Preheat the oven to 350°F.

Cut the vegetables for the roasting pan into chunks and spread them, with the thyme and bay leaves, in the pan. Set the ham on top and roast it for 3 hours. Check the vegetables in the pan from time to time and add a cup or so of water to the pan if they are sticking. Don't let them burn.

While the meat is cooking, prepare the onions, apples, and cabbage: Spoon 2 or 3 tablespoons of fat from the roasting pan into a large skillet or sauté pan and sauté the onions with the apples for 10 minutes, stirring frequently. Season with 2 teaspoons of salt and some pepper and add the wine and stock to the pan. Bring to a boil, cover the pan, and simmer until the apples are tender, 10 to 15 minutes. Trim the cabbage and cut it into 2-inch wedges. Cut out the core and slice the cabbage ½ inch thick.

After 3 hours, take the ham out of the oven. Set a baking sheet next to the roasting pan and, using pot holders or kitchen towels, pick up the ham and put it on the baking sheet. Pour off and discard the fat and vegetables in the roasting pan.

Prepare the sauce: Add the cider, wine, and stock to the roasting pan. Bring to a boil on top of the stove and deglaze the pan, scraping all browned bits into the liquid. Add the cabbage, spreading it to cover the surface of the pan, and pour the apple mixture over it. Toss everything together to combine evenly and lay the ham on top of the cabbage. Cover the pan with foil and roast 1 hour. Then uncover the pan and continue to roast the ham, stirring the exposed cabbage from time to time, until the cabbage is cooked and the ham is crisp and brown and has come to an internal temperature of 165°F on a meat thermometer, about 1 hour more.

Set the meat on a carving board for at least 1 hour; it will still be hot after 2 hours and it won't harm it a bit to wait that long. Using a slotted spoon, transfer the cabbage to a large, heatproof serving platter, season with salt and pepper, and keep warm in a low oven. Strain the pan juices into a saucepan, remove as much fat as you can and, skimming from time to time, reduce the sauce to 3 cups. Stir in the vinegar and simmer the sauce 5 minutes more. Taste and season with salt and pepper.

Cut off the crisp rind and cut it into small serving pieces. Carve the ham perpendicular to the bone into ¼-inch thick slices and arrange them over the cabbage. Scatter the crisp rind over the meat. Grate the unpeeled red apple and sprinkle it over the platter as garnish. Serve the meat and the cabbage together and pass the sauce in a sauceboat.

SPICED LOIN OF PORK
WITH BAKED ACORN SQUASH

This spicy roast is beautifully balanced by mellow acorn squash doused with bourbon. The vegetarian version of Braised Bitter Greens, page 222, is good with this.

Serves 6

FOR THE RUB
2 tablespoons coarse salt
½ teaspoon dried thyme
¼ teaspoon ground cloves
¼ teaspoon ground cinnamon
¼ teaspoon freshly grated nutmeg
2 bay leaves, crushed and chopped
1 heaping teaspoon black peppercorns, crushed or ground coarse

A 4-pound boneless pork loin roast, trimmed and tied

FOR THE SQUASH
3 small acorn squash, about 1 pound each
Coarse salt and freshly ground pepper
6 tablespoons unsalted butter, softened
1½ cups bourbon or brandy

½ cup Chicken Stock, page 31

Combine the rub ingredients and rub the mixture into every surface of the pork. Cover well and refrigerate at least overnight or for 2 days. Turn the meat over every 12 hours or so. Remove the meat from the refrigerator an hour before cooking, and put it on a rack in a roasting pan.

Preheat the oven to 350°F.

Prepare the squash: Cut the squash in half from stem to root end and remove the seeds. Score the flesh in the bowl of the squash in a crisscross pattern about ¼ inch deep, season with salt and pepper, and spread a tablespoon of butter in each half. Put an inch of water in a baking pan and set the squash, cut side up, in the pan. Pour ¼ cup bourbon into each squash half.

Put the pork and the squash in the oven at the same time. Roast the meat, uncovered, for 1½ hours. Baste occasionally, at first with half the chicken stock, later with the concentrated pan juices. Remove the roast to a warm platter and let it rest for 20 minutes. Turn off the oven and let the squash remain there until serving time.

Skim the fat from the roasting pan juices and, over medium heat, deglaze the pan with the remaining chicken stock. Simmer for a minute or 2. Cut the meat into ⅜-inch slices, arrange it in the center of a large platter, and pour the pan juices over it. Set the acorn squash around the meat. Serve with a mound of braised greens.

RACK OF LAMB
WITH WHITE BEANS
AND SWEET ROASTED GARLIC PUREE

This roast is festive and very easy to prepare. The beans, tomato compote, and garlic puree can be cooked a day ahead and the meat requires only a few minutes to get ready. It will cook in the time you need for a first course. A green salad completes the feast.

Serves 6

1 recipe White Beans, page 234, liquid reserved (Prepare a day in advance.)
½ cup Tomato Compote, page 293
1 recipe Roasted Garlic Puree, page 296
Coarse salt and freshly ground pepper
1 cup fresh white bread crumbs
2 tablespoons extra virgin olive oil
2 tablespoons extra virgin olive oil
2 racks of lamb, 1¼ pounds each, Frenched (ends of bones free of all fat and meat)
½ cup vegetable oil
3 tablespoons chopped parsley

Bring the cooked beans to a boil, add the Tomato Compote and 3 tablespoons of the garlic puree, and season with salt and pepper. Cover and let simmer gently while the lamb is cooking.

Preheat the oven to 400°F.

Using your fingers, combine the bread crumbs with the olive oil.

Set a plate lined with several layers of paper towels next to the stove. Season the lamb with salt and pepper. In a skillet, heat the vegetable oil until hot but not smoking and brown the lamb on all sides over high heat. Drain the lamb on the paper towels and discard the oil.

Spread the meat side of each rack of lamb with 2½ tablespoons of garlic puree. Sprinkle ½ cup of the bread crumb mixture over each, patting it into the garlic puree. Place the racks in a roasting pan, garlic side up. The meat can be prepared up to this point several hours ahead.

For medium-rare meat, roast the lamb 20 to 25 minutes, to an internal temperature of 130°F on a meat thermometer. Let stand for 10 minutes.

Stir the parsley into the white beans, reserving 1 tablespoon for garnish, and mound the beans in the center of a heated platter. Carve the racks into chops (6 chops per rack plus 2 ends) and arrange them around the beans. Sprinkle the platter with the remaining chopped parsley.

POTATOES, MUSHROOMS, CORN, & OTHER VEGETABLES

The only way to do justice to the wonderful vegetables of the Hudson Valley is to seek them out at the source. There are listings in the Sources section of this book, page 301, for New York City greenmarkets and for the Valley's community farmers markets, along with a sampling of farmstands throughout the region. But from May, when local asparagus becomes available, through Thanksgiving when the harvest season ends in a burst of gold, red, brown, and green, farmstands appear in every village and along every country road. Some are only a table or wagon offering the surplus from a family garden. Others sell honey, cider, fruit, and local breads and cheeses as well as an assortment of vegetables. It is a pleasure to drive through the lovely countryside looking for the tenderest new lettuces, the smallest, firmest, shiniest zucchini, tomatoes almost dripping with juice, or corn right from the field. If you imagine that all potatoes taste alike, just wait till you buy some freshly dug Yukon Golds or fingerlings. Fresh onions are sweeter, fresh garlic gentler, fresh herbs more fragrant than any you can get in the supermarket.

In this chapter you will find simple recipes that bring out the charm and freshness of the Hudson River Valley's bountiful produce, a great gift of nature.

LITTLE POTATOES

A few years ago, the burgeoning interest of chefs and consumers in unusual vegetables actually developed into a fad, and growers went so far as to produce what can only be called "designer" potatoes, giving fancy names to any potato that had an unusual shape or color and all but neglecting the plebeian potato that has fed us for centuries. One of the "discoveries," the Bintje potato, which was presented in bins like little jewels and priced accordingly, is actually the most widely consumed potato in the world. Like all fads, this one has largely faded, and we are the richer for the heirloom potatoes now being grown by some farmers with a genuine interest in reviving lost varieties. The little potatoes, such as Ozettes, fingerlings, and purple Peruvians now to be found in local markets, lend themselves particularly well to the treatments in the following very simple recipes.

The quantities given below are for 1 pound of small potatoes, to serve four, unless otherwise noted.

LITTLE POTATOES WITH CAVIAR

Use little potatoes of a uniform size, the diameter of a quarter.

Bake at 400°F until tender, about 30 minutes. Cut an X in the top and squeeze the potatoes. Remove a spoonful of potato and fill with a little sour cream, a sprinkling of chopped chives, and a small dab of caviar.

STEWED BINTJES

3 slices bacon, chopped
½ cup coarsely chopped onion
1 pound Bintje potatoes in their skins, scrubbed
Coarse salt and freshly ground pepper
1 cup Chicken Stock, page 31

In a saucepan, render the bacon and sauté the onion in the bacon fat until it is limp.

Toss in the potatoes, season with salt and pepper, add the stock, and bring to a boil. Cover the pot and simmer the potatoes until they are tender when pierced with a sharp knife, 20 or 25 minutes.

BRAISED FINGERLINGS

2 tablespoons unsalted butter
I pound fingerling potatoes, scrubbed
I teaspoon chopped rosemary leaves
2 cups Chicken Stock, page 31
Coarse salt and freshly ground pepper

Preheat the oven to 375°F.

Melt the butter in a flameproof casserole large enough to hold the potatoes in a single layer and toss in the potatoes and rosemary. Add stock to come ⅔ of the way up the sides of the potatoes, bring to a boil, cover the casserole, and bake until the potatoes are tender, half the stock has cooked away, and the remainder is slightly thickened. Season with salt and pepper.

STEAMED OZETTES

I pound little Ozettes, scrubbed
Coarse salt and freshly ground pepper
¼ cup Tomato Oil, page 290
I tablespoon Tomato Compote, page 293, or I small tomato, chopped

Put the potatoes in a saucepan and add cold water to cover the bottom ⅔ of the potatoes. Cover the pot and boil until the water has all evaporated. Season the potatoes with salt and pepper and garnish with the tomato oil and the tomato compote, or a small chopped tomato.

PURPLE PERUVIAN POTATOES BAKED IN THEIR SKINS

Choose potatoes the size of plum tomatoes, rub them with oil, sprinkle with coarse salt, and bake in a 400°F oven until they are tender, about 45 minutes. Cut a cross in the flat sides of the potatoes and scoop out some of the flesh. Season the potatoes with coarse salt and freshly ground pepper and fill with 2 teaspoons of some savory mixture to be found in this book. (Refer to Index for page numbers.) Some suggestions: Garlic and Onion Jam, Shallots Preserved in Red Wine with a dab of sour cream, Tomato Compote, Summer Vegetable Relish, or chopped Braised Wild Mushrooms.

MASHED POTATOES WITH VARIATIONS

Mashed potatoes may just be everybody's favorite food. This recipe is for basic mashed potatoes, with eight variations. Baking potatoes, which are starchier and have less sugar than boiling varieties, produce fluffy mashed potatoes with a nice grainy texture. Yukon Golds also make good mashed potatoes. To avoid overworking potatoes, incorporate all the ingredients at the same time. To turn mashed potatoes from a homely to an elegant dish, garnish them with Windowpane Potato Chips, page 189.

One large potato yields about 1 cup of mashed potatoes. This recipe can be adjusted up or down to serve any number of people.

Serves 6

2½ pounds baking potatoes, peeled and cut into chunks
Coarse salt and freshly ground pepper
6 tablespoons unsalted butter, at room temperature
⅓ cup heavy cream

Boil the potatoes in plenty of lightly salted water until they are tender throughout when pierced with a sharp fork or knife point. Drain the potatoes well and put them through a ricer or a food mill or press them through a sieve. Do not puree the potatoes in a food processor—they will become gluey.

Working the potatoes as little as possible and using a wooden spoon or a rubber spatula, beat in the butter and the cream and season the potatoes to taste with salt and freshly ground pepper. Serve immediately or set aside and reheat in a casserole in a 350°F oven.

This recipe for mashed potatoes can be varied endlessly.

⁓ Variations ⁊

FOIE GRAS MASHED POTATOES: Use ½ cup foie gras scraps, chopped into dice. Sear the scraps in a hot sauté pan, stirring until the foie gras is just cooked and has rendered some fat. Fold the liver and fat into the mashed potatoes instead of the butter.

ROASTED GARLIC MASHED POTATOES: Beat in 2 teaspoons Roasted Garlic Puree, page 296, when you add the butter.

HERBS AND CHEESE MASHED POTATOES: Add ½ cup grated Hawthorne Valley, Swiss, or Parmesan cheese and 3 tablespoons herbs (garlic, chives, and parsley, for example) chopped into a paste to the potatoes before seasoning them.

HORSERADISH MASHED POTATOES: Beat in 3 tablespoons prepared horseradish when you add the butter.

OLIVE OIL AND ROSEMARY MASHED POTATOES: Gently simmer 2 tablespoons chopped fresh rosemary in 4 tablespoons extra virgin olive oil for 5 minutes. Strain and add instead of the butter.

SORREL MASHED POTATOES: Beat in 2 tablespoons sorrel puree, page 63, (made from ¼ pound sorrel) when you add the butter.

TARRAGON AND TOMATO MASHED POTATOES: Beat in 1 tablespoon chopped fresh tarragon and 2 tablespoons Tomato Compote, page 293, when you add the butter.

YUKON GOLD AND DILL MASHED POTATOES: Add 2 tablespoons chopped fresh dill to the potatoes and substitute ⅓ cup sour cream for the heavy cream.

WINDOWPANE POTATO CHIPS

These translucent potato chips enclosing a sprig of herb leaves remind one of dried flowers framed in glass or a colorful autumn leaf pressed between layers of waxed paper and set in a window. They make a very dressy garnish for mashed potatoes. You will need a *mandoline* or other slicer to make the very thin slices required for this recipe.

Makes 12 windowpane potato chips

2 large baking potatoes, peeled
36 large unblemished tarragon leaves
Vegetable oil for frying

Trim one of the large surfaces of each peeled potato until it is flat. Using a *mandoline*, slice the potatoes lengthwise as thin as possible, about $\frac{1}{32}$ of an inch, keeping the slices in order so you can use matching slices to make the sandwiches. You will need 24 slices. Lay the potato slices on a surface in pairs. On the top half of one of each pair of slices arrange 3 tarragon leaves to look like *fleurs de lys*, with the point of the center leaf higher than the 2 on either side. Cover the leaves with the second slice of potato, set so that the 2 slices look like 1. Gently but firmly run the blunt side of a knife blade over the entire surface of the sandwich to ensure that the 2 slices will not separate when they cook.

Set a baking sheet lined with several layers of paper towels next to the stove. In a skillet, heat $\frac{1}{2}$ inch oil over medium-high heat and fry the potatoes, a few at a time, until they are evenly golden brown. Using tongs, remove them from the oil, tilting them to be sure any oil trapped inside can run out. Let the potatoes drain thoroughly.

Use the potato chips to garnish mashed potatoes, setting the leafless end of the chip into the mound of potatoes and hoping that the candles on the table will illuminate this tiny work of art.

POTATO AND BACON RAVIOLI

Any mixture thick enough to stick to a spoon can be substituted for the mashed potato filling in these ravioli. Some alternate fillings from this book (you'll find them in the Index): Summer Vegetable Relish, Garlic and Onion Jam, Baked Fava Bean Puree, or Seafood Mousse.

Makes 20 ravioli

FOR THE FILLING
2 cups mashed potatoes, page 187, without butter and cream
¼ pound sliced bacon, cooked until crisp and chopped
2 teaspoons bacon fat
2 tablespoons chopped parsley or chives or a combination of both
1 clove garlic, minced
1 shallot, minced
2 tablespoons unsalted butter
¼ cup heavy cream
2 tablespoons grated Coach Farm Aged Grating Stick
Coarse salt and freshly ground pepper

40 square wonton skins, purchased at an Oriental grocery
   (or use standard ravioli pasta already in your repertoire)
1 egg, beaten

GARNISH
½ cup hot Chicken Stock, page 31
3 tablespoons unsalted butter
1 tablespoon finely chopped chives

Combine warm mashed potatoes with all the filling ingredients and chill for 1 hour.

Lay 20 of the wonton skins on a flat surface and brush them all over with egg. Place a level tablespoon of filling in the center of each skin. Place a fresh skin on top of the filling, tamp down the edges with your fingers, sealing them, and press firmly but gently around the filling with the rim of a 2½-inch glass, being careful not to press through the dough. Cut out the ravioli with a round 3-inch cutter. Seal the edges well with your fingers, pressing out any air pockets. Arrange on a baking sheet, cover with plastic wrap, and refrigerate until serving time. This can be done 1 day in advance.

Bring a large pot of water to a boil, add a tablespoon of salt, and simmer the ravioli 6 or 7 minutes. Try to keep the water just at the boiling point; if it boils too rapidly, the ravioli may open and the filling leak out or become diluted with water. Drain the ravioli well and put them in a serving dish.

Prepare the garnish: Boil the stock with the butter and pour over the ravioli. Sprinkle with chopped chives.

SCALLOPED YUKON GOLD POTATOES

Yukon Golds contribute a lovely warm color as well as their rich flavor to this familiar dish.

Serves 6

5 cloves garlic
2 cups milk
1 cup heavy cream
1 bay leaf
4 large Yukon Gold or Yellow Finn potatoes, about 2½ pounds, peeled
6 ounces grated Hawthorne Valley medium Alpine cheese or Gruyère cheese
   (see Sources, page 301)
Coarse salt and freshly ground pepper

Cut 1 clove of garlic in half and with the cut side rub the bottom and sides of an 8-by-8-inch casserole. Rough chop the remaining garlic.

In a saucepan, combine the milk and cream with the bay leaf and all the garlic, bring it to a boil, turn down the heat, and simmer for 10 minutes. Strain the milk mixture and set it aside.

Preheat the oven to 350°F.

Using a *mandoline* or other vegetable slicer, slice the potatoes as thin as possible, approximately 1/16 inch thick. Layer the potatoes in the pan, sprinkling each layer with some of the cheese and adding a little of the liquid. Season every other layer with a little salt and pepper. Continue layering until all the potatoes are used, ending with a layer of cheese and pouring the remaining liquid over all. Press the finished casserole of potatoes firmly with your hands to saturate all the potatoes, cover the casserole with foil, and bake for 1 hour. Remove the cover and continue to bake for another 15 minutes, or until the potatoes are very tender. Serve very hot.

POTATO SALADS

As you can see by glancing at this group of potato salad recipes, variations on the basic theme are almost endless. It's important to choose and prepare the potatoes carefully, as directed. The instructions provide guidelines for proportions of dressings and flavorings to the potatoes. These recipes are intended to pique your imagination while giving you enough salads to last for a good long time.

General cooking instructions to be followed for all potato salad recipes:

For 6 average servings, use 4 large or 6 medium baking potatoes (preferred for cold salads) or 12 to 15 new potatoes (preferred for warm salads). All quantities in these recipes are for 6 servings, but potato salad is easy to make for a crowd and the leftovers keep well and are always welcome, so it may be a good idea to make a big batch—or even 2 different kinds— while you're boiling the potatoes.

Scrub the potatoes well, put them in a large pot, and cover them with cold water. Bring to a boil over high heat, turn the heat down a little, and boil the potatoes until they are tender when pierced with a sharp knife. Cooking time depends somewhat on the variety and size of the potatoes you are using, but very firm new potatoes can take surprisingly long. Keep an eye on the potatoes and test them from time to time. They should be thoroughly cooked— not al dente—but if overcooked they will fall apart and become waterlogged.

Make the dressing and prepare the other salad ingredients while the potatoes are boiling. When the potatoes are done, drain them and set them aside until they are cool enough to handle. Peel baking potatoes while they are still warm (leave small and new potatoes in their skins) and slice them into a salad bowl. Using your hands, gently mix the sliced potatoes with the dressing as directed below.

POTATO SALAD WITH RADISHES AND HERBS

This is a basic potato salad with a vinaigrette dressing. Vary the herbs you use, and try different vegetable (or even meat) garnishes.

For 4 large or 6 medium baking potatoes or 12 to 15 small new potatoes, boiled as directed above, use:

¾ cup Mustard Herb Vinaigrette, page 286, made without herbs
½ cup chopped mixed herbs: chives, parsley, basil, tarragon, and chervil
2 medium shallots
8 to 10 radishes
Coarse salt and freshly ground pepper

Prepare the Mustard Vinaigrette.

Cut the shallots and radishes into thin slices.

Slice the warm potatoes into a salad bowl and strew the herbs, shallots, and radishes over them. Pour on about ½ cup of the dressing. Using your hands, gently mix the salad until each slice of potato is coated with dressing and the herbs, shallots, and radishes are well distributed. Taste the salad and season it with salt and freshly ground pepper. Let the salad stand at least 1 hour. Taste the salad and add vinaigrette, salt, and pepper to taste.

POTATO SALAD WITH FIVE PEPPERS

For 4 large or 6 medium baking potatoes or 12 to 15 small new potatoes, boiled as directed above, use:

¾ cup Red Pepper Vinaigrette, page 288
1 medium sweet green pepper
1 medium sweet red pepper
1 medium sweet yellow or orange pepper
1 medium jalapeño pepper
Coarse salt and freshly ground black pepper

Prepare the Red Pepper Vinaigrette.

Cut the green, red, and yellow peppers into thin 2-inch strips. Wearing rubber gloves, cut the jalapeño pepper into very thin 1-inch strips.

Slice the warm boiled potatoes into a salad bowl, scatter the sliced peppers over them, and pour on about ½ cup of the vinaigrette. Using your hands, gently mix the salad until each potato slice is coated with vinaigrette and the peppers are well distributed. Taste the salad and season it with salt and freshly ground pepper (the fifth pepper). Let the salad stand at least 1 hour. Before serving, taste the salad again and add vinaigrette and seasoning to taste.

POTATO SALAD WITH HORSERADISH
AND RED ONION

For an elegant touch, cover a mound of this salad with small slices of smoked salmon and/or a little caviar before garnishing it with the onion rings.

For 4 large or 6 medium baking potatoes or 12 to 15 small new potatoes, boiled as directed
   above, use:
1 cup sour cream
2 to 3 tablespoons prepared horseradish
Coarse salt and freshly ground pepper
1 sweet red onion
6 scallions, including green tops

Mix the sour cream and horseradish and season generously with salt and freshly ground pepper.

   Slice half the onion into rounds and separate the rounds into rings. Cut the remaining onion and the scallions into thin slices.

   Slice the warm boiled potatoes into a salad bowl and scatter the sliced onion and half the sliced scallions over them. Add ¾ cup of the dressing to the bowl and, using your hands, gently mix the salad until each slice of potato is coated with dressing and the vegetables are well distributed. Let the salad stand at least 1 hour. Taste the salad and reseason it, adding more dressing, salt, and/or freshly ground pepper to taste. Garnish the salad with the onion rings and scatter the remaining sliced scallions over all.

POTATO AND GREEN BEAN SALAD
WITH YOGURT AND DILL

Serves 6

3 medium baking potatoes
1 pound green beans, cut into 1-inch pieces

YOGURT DRESSING
1 cup plain yogurt
¼ cup sour cream
3 tablespoons chopped fresh dill

I large clove garlic, minced
Coarse salt and freshly ground pepper

Boil the potatoes. When they are done, remove them from the pot with a slotted spoon and set them aside to cool. Bring the water back to the boil and cook the green beans in it until they are barely tender and still bright green, about 5 minutes. Drain the beans and plunge them in cold water to cool. Drain again. Peel the potatoes.

In a bowl, combine ¾ cup of the yogurt with 2 tablespoons of the dill and the remaining dressing ingredients. Slice the potatoes into the dressing while they are still warm. Add the beans and toss gently. Let the salad stand for I hour or so, then taste and reseason. Add a little more yogurt if there isn't quite enough dressing. Sprinkle the remaining tablespoon of dill over the salad before serving.

WARM POTATO SALAD WITH BACON AND SHALLOTS

Serves 6

12 to 15 small new potatoes, boiled in their skins and still warm
½ pound sliced bacon
8 shallots, sliced
½ cup Chicken Stock, page 31
4 tablespoons white wine vinegar
Coarse salt and freshly ground pepper

Cut the bacon crosswise into ½-inch strips and fry it in a frying pan large enough to hold the potatoes. When the bacon is almost crisp, add the shallots and cook for another minute or 2. Add the stock and vinegar and stir well. Slice the warm potatoes into the pan, season with salt and freshly ground pepper, and gently but thoroughly mix everything together until it is well combined and the potatoes have absorbed most of the liquid. Transfer to a salad bowl and serve at once, while still warm.

WARM NEW POTATO SALAD WITH PRESERVED SHALLOTS

Serves 6

12 to 15 small red-skinned new potatoes, scrubbed
⅓ cup white wine vinegar
¼ cup dry white wine
¼ cup Chicken Stock, page 31
½ cup extra virgin olive oil
3 to 4 tablespoons Shallots Preserved in Red Wine (page 294)
1 tablespoon chopped chives
1 tablespoon chopped chervil
Coarse salt and freshly ground pepper

Boil the potatoes in their jackets until they are tender. In a sauté pan, bring the vinegar, wine, stock, and olive oil to a boil. Over low heat, slice the warm potatoes ¼ inch thick into the pan, add the preserved shallots, the chopped herbs, and some salt and pepper, and toss gently to combine. Transfer the potatoes to a bowl and serve warm.

WILD MUSHROOMS

In everything I cook I try to have a number of well-matched flavors that you should be able to taste either all at once in harmonious combination or as a series of separate taste layers that appear while the food is on your tongue. Every distinguished cuisine has a recognizable, characteristic quality, a unifying factor, a common denominator that turns pedestrian dishes into something complex and memorable. If my cuisine has such a quality, the inclusion of wild mushrooms in so many dishes might account for it. Dried or fresh, wild mushrooms are a year-round part of my cuisine. I love the earthiness and roundness they give to so many of the dishes and sauces I cook. I love the way they add another taste layer to whatever they're cooked with. I'll tell you a secret: Into the mixture of salt and pepper I use when I cook, I mix morel powder, which I make by pulverizing dried morels. That's how I sneak an extra taste layer into all my cooking.

In the Hudson Valley most wild mushrooms are available fresh in fall, with a few in spring and summer. Some of my favorite local mushrooms are morels in the spring; hedgehog and hen of the woods in the summer; black trumpet, chanterelles, cauliflower fungus, and lobster mushrooms in the fall. Most of these mushrooms are gathered by professional foragers. Having spent some time with these professionals, gaining firsthand knowledge of how mushrooms are gathered in the wild, I've learned that you need to know a lot about mushrooms before you go foraging. Just because a mushroom looks like something you saw in the fancy food store, don't think you can pick and eat it. It's worth the expense of buying mushrooms to be sure of what you're getting. Even if you buy them, it's a good idea to cook wild mushrooms a minimum of 15 minutes before eating. See Sources, page 301, to order wild mushrooms.

To experience the pure, intense flavor of wild mushrooms, try Wild Mushroom Broth, page 48.

BRAISED WILD MUSHROOMS

Any combination of wild mushrooms or any single mushroom may be used in this versatile mixture. Halve, double, or triple the mushroom mixture when incorporating it in omelets, pasta, or rice dishes. Some of the many recipes in this book that call for this basic mixture are Asparagus with Morels, Onion Charlotte with Wild Mushrooms, Rabbit Pot Pies, and Boneless Quail Filled With Foie Gras and Black Trumpet Mushrooms (see Index for page numbers).

Makes 4 cups

½ cup plus 2 tablespoons unsalted butter
2 medium shallots, chopped fine
2 large cloves garlic, minced
I teaspoon fresh thyme leaves, chopped
I pound assorted wild mushrooms, cleaned and cut into large pieces
I cup dry white wine
I cup Chicken Stock, page 31
Salt and freshly ground pepper

In a large sauté pan, heat ½ cup of the butter as hot as possible without burning it. Toss in the shallots and garlic, then sprinkle on the thyme. Add the mushrooms and cook until they are lightly browned, 4 or 5 minutes, taking care not to burn the butter. Add the wine and boil until it is almost evaporated. Add the stock, stir well, and simmer the mushrooms until the liquid is reduced and has thickened slightly. Season the mushrooms with some salt and pepper and swirl in the remaining 2 tablespoons butter.

MUSHROOM AND ONION GRATINS

These stuffed onions are wonderful with any roast, especially the Roast Chicken with Maple and Walnut Glaze on page 131 or roast beef.

Serves 6

3 very large onions, peeled and cut in half crosswise
6 tablespoons unsalted butter
¾ pound mushrooms, chopped coarse
1 tablespoon fresh thyme leaves
Coarse salt and freshly ground pepper
¾ cup fresh white bread crumbs

Preheat the oven to 400°F.

Scoop out as much of the center of each onion half as you can and still leave a firm shell. Chop the centers coarse. In a sauté pan, melt half the butter and sauté the chopped onions and mushrooms with the thyme until the vegetables are limp and lightly browned. Season the insides of the onion shells with salt and pepper and fill each half with the mushroom mixture. Melt the remaining butter and combine it with the bread crumbs. Pat 2 tablespoons of the crumb mixture over each onion half.

Put the onions in a small baking pan and roast for about 1 hour, or until they are tender and the tops are well browned.

CORN

The Hudson Valley is one of the country's principal producers of sweet corn. The best is grown in the Rondout Valley in Ulster County, where the soil provides the best mineral tillage in New York State and the growers produce a full range of varieties, from old favorites such as Silver Queen to the latest super-sweet hybrids. The countryside around Stone Ridge (see succotash recipe, page 205) is fragrant with corn in bloom during July and August, and cornfields in various stages of maturity stretch out for miles in every direction.

CORN ON THE COB ROASTED IN ITS HUSK

Children love corn cooked this way. Holding the corn stalk like a giant popsicle stick, my son, Max, will make an entire meal of this, eating as many ears as we will give him. The corn cooks in its own juice; the moisture from the cob, the husk, and the silk cooks the kernels and the slight caramelization from the direct heat intensifies the flavor of the corn.

Leave about 2 inches of stalk attached to the corn. Remove 1 layer of the outermost leaves. Lay the ears on a medium-hot charcoal grill, cover the grill, and roast the corn 20 minutes, turning it once after 10 minutes. Wearing gloves, husk the corn while it is still hot, brush it with melted butter, and sprinkle it with coarse salt and freshly ground pepper.

FRESH CORN CUSTARD WITH SUMMER SALSA

Make this only when you have fresh sweet corn and juicy ripe tomatoes. The use of fresh coriander in the sauce reflects the evolution of farming in the Hudson Valley in the 1990s, where farms that used to produce only onions and potatoes now grow an undreamed-of variety of herbs, lettuces, and greens.

Serves 6

Soft unsalted butter for the casserole

FOR THE CORN CUSTARD
5 or 6 large ears fresh cooked corn, to yield about 4 cups corn kernels
3 extra-large eggs
2 cups heavy cream
2 tablespoons minced shallot
Salt and freshly ground pepper

FOR THE SALSA
3 large ripe tomatoes
2 tablespoons chopped sweet red onion
½ to 1 hot fresh red chili or jalapeño pepper, minced
1 to 2 tablespoons chopped fresh coriander (cilantro)
1 tablespoon fresh lime juice
Coarse salt

Preheat the oven to 350°F.

Cut the corn from the cobs, then run the dull side of the knife blade down the cobs to scrape out all the milky corn left behind. Butter a shallow 2-quart glass or ovenproof pottery casserole.

In a bowl, beat the eggs and stir in the corn, the cream, and the shallot. Season with salt and a little pepper and pour the mixture into the casserole.

Set the casserole in a roasting pan, add hot water to come halfway up the sides of the casserole, and bake about 40 minutes, until the edges of the custard are set and the center barely quivers when the casserole is shaken. Remove the custard from the oven; it is to be served warm, not hot.

Make the salsa: Peel and seed the tomatoes, chop them, and put them in a bowl. Stir in the remaining ingredients, adjusting the amounts of hot pepper, coriander, and lime juice to taste.

To serve, spoon a pool of salsa onto a medium plate. Using a large spoon, cut out a circle of custard and set it on top of the salsa. Pass the remaining salsa in a bowl.

SUCCOTASH WITH FAVA BEANS

The hundreds of different dishes called "succotash" all derive from a concoction American Indians made with "green" (as opposed to dried) corn and beans. Fava beans are particularly good combined with corn.

Serves 4 to 6

4 tablespoons unsalted butter
1 cup cooked fava beans, page 217
3 or 4 ears roasted corn, page 201, cut from the cobs to yield 2 cups kernels
1 cup green beans, diced and blanched
1 shallot, minced
½ cup Chicken Stock, page 31
¼ cup minced sweet red pepper
1 large tomato, peeled, seeded, and chopped
Coarse salt and freshly ground pepper

In a large sauté pan, melt the butter over medium-low heat and toss in the fava beans, the corn kernels, the green beans, and the shallot. Add the stock and simmer for 5 minutes.

Remove the pan from the heat, add the pepper and tomato, season with salt and pepper, and combine well.

STONE RIDGE SUCCOTASH

This succotash is a showpiece for perfect and perfectly ripe summer vegetables. Because it is so simple all the vegetables can be appreciated for themselves, while combining them in one bowl brings out all the contrasts of flavor and texture: They are at once crisp, tart, succulent, sweet, creamy, cold, hot, and buttery. This is a do-it-yourself dish, best served outdoors on a summer day just as hot afternoon gives way to cool evening. It's not hard to find cranberry beans, especially in Italian markets. They have long, light-green pods speckled with pink. If you can't get cranberry beans and have a garden, there is every reason to grow them yourself, for use in this succotash.

Serves 6 as a main course

5 pounds fresh cranberry beans, shelled
At least 12 ears sweet corn, shucked just before cooking
2 large, very sweet onions, preferably Italian red onions
8 to 10 large ripe, juicy tomatoes
Coarse salt
Unsalted butter

The beans can be cooked a few hours in advance, or can be started 2 hours before serving. In a large saucepan, cover the beans by 1 inch with water and bring to a boil. Turn down the heat, partially cover the pan, and simmer the beans for about 1 hour. Cooking time will vary depending on the age and freshness of the beans. They should be soft and creamy but still separate and intact. There should be at least a cup of juice left in the pan when the beans are cooked; watch carefully to see they don't burn and add more water if necessary. If you cook the beans in advance, reheat them gently in their juice.

Bring a big pot of water to a boil for the corn. Dice the onions and put them on the table in a bowl. Put a plate of tomatoes and a couple of dishes of butter on the table and make sure that some coarse salt is within everybody's easy reach. Each person should have a large soup bowl, a soup spoon, a sharp knife, and several napkins.

Just before serving, put the corn in the boiling water. As soon as the water returns to the boil, take out the corn, put it on a platter, and cover it with a clean towel to keep it hot. Put the hot beans into a serving bowl.

To prepare your own serving, put a large spoonful of beans and juice in your soup bowl. Next, stand an ear of corn on end in the bowl and cut the kernels into the bowl. Add a large piece of butter and let it melt while you cut a tomato into chunks and add it to the bowl. Sprinkle on plenty of chopped onion and salt and gently mix everything together. The first spoonful will taste heavenly, the next, sublime; then you will notice that you need a little more tomato or another dab of beans. The readjustment of ingredients continues as long as they last; then you can look forward to continuing the search for the perfect formula next time you have succotash.

SUPPAWN

In almost every culture there is a cornmeal mush of some sort, though only among the Indians of the Americas was it part of a truly ancient heritage. Grits in the South, scrapple among the Pennsylvania Dutch, polenta in Italy, mamaliga in Romania—even putu in Africa—are all basically the same dish.

Suppawn derives from a recipe I found in an old Hudson Valley cookbook. It was probably a staple in the diet of the Dutch peasants and farmers who were the region's earliest settlers. Since food was scarce, these farmers were grateful to the Indians of the region who introduced them to cornmeal, and before long they had begun to use it as a breakfast cereal, frying it into cakes in bacon fat. They flavored it with small bits of whatever they could find that reflected their own cooking culture, such as dried meats, sausages, game, and homemade cheeses.

I like suppawn because it seems to go with so many of the foods that flourish in the Hudson Valley. Crisply fried it works as an earthy accompaniment to venison chili; subtly seasoned, it is delicate and elegant when combined with lobster. Try serving it with all sorts of meat and game dishes, using the variations suggested in this book, and, as you come to appreciate how versatile suppawn is, start inventing your own combinations.

BASIC SUPPAWN
AND VARIATIONS

Serves 4 to 6

1 cup yellow cornmeal
3 cups Chicken Stock, page 31
½ cup heavy cream
3 tablespoons grated Coach Farm Aged Grating Stick
Coarse salt and freshly ground pepper

FOR FRIED SUPPAWN TRIANGLES
Vegetable oil for frying

In a heavy-bottomed saucepan, combine the cornmeal, the stock, and the cream. Whisking constantly, bring the mixture to a boil over medium heat. When the mixture has thickened, lower the heat and continue to cook for 5 minutes, stirring very frequently with a wooden spoon to be sure the suppawn is not sticking to the pan. Turn off the heat, add the cheese, and season with salt and pepper.

For *soft suppawn* serve immediately.

For *fried suppawn triangles*, line an 8-inch square baking pan with plastic wrap and spread the suppawn evenly in it. Cover the pan with plastic wrap, smoothing the wrap over the surface of the suppawn to keep it from drying out, and let it set for at least 2 hours (or in the refrigerator overnight). Cut the suppawn into 3 strips, cut each strip in thirds, and then in half into triangles. You should have 18 triangles.

Heat ½ inch of oil over medium heat until it is medium-hot, 325°F. Set a baking sheet lined with several layers of paper towels next to the stove. Add several triangles of suppawn before the oil reaches full temperature; it cooks better if the oil gets hot as it cooks. Watch and adjust the heat so the oil never gets much hotter. Cook the triangles, first on one side, then the other, until they are a rich golden brown. Drain well. Let the oil cool a bit before cooking the next batch of triangles.

Suppawn lends itself to many variations. Add one of the following to the hot suppawn before putting it in the dish to set.

Variations

FRESH CORN: Add ½ cup roasted fresh corn kernels.

BACON: Add 4 slices crisp bacon, chopped, 2 tablespoons bacon fat, and 2 tablespoons chopped chives.

TOMATO AND MUSHROOM: Add 2 tablespoons Tomato Compote, page 293, and ½ cup chopped Braised Wild Mushrooms, page 199.

GARLIC: Add 3 cloves garlic, chopped, and ¼ cup chopped parsley.

PEPPER: Add 1 jalapeño pepper, minced, and ¼ cup chopped roasted red pepper.

ASPARAGUS WITH MORELS

Asparagus and morels—this combination is the quintessence of spring. Asparagus, imported from wherever, gives the merest hint of the crisp, delicious seasonal sweetness of the local crop; dried morels are never the equal of delicate, succulent, slightly smoky-tasting fresh ones. The Hudson Valley is one of the few areas where lucky foragers can find wild morels; look for them at the edge of oak woods when the dogwood blooms. Serve this dish alone as an appetizer or with any simply broiled or roasted fish or meat.

Serves 4 to 6

½ recipe Braised Wild Mushrooms, page 199, using morels only
2 pounds fresh asparagus
Sprigs fresh thyme, for garnish

Prepare the braised morels.

If the asparagus spears are small (up to ½ inch in diameter), there's no need to peel them. Cut off the ends until the asparagus stalks are a uniform 6 inches long. If the stalks are thick, trim them to a uniform length and peel the bottom half of each stalk with a vegetable peeler.

Bring ½ inch of water to a boil in a large frying pan that has a tight-fitting lid. Lay the asparagus in the boiling water, cover the pan, and boil vigorously just until the bottom end of a stalk can easily be pierced with the point of a sharp knife, 4 or 5 minutes. Drain the asparagus on paper towels, divide it among 6 plates, and spoon the morels across the middle of the asparagus, making sure that each serving includes a spoonful or 2 of the pan juices. Garnish each plate with a sprig of fresh thyme and serve immediately.

ASPARAGUS WITH TOMATO VINAIGRETTE

Cold asparagus is just as good as hot, and is especially good with this tomato vinaigrette.

Serves 4 to 6

1 recipe Tomato Vinaigrette, page 289
2 ripe plum tomatoes, seeds removed, cut into ¼-inch dice
2 pounds fresh asparagus

Have the Tomato Vinaigrette and plum tomatoes ready.

Prepare and cook the asparagus spears according to the directions on page 210. Drain off the water, fill the pan with cold water and ice cubes, and run water into the pan until the asparagus is cool. Drain it on several layers of paper towels.

At serving time, divide the asparagus among 6 plates. Beat the vinaigrette with a fork to amalgamate it and spoon a band of it across the middle of the asparagus. Sprinkle a little diced tomato over each serving.

STIR-FRIED ASPARAGUS
AND RAMPS

Pungent ramps and sweet, nutty local asparagus are available for only a short time each year, so make the most of them while you can. This quick, simple stir-fry is a perfect way to enjoy these two seasonal treasures. Serve with buttered egg noodles or a plain omelet or alongside any grilled fish or meat. You can read more about ramps on page 37.

Serves 4 to 6

½ pound ramps or 2 large bunches scallions
2 pounds fresh asparagus
2 tablespoons extra virgin olive oil
Coarse salt and freshly ground pepper

Thoroughly trim and clean the ramps as you would the scallions they resemble. Trim off the woody bottoms of the asparagus and peel them. Slice the asparagus and ramps on the diagonal into 2-inch pieces. In a sauté pan, heat the olive oil over high heat, add the vegetables, and season sparingly with salt and pepper. Toss the vegetables almost constantly over high heat until they are beginning to caramelize and are tender but not soft, 7 or 8 minutes. This method of cooking will intensify the flavor of the vegetables; just be sure to keep tossing so they do not burn. Pile the vegetables on a platter and let them stand for 5 minutes; their own heat will cook them a bit more.

ROASTED BEETS ON BRAISED BEET GREENS

Roasting beets, as in this recipe, preserves all their sweetness and flavor. You'll never go back to boiling them after you taste these.

Serves 6

6 beets of uniform size, with their greens (2½ to 3 pounds)
2 tablespoons unsalted butter
Coarse salt and freshly ground pepper
3 tablespoons extra virgin olive oil
3 large cloves garlic, sliced thin
1 sprig fresh rosemary
½ cup Chicken Stock, page 31

Preheat the oven to 450°F.

Trim off the beet greens and reserve. Scrub the beets and cut off the roots. In a roasting pan, bake the beets until they are tender when pierced with a sharp knife point, about 1½ hours. Remove the beets from the oven, let them cool until you can handle them, and peel them. Return them to the roasting pan and dot them with a little butter. Ten minutes before serving, reheat the beets in a preheated 300°F oven.

Wash and blanch the beet greens according to the directions on page 221.

Heat the olive oil in a sauté pan and sauté the garlic slices until golden. Add the rosemary sprig, and sauté it for a minute. Take the pan off the heat, add the chicken stock, then boil the liquid for 5 or 6 minutes, reducing it by about ⅓. Remove the rosemary, season the stock, add the blanched beet greens, and cook over medium heat, covered, for 5 minutes. Uncover and continue to cook over medium heat until almost dry, 5 to 10 minutes.

Arrange the beet greens on a platter and set the roasted beets on top.

BRUSSELS SPROUTS WITH CHESTNUTS

This is a perfect vegetable dish for the Thanksgiving feast.

Serves 6

1 pound Brussels sprouts
½ pound chestnuts
¼ pound sliced bacon, cut into ¼-inch pieces
½ teaspoon chopped fresh rosemary
¼ cup Chicken Stock, page 31
Coarse salt and freshly ground pepper

Preheat the oven to 400°F.

Cut the bottoms off the Brussels sprouts and trim off any loose or discolored leaves. Blanch the sprouts in boiling salted water for 10 to 12 minutes. Drain the sprouts and plunge them into cold water. Drain.

Cut an X on the flat side of each chestnut, put the chestnuts in a single layer in a roasting pan, and roast for about 45 minutes. As soon as they are cool enough to handle, peel the chestnuts, removing both the shell and the reddish skin. Keep the unpeeled chestnuts covered as you work, so they remain hot. Crumble the chestnuts into 3 or 4 pieces each.

In a sauté pan, cook the bacon until it is brown and crisp. Remove the bacon from the pan and reserve. Pour off all but 2 tablespoons of the bacon fat, add the rosemary, and cook for 30 seconds. Add the chestnuts to the pan, toss them in the bacon fat, and cook until they are heated through. Add the stock and the Brussels sprouts, stir to combine, and cook for another 5 minutes. Put the vegetables in a serving dish and garnish with the reserved bacon.

CELERY ROOT PUREE

Celery root is highly prized in other parts of the world, but most Americans don't know how good it is. It has a distinct but delicate celery flavor and can be roasted alone or with other vegetables (page 228) or made into a creamy soup (page 39) or a puree that is excellent with beef and venison.

Serves 4

2½ pounds celery root, about 3 medium roots, weighed before peeling
3 tablespoons unsalted butter
½ cup heavy cream
Coarse salt and freshly ground pepper

Trim and peel the celery roots, cut them into quarters, then into ¼-inch slices. Put them in a saucepan with ½ cup water, cover the pot, and bring to a boil. Cook, covered, over medium-low heat for 30 minutes, then uncover and cook another 15 minutes, or until the liquid evaporates. Be careful not to burn the vegetable.

Puree the celery root in a food processor, add the butter and cream, and season with salt and freshly ground pepper. Put the puree in an ovenproof casserole, cover, and reheat in a 350°F oven for 15 to 20 minutes before serving.

CHESTNUT PUREE

Until early in this century chestnut trees grew so freely in the Hudson Valley that they were used to build log cabins. In 1904, chestnut saplings imported from Asia introduced a blight that killed off most of the region's magnificent chestnut trees. The area lost not only a main source of lumber but a treasured supply of food that was widely used by both the native American Indians and by European settlers. Chestnuts were used to make flour, were roasted over open fires (as they still are on the streets of New York City), and were frequently eaten with game (page 118), made into desserts (page 272), or used to make wonderful purees, both savory and sweet. North America is again producing some chestnuts from a few stands of trees in the Northwest that survived the blight, and perhaps it won't be long before they're back in the Hudson Valley.

Fortunately, it is now easy to buy fresh imported chestnuts of excellent quality and we can once again learn to make the dishes so loved by our Hudson Valley ancestors. Chestnut puree is a traditional garnish for venison, in particular; its sweet richness provides a perfect foil for that lean, juicy meat.

Serves 4

1 pound chestnuts
½ cup Chicken Stock, page 31
½ cup heavy cream
2 tablespoons brandy
Coarse salt

Preheat the oven to 400°F.

To peel the chestnuts, cut an X in the flat side of each chestnut, put the chestnuts in a single layer in a roasting pan, and roast for 45 minutes. As soon as they are cool enough to handle, peel the chestnuts, removing both the shell and the reddish skin. Cover the unpeeled chestnuts as you work, to keep them warm.

Put the chestnuts in a saucepan with the stock, bring to a boil, and simmer, covered, until the chestnuts are soft, 10 or 15 minutes. In a food processor, puree the chestnuts, using the stock to make a very smooth puree. Add the cream and the brandy and process another minute. Season the puree to taste with salt.

Put the puree in a casserole, cover, and reheat in a 350°F oven for 15 to 20 minutes before serving.

BAKED FAVA BEAN PUREE

This puree goes well with lamb and roasted game birds and makes a good filling for zucchini blossoms. You can make it a day ahead and reheat it. Fava beans must be peeled twice. First remove them from the pods, then blanch and peel them as described below. Three pounds of fava beans will give you three cups of shelled, but only two cups of peeled beans.

Serves 6

3 pounds fresh fava beans
1 tablespoon Roasted Garlic Puree, page 296
¼ cup Chicken Stock, page 31, or fava bean cooking liquid
¼ cup heavy cream
1 egg white
Coarse salt and freshly ground pepper
1 clove garlic, halved

Half fill a 3-quart pot with water and bring it to a boil. Shell the fava beans and drop them into the boiling water. Return the water to the boil and continue to boil the beans for 5 minutes. Drain them, reserving ½ cup of the cooking liquid, and put them in a large bowl of cold water.

When the beans are cool, drain and peel them. Holding the seamed end of a bean between 2 fingers, nick the opposite, smooth end with a fingernail. Gently squeeze the bean from the pod. It will pop right out.

Put the peeled beans in the bowl of a food processor. Add the remaining ingredients and process until smooth. Taste for seasoning. Rub a 3- to 4-cup baking dish, preferably earthenware, with the cut clove of garlic and put in the bean puree.

Half an hour before serving, preheat the oven to 350°F. Bake the puree for 15 to 20 minutes and serve hot.

BRAISED FENNEL

This wonderful vegetable is underused and underappreciated, although it's readily available. Fennel has a particular affinity with fish dishes, especially striped bass, page 88.

Serves 4

4 bulbs fennel
2 tablespoons olive oil
¾ cup Chicken Stock, page 31

Preheat the oven to 350°F.

Trim the fennel, removing leaves and stems. Cut the bulbs into quarters. Heat the oil in a sauté pan large enough to hold the fennel in one layer and brown the cut sides of the fennel very thoroughly over medium-low heat until the fennel has begun to caramelize and soften. This will take at least 15 minutes.

Put the fennel in a casserole large enough to hold it in one layer. Bring the stock to a boil, season it with a little salt and pepper, and pour it over the fennel. Cover the pan loosely with foil and braise the fennel until it is quite soft, about 1 hour and 15 minutes.

THE HUDSON RIVER VALLEY COOKBOOK

SPICY FENNEL AND CABBAGE SLAW

It's hard to know if fennel tastes better raw or cooked. This spicy slaw is especially good with cold fish.

Serves 6

1 large bulb fennel
¾ pound green cabbage
1 small sweet red pepper
1 small sweet green pepper
2 small Thai bird or other hot chili peppers
1 tablespoon chopped dill or fennel tops
½ cup white wine vinegar
½ cup extra virgin olive oil
Coarse salt and freshly ground pepper
1 teaspoon fresh lime juice

Trim the fennel and quarter it lengthwise. Cut out the core and shred the fennel fine. Core and shred the cabbage fine. Sliver the red and green peppers and, wearing rubber gloves, mince the chilis.

Combine all the ingredients and mix together very thoroughly, using your hands. Let the slaw rest for 1 hour, stir again, and taste for seasoning before serving.

BITTER GREENS

There are fresh local greens to be had all through the fall and sometimes, if the weather is mild enough, right up to Christmas. Farm market bins are filled high with big bunches of collards, mustard greens, turnip greens, escarole, chicory, broccoli rabe, dandelion, watercress, and spinach in all shades of green, along with frilly blue kale and deep red Swiss chard. Unlike salad greens, most of these are at their best cooked, either one at a time or in combination with each other and/or other vegetables. Braised bitter greens cooked with bacon are especially good with roasted meat, poultry, or game. Baked with potatoes, they are an excellent main course dish. Sautéed watercress and spinach take about five minutes to cook and provide a lively accent to winter meals. These greens must be very carefully washed and most of them benefit from blanching before cooking. Directions for both these procedures follow, along with six recipes for cooking bitter greens.

WASHING AND BLANCHING GREENS

There are several reasons to blanch greens. Blanching gives greens an extra cleaning; it takes away some of the bitterness of strong greens like kale or mustard; it greatly reduces their volume and the amount of liquid the greens give off when they are cooked, making it much easier to use them in a dish such as Bitter Greens and Potatoes. So it's a good idea to blanch bitter greens when they are very gritty, very bitter, or when you don't want to deal with a big pile of leaves. There's no need to blanch the more delicate greens that can be sautéed in a minute or 2, or those you will use in a soup or a juicy stew.

WASHING GREENS

Greens must be very thoroughly washed before blanching. Washing is simpler and more effective if the greens are first trimmed and cut up. Use slightly warm water when washing greens, especially if you intend to cook them. It seems to be more effective than cold water for dislodging sand (and it's a lot easier on your hands). Slightly warm water also works well for cleaning leeks. Use this method for all bitter greens.

If you intend to blanch the greens, bring a large pot of water to a boil while you are cleaning them.

Trim off any limp or yellowed leaves. Starting at the tips of the leaves, cut heads or bunches of greens into 1-inch strips, up to but not including stems. Discard the tough stems and roots. For greens with tender, edible stems, such as broccoli rabe or Swiss chard, cut the stems into 1-inch pieces too. Fill the sink with slightly warm water (the more water the better) and put in the greens. Swish them around vigorously to dislodge all dirt, then lift the greens out of the water and into a colander. All the dirt will have sunk to the bottom. For very sandy or muddy greens, repeat the process.

BLANCHING GREENS

When the pot of water comes to a boil, add a tablespoon of salt and then the greens. Cover the pot. As soon as the water returns to the boil, lift the greens out with a slotted spoon, drain them in a colander, and press them as dry as possible.

BRAISED BITTER GREENS WITH BACON

For a vegetarian version of this dish, substitute 2 tablespoons of extra virgin olive oil for the bacon and use more garlic.

Serves 4

1 pound dandelion greens
¼ pound turnip greens
¾ pound spinach
¼ pound sliced bacon, cut into 1-inch strips
1 large clove garlic, sliced
1 cup Chicken Stock, page 31
Coarse salt and freshly ground pepper

Wash and blanch the dandelion greens, turnip greens, and spinach following the directions on page 221.

In a heavy-bottomed saucepan, render the bacon with 2 tablespoons of water. When the water has evaporated, the fat is boiling and the bacon is beginning to brown, stir in the sliced garlic and continue to cook over medium-high heat until the garlic is browned but not burnt and the bacon is completely rendered. Pour off all but 2 tablespoons of the fat.

Add the stock to the bacon, bring to a boil, and add the blanched and drained greens. Season with salt and pepper, mix to combine well, and cook over high heat for a minute or 2. Turn down the heat and simmer over low heat, uncovered, 20 to 25 minutes. Stir well and serve hot.

BITTER GREENS WITH POTATOES AND ONIONS

Serves 6

3 pounds mixed bitter greens, including at least 3 of the following: mustard greens, Swiss
    chard, turnip greens, collards, escarole, chicory, broccoli rabe, kale, dandelion, or spinach
2 large onions, sliced
1 clove garlic, sliced
6 tablespoons unsalted butter
1½ cups Chicken Stock, page 31
Coarse salt and freshly ground pepper
1½ pounds Yukon Gold potatoes, peeled and sliced

Wash and blanch the greens, following the directions on page 221.

Preheat the oven to 375°F.

In a large sauté pan, sauté the onions in 4 tablespoons of the butter until they are softened
and just beginning to brown, about 10 minutes. Add the chicken stock and bring to a boil.
Season with about 1 teaspoon of salt and plenty of freshly ground pepper.

Combine the greens and potato slices with the onion mixture and transfer the vegetables
to a gratin dish, pressing them down firmly. Dot the vegetables with the remaining butter,
cover the pan tightly with foil, and bake for 30 minutes. Remove the foil and bake 15
minutes more, or until the potatoes are very tender.

BROCCOLI RABE
WITH SHALLOTS

These bitter greens have a distinctive flavor that combines especially well with grilled sausage and pasta.

Serves 4 to 6

2 pounds broccoli rabe
4 tablespoons extra virgin olive oil
4 large shallots, sliced thin
4 cloves garlic, sliced very thin
Coarse salt and freshly ground pepper

Trim the broccoli rabe of all tough stems, cut it on the diagonal into 2-inch lengths, and wash it. Blanch according to the directions on page 221 and spread it out on a towel to drain very thoroughly.

Heat the oil in a sauté pan and sauté the shallots and garlic until they soften and just begin to brown. Add the broccoli rabe, toss, and sauté until it is heated through. Season the broccoli rabe with salt and pepper and transfer it to a platter or bowl.

SWISS CHARD WITH GOLDEN ONIONS

Serves 4 to 6

2 pounds Swiss chard
4 tablespoons rendered duck fat, foie gras fat, or chicken fat
1 large onion, cut into ¼-inch julienne sticks
½ cup Chicken Stock, page 31
Coarse salt

Wash the chard but do not blanch it, and cut the leaves in 1-inch strips.

Heat the fat in a sauté pan and cook the onion slivers over medium-low heat until they are very limp and golden brown, at least 15 minutes. Don't try to hurry this process; the onions will burn if you turn up the heat. Add the stock and cook over medium-high heat for another 5 minutes or so until the stock is syrupy and almost cooked away. Add the chard and a little salt, cover the pan, and wilt the chard over high heat, mixing it into the onions after a minute or 2. Cook for 4 or 5 minutes. Transfer to a serving dish and serve hot.

SAUTÉED SPINACH
WITH GARLIC

Serves 4 to 6

2 pounds spinach
3 tablespoons extra virgin olive oil
3 cloves garlic, sliced
Coarse salt and freshly ground pepper

Wash and blanch the spinach, following the directions on page 221. Immediately plunge it into a bowl of ice water, swish it gently, and drain thoroughly. Squeeze the spinach as dry as possible and chop it coarse.

Heat the oil in a sauté pan over medium heat. Add the garlic and cook for a minute or 2, until it is just tinged golden. Add the spinach and toss to warm it, combining it thoroughly with the oil and garlic. Season to taste with salt and pepper.

SAUTÉED WATERCRESS

Serves 4 to 6

2 bunches watercress
2 tablespoons extra virgin olive oil
1 clove garlic, minced
Coarse salt

Cut off the bottom inch of the watercress stems. Cut the bunches of watercress in thirds, wash, and drain but do not blanch.

In a sauté pan, heat the oil over medium-high heat, add the garlic, and cook for 30 seconds. Add the watercress and a little salt, turn up the heat to high, and cook, tossing constantly, just until it is wilted, 2 or 3 minutes. Serve hot.

ROASTED ROOT VEGETABLES

Root vegetables combine harmoniously both with each other and with many meat or fish dishes. Choose the ones you like best but remember that variety lends both complex flavor and appealing color to the mixture. The vegetables also make a very good puree (see end of recipe).

Use a few of these vegetables, or some of each:

1 parsnip
2 carrots
1 celery root
½ rutabaga
1 turnip
3 thin salsify roots, blanched, page 221
Olive oil
1 cup Chicken Stock, page 31, heated
2 tablespoons unsalted butter, cut into pieces, optional

FOR A PUREE
A pinch nutmeg
3 tablespoons unsalted butter
¼ cup heavy cream

Preheat the oven to 350°F.

Peel the vegetables and cut them into ½-inch dice.

Choose a roasting pan or casserole that will hold the vegetables in a 1½-inch-deep layer. Film the pan with olive oil, add the vegetables, and toss them in the oil. Roast the vegetables, turning once or twice, for about ½ hour.

Pour the hot stock over the vegetables and dot them with butter. Cover the pan, raise the temperature to 375°F, and continue to roast for about 1 hour, or until the vegetables are soft. Uncover the pan and continue to cook until all the liquid has evaporated.

If necessary, reheat the vegetables in a 350°F oven or toss them in a sauté pan with a little chicken stock.

To puree the vegetables, put them through a food mill or puree them in a food processor, adding nutmeg, butter, and cream to taste. Put the puree in a casserole and reheat in a 350°F oven.

SALSIFY GRATIN WITH LITTLE RAINBOW RICOTTA

Salsify, also called "oyster plant," appears regularly in nineteenth century cookbooks and menus and is standard fare in northern Europe, but it is almost forgotten in this country. It is a root vegetable similar to carrots and parsnips, but with a dark brown skin. When you peel salsify, it is glistening white. It does not taste the least bit like oysters. Salsify is available at farm markets from late summer to early winter and is well worth trying. This way of cooking salsify brings out its very delicate flavor. It tastes even better if you make it in advance and reheat it.

Serves 6

2 lemons
Coarse salt
2 pounds salsify
¾ cup Little Rainbow ricotta or ordinary ricotta
2 tablespoons extra virgin olive oil
½ cup heavy cream
Freshly ground pepper
2 tablespoons unsalted butter
2 large cloves garlic, sliced thin

Squeeze 1 of the lemons into a large bowl of cold water. As you peel the salsify, drop it into the bowl of acidulated water.

Bring a large pot of water to a boil, salt it generously, and squeeze in the juice of ½ a lemon. Trim the salsify, cut it into 2-inch pieces, and put it in the boiling water. Cook the salsify for 15 to 20 minutes, or until it is very tender and the point of a knife easily pierces the thickest piece. Drain the salsify.

Preheat the oven to 325°F.

In a bowl, whisk together the ricotta, the olive oil, and the cream until smooth and season with salt and pepper.

Melt the butter in a sauté pan. Add the salsify and sliced garlic and sauté until lightly browned, 5 minutes or so. Put the vegetables in a shallow casserole and spread the cheese mixture over them. Bake the casserole for 1½ to 2 hours, until the salsify is very soft and has a golden crust.

BUTTERNUT SQUASH AND SWEET POTATO PUREE

You can make this puree using all squash or all sweet potatoes, but the combination is particularly intense.

Serves 4

2 large sweet potatoes
A 1-pound butternut squash
1 cup fresh orange juice
1 tablespoon unsalted butter
A 2-inch piece of cinnamon stick
Coarse salt and freshly ground pepper

Preheat the oven to 375°F.

Cut the sweet potatoes in half. Cut the squash in half vertically and scrape out the seeds. Put the vegetables, cut side up, in a baking pan, sprinkle with salt and pepper, and bake, uncovered, until they are very soft, at least 1½ hours. Scoop the potato and squash out of the skins, combine them, and mash until smooth.

Put the orange juice, the butter, and cinnamon stick in a small saucepan and reduce until it is about ¼ cup syrup. Discard the cinnamon stick. Stir the orange syrup into the mashed vegetables, season with salt and pepper, transfer to a small casserole, and reheat gently in the oven or on top of the stove.

BABY TURNIPS AND CARROTS CARAMELIZED IN BUCKWHEAT HONEY

The many honey farms in the Hudson Valley range from a few hives on a vegetable farm or in somebody's backyard to a seedy extravaganza of bear shows and souvenirs. Flavors range from clover honey to herbs. The buckwheat honey used here has a dark color and an unusual yeasty aftertaste.

Serves 4

½ pound baby turnips, stems left on, peeled and trimmed
½ pound baby carrots, peeled and trimmed
2 tablespoons buckwheat or other strong-flavored honey
2 tablespoons unsalted butter
Coarse salt and freshly ground pepper

Parboil the vegetables in lightly salted water for 4 minutes and drain.

In a saucepan, cook the honey and butter together over high heat until bubbling. Stir in some salt and pepper and add the vegetables. Toss them in the honey butter and cook until the liquid is a thick, light brown syrup that lightly coats the vegetables.

GREEN BEANS

When I started cooking in the Hudson Valley 15 years ago, farmers grew massive amounts of what were called "soup quality" green beans. They must have called them that because they were too big, tough, and stringy to eat unless they were ground up in a soup. As local chefs and consumers became more demanding, the picture began to change. A grower who was stuck with 600 acres of green beans he could no longer sell cautiously tried putting in 20 acres of thin haricots verts (French green beans) and now has 300 of his acres planted with this delicious, tender bean. When my daughter, Merrill, went to nursery school and was served frozen green beans, she didn't know what they were and insisted they were not green beans. She took haricots verts to school with her and they became the snack of choice.

Any green bean is good as long as it's picked when it's young and tender; it doesn't have to be a French bean. Fresh from the garden, green beans are at their best eaten hot or at room temperature with a little extra virgin olive oil, or hot with butter and a chopped shallot or a squeeze of lemon. Thyme is a good complementary flavor; put in a sprig or two when you steam or blanch the beans. Two good simple recipes in this book using green beans are: Chopped Fresh Green Beans with Cured Duck, page 27, and Green Bean and Potato Salad with Yogurt and Dill, page 195.

WHITE BEANS

Serve these beans with rack of lamb, page 180, and use them in White Bean Strudel with Duck, page 28.

Makes about 6 cups beans

1 pound Great Northern beans
1 smoked ham hock or ¼ pound salt pork
6 cups chicken stock, page 31
1 onion
herb sachet: 1 tablespoon black peppercorns ⎫
             1 bay leaf   ⎬ Tied together in a
             ½ teaspoon dried thyme   double layer of cheesecloth
             2 cloves garlic, smashed ⎭

2 teaspoons coarse salt

Soak the beans overnight in cold water to cover.

Drain the beans and combine all the ingredients in a heavy-bottomed soup pot. Bring to a boil and simmer, with lid slightly ajar, until the beans are tender but not mushy. After an hour, taste the beans frequently to avoid overcooking. When the beans are done, stir in the salt. Drain the beans and reserve the liquid.

CHARCOAL GRILLED VEGETABLES

Simply seasoned with a few drops of olive oil, some coarse salt, and freshly ground pepper, grilled vegetables go beautifully with charcoal grilled buffalo steak, duck, or salmon. Serve hot or at room temperature. Also see Corn on the Cob Roasted in Its Husk, page 201.

ASPARAGUS

Choose large, thick spears with tightly closed tops, 4 or 5 per serving. Cut off the woody bottoms and peel the stalks. Brush with olive oil and grill over medium-hot coals, 3 to 4 minutes per side, turning once. Put the asparagus on a platter and season with coarse salt, freshly ground pepper, and a little fresh lemon juice.

FENNEL

Plan on ½ a medium bulb of fennel per serving. Trim the bulbs, being careful to leave the bottoms intact, and cut them in quarters vertically. Blanch the fennel quarters in boiling salted water for 15 minutes. Using tongs, remove them carefully from the water and drain on paper towels. Brush the cut sides of the fennel with olive oil and grill, cut sides down, turning once, for about 5 minutes on each side.

GARLIC

Plan on ½ a head of garlic per person. Slice off the top ½ inch of the heads of garlic. Blanch the heads in boiling salted water for 30 minutes, remove them from the water, and drain on paper towels. Brush the cut side of the garlic with olive oil and put them on a grill, cut side down. Grill the garlic, turning once, about 10 minutes on the first side, 5 minutes on the second. Let the garlic cool a bit and squeeze the soft garlic cloves out of the skins. Spread on bread or potatoes or eat as a garnish with grilled meat.

MUSHROOMS

Plan on 4 to 6 large mushrooms per serving. Cut off the stems. Toss the mushrooms with 1 teaspoon chopped fresh coriander per serving, plenty of freshly ground pepper, and enough olive oil to coat them completely. Grill the mushrooms over moderate heat upside down for the first 5 minutes, then right side up for 5 minutes more.

ONIONS

Plan on ½ a medium onion per person. Peel the onions and cut them in half root end to stem end. Blanch them in boiling salted water for 15 minutes. Using tongs, remove them carefully and drain on paper towels. Brush the cut side of the onions with olive oil and grill them, cut side down, turning once, until they are lightly browned, about 5 minutes on each side.

PEPPERS

This is a good vegetable to grill, put on a platter, and offer to guests while the meat is cooking. Get a combination of red, green, and yellow peppers. Seed them and cut them vertically into 2-inch strips. Brush with olive oil and grill over moderate heat 3 or 4 minutes on each side.

POTATOES

Boil tiny potatoes in their skins until they are tender. Put the potatoes on metal or wooden skewers or thread them on branches of rosemary. Drizzle olive oil over them and grill for 7 or 8 minutes, turning once.

SUMMER SQUASH

Choose zucchini or yellow squash not larger than 1½ inches in diameter. Cut them on the diagonal into ½-inch slices, brush with olive oil, season with coarse salt and freshly ground pepper, and grill 2 to 3 minutes on each side.

GRILLED VEGETABLES
WITH ANGEL HAIR PASTA

If you're lucky, you'll be able to grill these vegetables right from your own garden. If not, harvest them from the summer cornucopia offered at local farmstands and markets.

Serves 4 as a lunch main course or a dinner appetizer

Olive oil
2 medium zucchini, sliced on the diagonal ¼ inch thick
2 medium yellow squash, sliced on the diagonal ¼ inch thick
2 medium tomatoes, sliced ¼ inch thick
2 medium onions, halved and sliced into ¼-inch half-circles

FOR THE PASTA SAUCE
1 sweet red pepper, roasted, peeled, seeded, and rough chopped
4 large ripe tomatoes, peeled, seeded, and rough chopped
1 fresh hot pepper, chopped fine
1 shallot, chopped
⅓ cup olive oil

½ pound angel hair pasta

GARNISH
Crisp Fried Shallots, page 239

Spread 2 or 3 cookie sheets lightly with olive oil. Lay the sliced vegetables on the sheets, brush on a little oil, and set the oven rack 6 inches from the element. Broil the vegetables; as soon as the first side is lightly browned, turn the vegetables, using tongs or a spatula, and cook until the second side is lightly browned. Cooking time varies widely, depending on your broiler. The only way to grill vegetables properly is to watch them closely.

Let the vegetables cool on the sheets, then arrange them decoratively around the edge of a large round platter.

Make the pasta sauce: Put all the sauce ingredients in a pot, cover, and cook over high heat, stirring from time to time, until all the vegetables are soft. Strain the sauce and return it to the pot.

Prepare the Crisp Fried Shallots.

Boil the pasta in plenty of salted water for 2 or 3 minutes, until it is done al dente. Drain and toss with the sauce. Taste for seasoning. Put the pasta in the center of the ring of grilled vegetables, garnish with the fried shallots, and serve immediately.

CRISP FRIED SHALLOTS

Use these fried shallots as a garnish on diverse dishes, ranging from pasta to steak, stew, or mashed potatoes. You can prepare them a couple of hours in advance of serving, and there's no need to reheat them.

Makes 1 cup

Vegetable oil for frying
Flour for dredging
1 cup sliced large shallots, cut ⅛ inch thick

Heat about 1½ inches vegetable oil in a saucepan. Put the flour on a plate and toss the shallots in it, breaking the slices into rings. Each ring should be thoroughly coated with flour. Put the shallots in a sieve and shake out any excess flour. When a pinch of flour sizzles and browns in the hot oil, put in the shallots and fry them over high heat until they are crisp and brown, 3 or 4 minutes. Drain on paper towels.

APPLES,
BERRIES,
&
OTHER
DESSERTS

CREATING DESSERTS

In developing this chapter I was lucky enough to have two collaborators. Martin Howard, my colleague for ten years and one of the best pastry chefs working today, brought his elegant and sometimes wild imagination and his expertise, with chocolate in particular, to the project. My co-author, Molly Finn, contributed a refined sensibility, an emphasis on purity and simplicity, and a much-needed down-to-earth approach. These qualities meshed beautifully with the subtle blendings and contrasts of my own work, along with my desire to present distinctive recipes for delicious desserts. Each of us contributed to the others' recipes; we shared a respect for tradition and a commitment to using the finest ingredients, especially the fruits of the region at the peak of their flavor. Way back somewhere, many of these recipes were inspired by Martin's and my mentor, Albert Kumin. With all these influences at work, I feel we have created a group of wonderful desserts for you to enjoy.

APPLES

In October, the Union Square Greenmarket in New York City is a festival of apples. They are clearly labeled—Opalescent, Jonagold, Northern Spy, Baldwin, Gravenstein, King Luscious, Golden Russet, Esopus Spitzenberg, and thirty, or maybe even forty, more—and it's fun to buy small bags of a number of varieties, marking them as you go and taking them home for a delicious afternoon of tasting your way through them. There are enough different kinds of apples to keep you tasting and learning for the whole month. Farmers are delighted to talk apples with you and offer cider, homemade applesauce, baked goods, and recipes.

Even though apples are a seasonal fruit, at their peak of flavor and texture when freshly picked, (between mid-September and mid-November in the Hudson Valley), if you go into a supermarket or even a fruit and vegetable store during those months you will find the same apples that are available year round—Red Delicious, Golden Delicious, Granny Smith, McIntosh, and Rome. Known as the "top five," these apples are grown primarily for their uniformity of color, size and shape, and the ease of storing and shipping them, not for their flavor. Lots of these apples are grown in New York State, which is the second largest producer of apples in the U.S. The Hudson Valley is a center of "top five" apple production, but it is also home to a small number of adventurous fruit growers who have revived many choice varieties of apples that were readily available early in this century but had virtually disappeared from the market.

Elizabeth Ryan and Peter Zimmerman grow forty-five varieties of "rare, unusual, and special" apples, many of these antique apples, on their farm, Breezy Hill Orchard, in Dutchess County. They are among a handful of growers who are intent upon making available again the entire spectrum of apple flavors that range from "sweet with a juicy perfume" through "tart and spicy," "musky," "sweet tart honeyed flavor," "aromatic," and "rich." Country farmstands and the greenmarkets in New York City are almost the only way farmers have of distributing these special apples. It's a struggle all the way. In an effort to find a wider market and more effective distribution, especially in the restaurant community, where food trends are developed and tested, Hudson Valley growers have formed the Hudson Valley Marketing Association, a cooperative designed to pool and sell small quantities of unusual fruits and vegetables. Supporting local farmers by shopping at farmstands in the country and greenmarkets in the city is the best way to provide yourself with the best foods available and to insure future crops of delicious and uncommon fruits and vegetables.

The apple recipes that follow are intended to show off the whole range of Hudson Valley apples. During the apple season, different varieties ripen and are picked at different times. Ask for the apple that is being harvested that week; it will be at its peak.

APPLE PIE WITH
A CHEDDAR CRUST

Apple pie without cheese
Is like a kiss without a squeeze.
—Waldense D. Malouf, Sr.

Makes a 9-inch pie

1 recipe Pie Crust, page 258
1 cup grated sharp New York State cheddar cheese (¼ pound)

FOR THE FILLING
5 or 6 large tart apples such as Macoun, Jonagold, or Cortland, peeled, cored, and sliced thin
Juice of ½ lemon
½ teaspoon coarse salt
¾ cup brown sugar
2 tablespoons flour

Make the crust according to the directions on page 258, blending the cheese with the flour until it is finely chopped and evenly distributed before adding the butter.

Remove the pastry from the refrigerator ½ hour before baking. Preheat the oven to 375°F.

Make the filling: Put the apples in a bowl, squeeze the lemon over them, and sprinkle on the salt, sugar, and flour. Using your hands, mix the filling thoroughly and put it into the pie crust. Cover the apples with the top crust. Dip your finger in water and run it along the pie plate between the two crusts, then crimp the edges. Trim the crust and slash the top crust or cut a decorative shape out of the pastry to allow steam to escape.

Bake the pie on the bottom shelf of the oven for ½ hour. Lay a piece of foil loosely over the pie and bake for another 20 to 25 minutes, or until the juices are bubbling and the fruit is tender (stick a knife into it through the opening in the crust to see if it is done). Serve warm, with or without extra cheese.

APPLE BREAD PUDDING

The melted caramel at the bottom of this pudding makes a lovely contrast with the unsweetened custard. The pudding can stand by itself or it can be served with ice cream or whipped cream.

Serves 6 to 8

4 or 5 tablespoons unsalted butter, softened
1 cup brown sugar
A 7- or 8-ounce loaf French-style bread, sliced
2 Jonagold or Golden Delicious apples, peeled and cut into ½-inch dice
3 cups milk
3 eggs
1 teaspoon vanilla extract

Preheat the oven to 350°F.

Butter a 2-quart casserole or soufflé dish and spread the brown sugar evenly over the bottom. Butter the bread generously, stack it, and cut it into 2-inch squares. Toss the bread with the apples and put them in the casserole on top of the sugar. Whisk the milk, eggs, and vanilla together and pour over the bread. Bake the pudding 40 to 45 minutes, until a knife inserted in the center comes out clean. Baking time varies with the depth of the baking dish. The brown sugar will have melted into a delicious caramel; be sure to include some of it in each serving.

APPLE CHARLOTTES WITH SHERRY SYLLABUB

This charlotte is a modern version of one that might have been served in the nineteenth century at a formal dinner in one of the great Hudson Valley mansions. Use a mixture of Hudson Valley apples for the filling. Syllabub, here used as a sauce, is of English origin and was the dessert of choice in the days before ice cream. It was sold by street vendors, eaten by children and adults, and served at elegant banquets. Syllabub was sometimes made with whiskey, sometimes with wine. In olden days a recipe for syllabub might have read "Combine the lemon, sherry, brandy (or whiskey) and sugar in a bowl and let stand overnight. In the morning, take the bowl to the barn and milk the cow into it, creating as much foam as possible. Let the mixture stand until dinner."

Serves 6

Equipment: Six 5-ounce ramekins

FOR THE SYLLABUB
Grated zest and juice of 1 lemon
6 tablespoons good-quality cream sherry
2 tablespoons good-quality brandy
4 tablespoons superfine sugar
1¼ cups heavy cream

FOR THE CHARLOTTES
8 Winesap, Monroe, and Jonagold apples, peeled, cored, and sliced ¼-inch thick
½ cup sugar plus additional for dusting the ramekins
One 3-inch cinnamon stick
½ lemon
¼ cup raisins
12 slices good-quality white bread
½ cup unsalted butter, melted

GARNISH
Apple slices
Fresh mint leaves

A day ahead, begin making the syllabub. Combine the lemon zest and juice, the sherry, brandy, and sugar in a nonreactive bowl. Refrigerate the mixture overnight.

Prepare the charlottes: Put the apples, sugar, cinnamon, lemon, and raisins in a heavy-bottomed saucepan and cook over low heat, stirring from time to time, for 15 or 20 minutes, or until the fruit is completely cooked and reduced to a thick puree. Remove the lemon and cinnamon stick and taste; add more sugar if the mixture is too tart. Set the filling mixture aside.

Using a pastry brush, butter the bottoms and sides of six 5-ounce ramekins and sprinkle them with sugar. Trim the crusts off the bread. Cut 6 of the slices into 4 equal strips each, then cut the strips in half crosswise, creating 48 strips. Cut the remaining 6 slices of bread into 6 rounds a little smaller than the inside diameter of the ramekins. Dip each strip of bread in the melted butter and press it onto the side of a ramekin. Continue until all the ramekins are lined, then dip the rounds in butter and place one in the bottom of each ramekin. Divide the apple puree equally among the ramekins.

Preheat the oven to 325°F. Place the charlottes on a cookie sheet and bake for 25 to 30 minutes. Remove and keep warm.

While the charlottes are baking, finish the syllabub. In a mixing bowl, whip the cream until soft peaks form. Strain the lemon mixture and whip it into the cream. Keep the syllabub chilled or freeze it for ½ hour or so until it forms a soft slush.

To serve, invert the charlottes onto plates and remove the ramekins. Place 2 or 3 tablespoons of syllabub on each portion and garnish the plates with apple slices and mint leaves.

APPLE CREPES WITH CANDIED WALNUTS

Apples, brown sugar, nuts, and cream . . . what could be better? Use your favorite ice cream on the crepes.

Serves 6

Equipment: 1 heavy 6-inch nonstick crepe pan or skillet with
                      sloping sides
                2 nesting cookie sheets
                baking parchment

FOR THE CREPES
1 extra-large egg
1 tablespoon sugar
4 tablespoons flour
½ cup milk
½ teaspoon vanilla extract
A pinch ground cinnamon
1 tablespoon unsalted butter, melted

FOR THE APPLE FILLING
2 tablespoons unsalted butter
2 tablespoons honey
½ cup brown sugar
6 Cortland and/or Northern Spy apples, peeled, cored, and cut into 12 wedges each
1 pint good-quality vanilla ice cream

1 recipe Candied Walnuts, page 300, chopped coarse

Make the crepes: Combine all the ingredients in the bowl of a food processor or blender and blend until the mixture is perfectly smooth. Set a plate for the crepes next to the stove. Heat a heavy, nonstick 6-inch pan with sloping sides over medium heat and add about ⅛ cup of the crepe batter. Tilt the pan immediately to coat the entire bottom with batter. When the bottom of the crepe is golden brown, in about 1 minute, turn it over, using your fingers or a spatula (the long, skinny kind is most convenient) and cook the other side for about ½ minute. Turn the crepe out onto the plate. Continue to make crepes until all the batter is used, adding a little butter or nonstick spray to the pan only if the crepes are sticking. You should have 8 crepes.

Make the apple filling. Melt the butter in a large sauté pan, add the honey, then the brown sugar and cook, stirring frequently, until the sugar is dissolved. Add the apples and cook, stirring and tossing them frequently, until they are almost completely cooked. The slices should retain their shape and remain slightly firm in the center. Turn off the heat and cover the pan; their own heat will finish cooking the apples.

Cut 2 of the crepes into quarters. Line a baking sheet with parchment and lay the 8 quarters on it. Nest a second baking sheet on top of the crepes and put them in a 225°F oven for 45 minutes to dry out until they are crisp and golden brown. They will be used as garnish.

To serve, place a crepe on a large dessert plate and arrange apple slices around its circumference. Drizzle a little of the apple pan juices over the crepe. Set a scoop of the ice cream in the center of the crepe and stand 2 quarters of toasted crepe on opposite sides of the scoop of ice cream. Sprinkle each serving with candied walnuts and serve immediately.

WARM APPLE SACKS
WITH CLABBERED CREAM

These pretty, light, and appealing warm pastries are named after the beggar's purses they resemble. They look impressive and are very easy to make; you can bake them ahead and reheat just before serving. Clabbered Cream is a thick cultured cream produced by Egg Farm Dairy in Peekskill, New York. The new dairy, which boasts that it has "taken the dairy industry back 100 years," makes old-fashioned products such as hand-churned butter and buttermilk pot cheese as well as aged cheddar, mascarpone, and many other cheeses (see Sources, page 301).

Serves 8

Equipment: a baking sheet
                baking parchment

FOR THE FILLING
1 recipe apple filling for crepes, page 248
1 cup dried cranberries
1 teaspoon grated lemon zest

12 sheets phyllo pastry
6 tablespoons unsalted butter, melted
Freshly ground nutmeg
Sugar to sprinkle the pastry
1 cup Egg Farm Dairy Clabbered Cream

Make the apple filling according to the directions on page 249, cutting the apples into small chunks and cooking the dried cranberries and lemon zest along with the apples. Raise the temperature at the end to reduce and thicken the pan juices to a syrup.

Preheat the oven to 350°F.

Line a baking sheet with parchment paper and set it next to you. Using a slotted spoon, transfer the apple mixture into a bowl. Lay a sheet of phyllo pastry on a work surface, brush it with butter, grate on a little nutmeg, and sprinkle with sugar. Cut the sheet of pastry in half and lay one half crosswise over the other. Brush a second sheet with butter, sprinkle it with sugar, cut it in half, and lay ½ of it diagonally across the 2 prepared layers. Put a generous ½ cup of the filling in the center of the pastry and gather the edges together to form a sack, squeezing the neck of the sack securely closed. Put the sack on the prepared baking sheet and continue, making 8 sacks in all. Brush the outsides of the sacks lightly with butter and sprinkle them with sugar.

Bake 20 minutes, until the sacks are crisp and brown. Serve warm with the ice cream.

BERRY SHORTCAKE WITH WHITE CHOCOLATE MOUSSE

Replacing the usual whipped cream with white chocolate mousse takes this classic into another dimension. In the Hudson Valley you can find all kinds of wonderful berries, both wild and cultivated.

Makes one 9-inch shortcake

Equipment: a 9-inch cake pan

FOR THE SHORTCAKE

1¼ cups flour

3 tablespoons sugar plus a little additional to sprinkle on the shortcake

1 tablespoon baking powder

½ teaspoon salt

6 tablespoons cold unsalted butter, cut into bits

¾ cup heavy cream

2 tablespoons unsalted butter, melted

FOR THE BERRIES

4 pints mixed berries such as strawberries, raspberries, blueberries, and blackberries

3 or 4 tablespoons sugar

2 tablespoons orange- or raspberry-flavored liqueur

FOR THE MOUSSE

3 extra-large egg yolks

2½ tablespoons sugar

¼ cup dry white wine

7 ounces white chocolate, chopped

2 cups heavy cream, very cold

1 teaspoon vanilla extract

1 tablespoon orange- or raspberry-flavored liqueur

Preheat the oven to 375°F.

Make the shortcake: Put the dry ingredients and the cold chopped butter in the bowl of a food processor or cake mixer and combine until the mixture is sandy. Stop the machine, add the cream all at once, and continue to mix just until the cream is incorporated. Gather the dough into a ball, put it on a floured board, and pat it into a ¾-inch-thick round. Fit the round of dough into a 9-inch cake pan and pat it to fill the pan. Brush the shortcake with the melted butter and sprinkle it with sugar. Bake the shortcake for 20 minutes, or until it is golden and firm to the touch.

While the shortcake bakes, prepare the berries: Wash and hull them. Cut strawberries in half and leave other berries whole. Sprinkle them with the sugar and liqueur and toss well. Leave them at room temperature, tossing them from time to time, while you prepare the mousse. When the mousse is done, refrigerate it and the berries.

Bring several inches of water to a boil in the bottom of a double boiler. In the top of the double boiler whisk together the egg yolks, sugar, and wine. Put the top over the boiling water and whisk the mixture constantly and very vigorously until it is very foamy and thickened. Don't stop whisking or the eggs will curdle. When the custard has thickened, remove it from the heat and continue to whisk for another minute or two. You have just made a sabayon sauce.

Melt the chocolate over the boiling water. Little by little, whisk the melted chocolate into the sabayon.

Whip the cream. When it is half-whipped, add the vanilla and the liqueur and continue to whip just until the cream holds its shape. Do not overwhip. Whisk ⅓ of the cream into the sabayon, then fold in the remaining cream gently but thoroughly. Chill the mousse, covered, for at least 2 hours.

To serve, put the shortcake on a cake plate and split it horizontally. On the bottom half, spread some mousse, add a few spoonfuls of berries, and put the top of the shortcake back on. Spoon on some more mousse and top with more berries and some juice.

WILD HUCKLEBERRY
CUSTARD PIE

Huckleberries are one of the delights of summer. They grow only in the wild, they look like small blueberries, and have a very intense flavor. Early in this century they were available by the truckload, and you could pick enough for a pie in a few minutes. You still might be able to pick them yourself in the woods if you know where to look, and occasionally they turn up at small local farm stands. During the last few years you can sometimes find frozen huckleberries in specialty food stores, or by mail order (see Sources, page 301). If you're not lucky enough to find wild huckleberries, you may substitute blueberries.

Makes one 9-inch pie

I recipe Pie Crust, page 258
I teaspoon grated lemon zest
2 cups huckleberries
2 tablespoons sugar

FOR THE CUSTARD
3 extra-large eggs
3 tablespoons sugar
I cup heavy cream
I teaspoon vanilla extract
2 tablespoons brandy or cognac

Make the pastry following the directions on page 258, incorporating the lemon zest into the dough with the butter. Pat the dough into the pan, crimp the edges, and chill as directed. Freeze the remaining dough for another use.

Preheat the oven to 375°F.

Line the pie crust with foil and fill it with pie weights, raw rice, or dried beans. Bake the crust for 10 minutes, remove the foil and weights, and bake the crust 5 minutes more. Take the crust out of the oven and let it cool in the pan on a rack for 15 minutes; leave the oven on.

Toss the huckleberries with the sugar and put them in the baked pie crust.

In a bowl thoroughly combine the custard ingredients and pour over the berries.

Put the pie on a baking sheet on the middle rack of the oven. After 35 minutes, start checking to see if the custard filling is done. When the edge of the custard has set and the berries have begun to boil and give up their juices, take the pie out of the oven and put it on a rack to cool. The heat of the pie will complete the cooking of the custard.

Serve at room temperature. If the pie has been refrigerated, let it come back to room temperature before serving.

INDIVIDUAL DEEP-DISH SUMMER FRUIT PIES

This is an easy, seasonal dessert that everyone loves. With a one-time investment in six deep ramekins, you can make it a tradition in your household. You need five cups of fruit for the filling. In summer, use berries of all kinds, peaches, plums, and nectarines, alone or in various combinations. In spring, use rhubarb, with or without strawberries; in the fall, apples and pears are a natural. The fruits you get in winter may not be seasonal, but you can still use them to make a good deep-dish pie.

Makes 6 individual pies

Equipment: Six 8-ounce ramekins (the kind that look like small
            white soufflé dishes)

FOR THE FRUIT FILLING
1 cup blackberries
1 cup blueberries
2 peaches
2 nectarines
½ to 1 cup sugar, depending on the tartness of the fruit
2 tablespoons flour

1 recipe Pie Crust, page 258
1 egg

GARNISH
Sprigs of mint

Prepare the fruit filling: Wash the berries, removing any leaves and stems; peel, pit, and slice the peaches and slice the nectarines. If you don't have quite 5 cups, add a little more fruit. Put the fruit in a bowl and sprinkle the sugar and flour over it. Using your hands, combine well. Divide the fruit evenly among six 8-ounce ramekins.

Make the pastry following the directions on page 258 to the point of working the dough into a ball. Cut the ball of dough into 6 equal parts and form each of these into a ball. On a lightly floured board, press the balls of dough flat and roll them into ¼-inch-thick circles. Moisten the rims of the filled ramekins and fit a circle of dough on each one, pressing it over the rim to form a tight seal. Trim the edges. Cut a decorative star or flower into the center of each pie crust to serve as a steam vent. Refrigerate the pies for at least 1 hour.

Preheat the oven to 375°F.

Beat the egg with 1 tablespoon of water and brush some of it over the top of each pie. Bake the pies on a baking sheet in the middle of the oven for about 40 minutes, until the crust is golden brown. Remove the pies from the oven and let them cool on a rack. Stick a little sprig of mint into the steam vents and serve them warm or at room temperature.

PIE CRUST

This is as easy to make as a pie crust can be. It can be seasoned with cheese (page 244), lemon zest (page 254), or with chopped toasted nuts (¼ cup), toasted sesame seeds (2 tablespoons), caraway or poppy seeds (2 teaspoons) to complement a sweet or savory filling. For whole wheat pastry, substitute ½ cup whole wheat flour for ½ cup white flour. This recipe makes enough dough for a 2-crust 9-inch pie. If you're making a 1-crust pie, prepare the whole recipe and freeze what's left, well wrapped, for up to 1 month.

Makes dough for a double-crust 9-inch pie

1½ cups flour
¼ teaspoon coarse salt
½ cup (1 stick) cold unsalted butter, cut into 8 pieces
1 egg

Put the flour, salt, and butter in the bowl of a food processor and pulse a few times until the mixture has the consistency of meal. Do not overprocess to make the mixture completely smooth. Transfer the mixture to a bowl. Make a well in the center of the flour, break in the egg, and, using a fork, stir the egg into the flour mixture. Press down the dough to force it into a mass, then gather it up and work it into a ball. Don't be afraid to knead the crust for a minute or 2 until it is well combined and pliable; because it is made with egg, kneading will not toughen it. Break off a little more than half the dough and, using your fingers, pat it into a 9-inch pie plate. If you prefer, roll the dough about ¼ inch thick between 2 pieces of wax paper and fit it into the pie plate. Between 2 pieces of wax paper, roll the remaining dough into a top crust a little less than ¼ inch thick and lay it over the bottom crust. Cover well and refrigerate or freeze the pastry for at least 2 hours.

Remove the pastry from the refrigerator ½ hour before baking. Fill the bottom crust and lay the top crust over the filling. Dip your finger in water and run it along the pie plate between the 2 crusts, then trim the crust and crimp the edges. Slash the top crust or cut a decorative shape out of the pastry to allow steam to escape.

BLUEBERRY BETTY

A "betty" is one of the three old-fashioned baked fruit desserts that were most popular in colonial America. All are farm food and are made from the same four ingredients—fruit, sugar, flour, and butter. The simplest of the three is the "crisp" (see Rhubarb and Strawberry Crisp, page 262) baked fruit with a crumb topping. The betty adds bread crumbs to thicken the fruit; and the "cobbler" on page 261 has a batter rather than a crumb topping. They can all be made with any fruit in season and are easy to put together, comforting, and delicious.

Serves 6 to 8

FOR THE TOPPING
½ cup brown sugar
½ cup flour
4 tablespoons unsalted butter

Juice and zest of I large orange
2 pints blueberries
I cup fresh bread crumbs
5 tablespoons brown sugar
2 tablespoons white sugar
5 tablespoons unsalted butter, melted
Pinch cinnamon
Pinch freshly grated nutmeg

Preheat the oven to 350°F.

Using your fingers, work the topping ingredients together in a bowl until they are evenly blended. Refrigerate the topping while you prepare the fruit.

Using a vegetable peeler, peel the zest from the orange and cut it into very thin I-inch strips. Squeeze the juice from the orange. Put the berries in a large bowl and combine them with the orange juice and zest, the crumbs, both sugars, all but I tablespoon of the butter, and the spices. Spread the remaining melted butter over the bottom and sides of a 10-inch pie plate or shallow baking dish. Pour in the berry mixture and sprinkle the topping mixture evenly over it.

Bake the betty for 1 hour, or until the fruit juices are bubbling around the edges and in the center of the dish and the topping is crisp. Serve warm or chilled, with or without cream, whipped cream, or vanilla ice cream.

WHITE PEACH AND RASPBERRY COBBLER

Toward the end of July or the beginning of August there is nothing better than finding perfectly ripe, fragrant white peaches at a farmstand in Ulster or Dutchess County. At that time in summer, raspberries are sure to be close by. Pick up a good supply of both so you have some left to make this cobbler when you get home.

Serves 6 to 8

3 very ripe peaches, peeled and sliced
1 cup raspberries
3 tablespoons sugar

FOR THE BATTER
½ cup sugar
1¼ cups flour
2 teaspoons baking powder
1 tablespoon unsalted butter, melted
½ cup milk

In a 1½- to 2-quart shallow flameproof casserole, combine the peaches and raspberries with the sugar.

Preheat the oven to 350°F.

Make the batter. In a bowl, combine the sugar, flour, and baking powder and mix in the butter and milk.

Put the casserole over medium-low heat and gently heat the fruit, stirring it gently as the sugar melts and the peaches and raspberries begin to give up their juice. When the fruit has softened, drop the batter by the tablespoon into the casserole. Place the cobbler in the oven and bake for about 35 minutes, until the fruit is bubbling and the top is firm and lightly browned. Serve on its own or with whipped cream or vanilla ice cream.

RHUBARB AND STRAWBERRY CRISP

Simplicity itself, this dessert works well with any kind of summer or autumn fruit. The best ones, though, are this one in early summer and the classic apple crisp of fall, made, of course, with a variety of Hudson Valley apples such as Northern Spy, McIntosh (but only when they're at their best, from September through mid-October), or Mutsu.

Serves 8

FOR THE TOPPING
½ cup flour
½ cup brown sugar
4 tablespoons unsalted butter, cut in bits

1 pound rhubarb stalks, trimmed
1 quart strawberries
½ cup sugar
Heavy cream or vanilla ice cream for serving

Preheat the oven to 350°F.

Make the topping: Using your fingers, work the topping ingredients together until they are evenly blended. Refrigerate while you prepare the fruit.

Cut the rhubarb into 1-inch pieces. Hull the strawberries and cut them in half. In a bowl, combine the fruit with the sugar. Pour the fruit into a 10-inch pie plate or shallow casserole of similar size. Sprinkle the topping evenly over the fruit. Put the casserole on a baking sheet and bake the crisp in the middle of the oven for about 1 hour, until the juices are bubbling around the edges and in the middle of the dish, and the topping is crisp. Serve warm with heavy cream or vanilla ice cream.

STEWED SUMMER FRUITS WITH FRESH FARM-MADE CHEESE

This dessert is a simple, light, and refreshing way to end a meal when summer fruits are at their peak. Visit farmstands to find the ripest, most flavorful fruit rather than the most beautiful. A few bruises won't do any harm; you'll trim them away when you prepare the fruit for cooking. Also available at farmstands, and at specialty and health food stores as well, are fresh farm-made cheeses that make the cream cheese, cottage cheese, and farmer's cheese of the grocery store seem bland and uninteresting. These cheeses and fresh fruit compotes were made for each other.

Serves 8

1 cup good-quality white wine
1 cup brewed tea
1 cup sugar
2 tablespoons honey
One 3-inch cinnamon stick
4 whole cloves
3 to 4 pounds mixed summer fruits such as peaches, nectarines, plums, and apricots, pitted
    and cut into 1-inch wedges

FOR THE CHEESE
6 ounces fresh Hollow Road Farms ricotta or other good-quality ricotta
6 ounces Coach Farm Fresh Curd cheese or other "farmer's" cheese
2 tablespoons honey

GARNISH
Fresh mint sprigs

In a 3-quart saucepan, boil the wine, tea, sugar, honey, and spices for about 10 minutes. When the large bubbles on the surface of the mixture turn to foam when you stir it, a light syrup has formed. Add the fruit, cover, and bring to a boil. Remove the lid, stir the fruit, and let it simmer another 10 or 15 minutes, until it is cooked but not mushy, and still in recognizable slices. Let the fruit cool, then chill it.

Combine the cheese ingredients in the bowl of a food processor and process until it is very smooth. Chill, covered.

To serve, put about 1 cup of the fruit in elegant stemmed glass bowls or brandy snifters. Using 2 spoons, form the cheese into egg-shaped balls and place one on each serving. Decorate with fresh mint.

SUMMER PUDDING

This simple, intensely-flavored pudding makes the most of the Hudson Valley's abundance of berries and its modest supplies of red currants. In the 1920s there were 500 farms growing red currants in Ulster County alone. Today it's rare to find them at farmstands in the height of the season. Small amounts of other summer fruits make a nice accent.

Serves 8

A 1-pound loaf good-quality sliced white bread, crusts removed
1 large peach, peeled, pitted, and cut into wedges
2 large plums, pitted, and cut into thin wedges
6 tablespoons sugar
2 cups raspberries
2 cups red currants, leaves and stems removed
1 cup blueberries

OPTIONAL GARNISH
Heavy cream

Line the bottom and sides of a 6-cup bowl with bread, cutting the bread so the pieces cover the surfaces completely, with no gaps.

Put the peach and plums in a saucepan with the sugar and 2 tablespoons of water and gradually bring to a boil, taking care not to burn the fruit. Simmer and stir the fruit until it is just tender, about 5 minutes, then add the berries and currants, bring to a boil, and simmer, stirring, for another 4 or 5 minutes. Turn off the heat. Taste the fruit; it should be deliciously tart. If too tart, add a little more sugar.

Using a slotted spoon, spoon the fruit into the bread-lined bowl and cover the top completely with more pieces of bread, being sure to leave no space between the pieces. Reserve and refrigerate the juices remaining in the saucepan. Cover the dish with a plate that just fits inside it and weight the pudding with a heavy can. Refrigerate overnight.

Unmold the pudding several hours before serving. Run a knife carefully around the inside of the bowl and invert the pudding onto a serving dish. Spoon the reserved juices over the pudding to saturate the bread completely. Serve wedges of pudding and pass a pitcher of heavy cream for those who want it.

POACHED PEARS WITH TEAR OF THE CLOUDS SABAYON

The true source of the Hudson River, in the Adirondacks, was discovered and poetically named in 1872 by a New York state surveyor who wrote in his report to the state legislature:

> Far above the chilly waters of Lake Avalanche . . . is Summit Water, a minute, unpretending tear of the clouds, as it were—a lovely pool shivering in the breezes of the mountains, and sending its limpid surplus through Feldspar Brook and to the Opalescent River, the wellspring of the Hudson.

Rivendell Vineyards named one of its lovely late-harvest dessert wines for this little lake. Here it is used to poach the pears and in a light and elegant sabayon sauce instead of the usual Madeira.

This versatile dessert is easy to prepare in advance. Both the pears and the sauce can also be used in other desserts: You can serve the sabayon warm or cold; it is excellent with berries and other fruit. The pears can be served on their own or with ice cream.

Serves 8

FOR THE PEARS
One 12.7-ounce bottle Rivendell Tear of the Clouds Late Harvest dessert wine
    or Clinton Vineyards Late Harvest Riesling
1 cup sugar
Two 1-inch strips orange zest
Two 1-inch strips lemon zest
A 1-inch piece of cinnamon stick
1 whole clove
8 large ripe Bosc pears

FOR THE SABAYON
6 extra-large egg yolks
5 tablespoons sugar
1½ cups heavy cream

GARNISH
Mint leaves
Crisp cookies

Pour off 5 ounces of the wine and set it aside for the sabayon sauce. Put the rest of the wine, 3 cups of water, the sugar, the zest, and the spices in a pot large enough to hold the pears in one layer. Bring to a boil and simmer the syrup over low heat while you peel the pears. Peel them carefully to retain the shape, leaving the stems on. Slice a piece off the bottom of each pear and stand them in the hot syrup. Cover the pan, let the syrup return to the boil, turn down the heat and poach the pears over low heat until they are tender when pierced with a sharp knife point, about 30 minutes. Remove the pears from the syrup and set them on a platter or in a shallow bowl. Remove the zest and spices, return the syrup to the boil, and reduce it until you have about 1½ cups. This should take about 15 minutes. Pour the syrup over the pears. As the pears cool, lay them in the syrup and turn them from time to time so they absorb as much of the syrup as possible.

Make the sabayon: In a nonreactive bowl, over a double boiler, beat the egg yolks, sugar, and wine with a wire whisk or hand beater until the mixture is light yellow and thick. Remove from the heat and continue beating until cool. (Beating should take 5 to 10 minutes.) Set aside. Whip the cream until stiff and fold it into the egg-wine mixture. Refrigerate the sauce.

To serve, spoon 4 tablespoons of sabayon in the center of each of 8 dessert plates. Place a poached pear on top and garnish with a mint leaf. Serve with crisp cookies, if you wish.

MINIATURE PUMPKIN SOUFFLÉS

People love being served a whole pumpkin with a browned soufflé rising out of it. Using cute little pumpkins as the actual soufflé dish adds both flavor and substance to this unusual dessert. Don't be intimidated at the idea of making a soufflé; this one is foolproof. Most of the work for this dessert can be done in advance, and the last phase of preparation takes only ten minutes and can be done half an hour before serving.

Serves 8

8 miniature pumpkins, ¾ to 1 pound each, as uniform in size as possible
4 tablespoons unsalted butter
½ cup maple syrup
Spice mixture: 1 teaspoon cinnamon, ½ teaspoon allspice, ½ teaspoon mace, ¼ teaspoon
    nutmeg, ⅛ teaspoon cloves, mixed together
½ teaspoon grated peeled fresh ginger
1 cup canned pumpkin puree
½ cup good-quality brandy

FOR THE PASTRY CREAM
1½ cups milk
A 2-inch piece of vanilla bean
½ cup sugar
4 extra-large egg yolks
⅔ cup flour
4 extra-large egg whites
1 teaspoon fresh lemon juice
7 tablespoons sugar

GARNISH
Vanilla ice cream

FALL MENU

Onion
Charlotte
with Wild
Mushrooms

Spiced Loin of
Pork with
Baked Acorn
Squash

Swiss Chard
with Golden
Onions

Miniature
Pumpkin
Soufflés

Preheat the oven to 400°F.

Using a grapefruit knife, remove enough of the stem end of each pumpkin to create an opening at least 3 inches in diameter. Using a grapefruit spoon, scrape out the seeds and enough of the pumpkin flesh to create a straight-sided bowl. Be careful not to cut through the bottom and sides of the pumpkins.

The day before serving, or early in the day of serving, put the pumpkin bowls in a baking pan, put ½ tablespoon butter and 1 teaspoon of maple syrup in each one, and sprinkle 1 teaspoon of the spice mixture over all the pumpkins. Put 1 cup of water in the pan to keep the pumpkins from burning, and bake until the pumpkins are very tender, about 1¾ hours, adding more water to the pan if necessary to keep them from sticking. When the pumpkins are done, set them aside in the pan.

In a small, heavy-bottomed saucepan, combine the remaining spices, the brandy, and the pumpkin puree. Cook over the lowest possible heat, stirring frequently, for 20 to 30 minutes, until the puree is very thick and reduced.

Make the pastry cream: Scald the milk with the vanilla bean in a heavy-bottomed saucepan. In a bowl, beat the sugar and yolks until they are light and creamy, then blend in the flour. Gradually beat in the hot milk, then return the custard to the pot and cook it over moderate heat, without boiling, until it is very thick and smooth and has no flour taste. Remove the vanilla bean and add the reduced pumpkin mixture to the pastry cream. Scrape the mixture into a bowl that will be big enough to hold all the egg whites when beaten.

Forty-five minutes before serving, preheat the oven to 350°F and beat the egg whites. As they begin to thicken, add the lemon juice and the sugar, a spoon at a time, and continue beating until stiff peaks form. Stir ⅓ of the beaten whites into the pumpkin mixture, then gently fold in the remaining whites. Fill the pumpkins with the soufflé mixture. Tap the bottom of each one firmly on a hard surface to settle the mixture and eliminate air pockets. Put a little more of the mixture in each pumpkin and swirl the top with your finger. Return the pumpkins to the pan.

Place the pan of pumpkins in the oven. The soufflés will take 25 to 30 minutes to cook. They will rise at least 1 inch above the tops of the pumpkin and have browned crusts. Serve immediately and at the table float a tablespoon of vanilla ice cream in the center of each soufflé.

INDIAN PUDDING WITH BUTTERSCOTCH SAUCE

Because cornmeal, or Indian, pudding was so quickly prepared, it was also known in colonial days as "hasty pudding." Versions of the dish ranged from basic to luxurious. This version is definitely on the luxurious side, with its abundance of eggs and the delicate flavors of fresh ginger and pear, and it takes longer to prepare than traditional hasty pudding. To make it even more luxurious, serve it with a small scoop of vanilla ice cream. The corn bread for this recipe makes an excellent spiced cake; make it a day ahead. You will need only half of it for the pudding, so enjoy eating the rest while it's fresh.

Serves 8

Equipment: Eight 6-ounce pudding molds or ramekins
          nonstick spray

FOR THE CORNBREAD
¾ cup buttermilk
¾ cup cornmeal
1 extra-large egg
1 cup flour
1½ teaspoons baking powder
1 teaspoon coarse salt
½ cup sugar
4 tablespoons unsalted butter, melted
¼ cup sour cream
1 teaspoon powdered ginger
1 teaspoon ground cinnamon

FOR THE PUDDING
1 quart milk
¼ cup peeled, sliced fresh ginger
1 recipe spiced corn bread
5 extra-large eggs

8 extra-large egg yolks
⅔ cup molasses
1 pear

FOR THE BUTTERSCOTCH SAUCE
⅓ cup light corn syrup
¾ cup brown sugar
4 tablespoons unsalted butter
½ cup heavy cream
2 tablespoons brandy

Preheat the oven to 375°F.

Make the corn bread: Combine the buttermilk and cornmeal and let it soak for 5 minutes. Stir in the remaining ingredients and combine well. Spray an 8-inch-square baking pan with nonstick spray, spread the batter in the pan, and bake for 30 minutes. Let half the corn bread dry out and turn it into crumbs in a food processor.

Make the pudding: Put the milk in a saucepan, add the ginger, and bring to a boil. Turn off the heat, cover the pan, and let the mixture steep while you proceed with the recipe. In a bowl combine the eggs and yolks with the molasses. Put the corn bread crumbs in a bowl. Bring the milk back to the boil and whisk it gradually into the egg mixture. Strain the mixture over the crumbs and stir to combine.

Reduce the oven to 325°F.

Peel, core, and cut the pear into ½-inch dice and add it to the pudding mixture. Spray the pudding molds with nonstick spray, fill them to within ½ inch of the top, and put them in a baking pan. Add water to come ⅓ of the way up the sides of the molds, cover the pan tightly with foil, and bake for 55 minutes. The puddings will feel firm to the touch when they are done.

While the puddings bake, make the butterscotch sauce: Combine the corn syrup, brown sugar, and butter in a 2-quart saucepan and stir over high heat until the butter is melted and the mixture comes to a boil. Add the cream, turn the heat to medium, and bring back to the boil. Simmer until the temperature reaches 240°F on a candy thermometer, or until the sauce thickens slightly, about 10 minutes. Turn off the heat and stir in the brandy.

To serve, invert the molds and turn out the puddings onto individual dessert plates. Spoon a little sauce over the tops of the puddings and scatter zigzag lines of it decoratively around the plate.

BROWN SUGAR AND CHESTNUT PUDDING

This variation on a farm-style brown sugar pudding is essentially a cobbler with a brandy sauce instead of fruit. For a fruit cobbler, see White Peach and Raspberry Cobbler, page 261. Old Hudson Valley recipes for special winter occasions often called for tropical fruits, a great treat brought up the river by trade ships. Garnishing this pudding with orange segments would have turned it into a very festive dessert.

Serves 6 to 8

FOR THE BATTER
1 cup candied chestnuts *(marrons glacés)*, plus 6 or 8 more for garnish
½ cup brown sugar
1¼ cups flour
2 teaspoons baking powder
1 tablespoon unsalted butter, melted
½ cup milk

FOR THE BRANDY SAUCE
¼ cup brandy
½ cup unsalted butter
1 cup brown sugar

GARNISH
¼ cup Candied Walnuts, page 300
½ cup heavy cream
1 tablespoon molasses
6 to 8 whole candied chestnuts
Orange segments from 2 navel oranges

Preheat the oven to 350°F.

Make the batter: Chop the chestnuts coarse. In a bowl, combine the sugar, flour, and baking powder and mix in the butter, milk, and chestnuts.

Make the sauce: Combine the brandy, butter, and brown sugar with 1¼ cups water in a saucepan and bring to a boil. Simmer for 2 minutes and remove from the heat. Pour the sauce into a 2-quart shallow casserole.

Drop the batter by the tablespoon into the sauce. Bake the pudding for 35 minutes, until the sauce is bubbling and the top is firm and lightly browned. Remove the pudding from the oven and let it stand for 1 hour before serving.

Make the garnish: Chop the walnuts fine. Whip the cream until soft, add the molasses and walnuts, and whip until stiff.

To serve, spoon the pudding onto dessert plates and garnish each serving with walnut cream, a whole candied chestnut, and some orange segments.

FRUITCAKE

We looked forward all year to Grandma Harris's fruitcake. Unlike most fruitcakes that you dread being given, hers was light rather than dark, light rather than dense, and truly a gift. This is a cake that would be good at any time of year, but of course Grandma never baked it any time but Christmas and neither do I. Doris Harris, my maternal grandmother, is a Massachusetts Yankee and she got this recipe from her grandmother. The original recipe has undoubtedly gone through some changes over the years, but essentially it tastes the same as the fruitcake I loved as a child. When you buy the fruit for this cake, please don't get it at the grocery store; go to a specialty food store and get the unusual fruits you need to make the cake that's been in my family for five or six generations.

GRANDMA HARRIS'S FRUITCAKE

Equipment: a 9-inch springform pan or an angel food cake pan

½ teaspoon baking soda
I cup buttermilk
I cup dried pitted cherries
½ cup dried cranberries
½ cup golden raisins
I cup good-quality brandy
Soft butter and flour for the cake pan
I cup unsalted butter, at room temperature
2 cups sugar plus 3 tablespoons sugar to sprinkle on top
2 extra-large eggs
3 cups flour
I teaspoon coarse salt
I teaspoon freshly grated nutmeg
I cup candied lemon and orange rind, chopped coarse
¾ cup hazelnuts, toasted in the oven for 10 minutes and chopped coarse

Preheat the oven to 325°F.

Put the baking soda in a 2-cup measure and add the buttermilk. Stir well with a fork and set aside. (The soda will make the buttermilk foam and rise.)

Combine the dried cherries, cranberries, and raisins with the brandy in a small saucepan. Bring to a boil, simmer for 5 minutes, cover the pan, and let the fruit steep.

Butter and flour a 9-inch springform pan or angel food cake pan. Tap out any excess flour.

Cream the butter and sugar together until light and fluffy and beat in the eggs. Combine the flour with the salt and nutmeg and sift the dry ingredients together. Beat the flour mixture into the butter mixture in thirds, alternating with the buttermilk mixture. Scrape the bowl as necessary. Fold in the fruit, the candied rind, and the nuts, making sure they are evenly distributed through the batter. Spoon the mixture into the cake pan, smooth the top, and sprinkle it evenly with the remaining 3 tablespoons of sugar.

Bake 1 hour and 40 minutes. Let the cake cool on a rack for an hour. Carefully turn it out of the pan and invert it onto a cake plate, sugared side up. Serve right away or wrap tightly in several layers of plastic wrap and store in an airtight container 2 weeks at room temperature, 1 month in the refrigerator.

MARTIN'S INCREDIBLE FLOURLESS CHOCOLATE CAKE WITH ENGLISH CUSTARD SAUCE

Martin Howard's chocolate work is legendary. Over the years he has created thousands of spectacular, sometimes whimsical desserts and cakes that always surprise and astonish and often elicit awe from those lucky enough to see and to taste them. Amazingly, Martin's desserts always taste as good as they look. Martin draws inspiration from everything: the sea, the skyline, a sunrise, or even the Statue of Liberty. Often his elaborate creations incorporate three or four of the desserts in this chapter that are here offered as separate recipes.

Almost pure chocolate, the intensity of this cake puts chocolate lovers in seventh heaven. The vanilla sauce provides a stunning contrast.

Makes one 9-inch cake

Equipment: a 9-inch cake pan, 2 inches deep
      nonstick spray
      baking parchment

1¼ cups sugar
4 ounces bittersweet chocolate, Valrhona or comparable quality, cut into small chunks
8 ounces unsweetened baking chocolate, cut into small chunks
½ pound unsalted butter at room temperature, cut into small chunks
1 tablespoon Grand Marnier
7 extra-large eggs
1 recipe English Custard Sauce (recipe follows)

Preheat the oven to 300°F.

Cut a piece of parchment to fit the bottom of the cake pan, spray the pan with nonstick spray, and line it with the paper. Press the paper flat and spray the top surface.

Put 1 cup of the sugar in a saucepan with ¼ cup water and bring to a boil over medium heat, stirring to dissolve the sugar. Turn off the heat.

Heat water in the bottom of a double boiler over medium heat, put all the chocolate in the top, and melt it over hot water, stirring so it melts evenly. Make sure all the chocolate is melted. Remove the chocolate from the heat and, stirring constantly with a rubber spatula, add the butter bit by bit until is has melted smoothly into the chocolate. Make sure all the butter has melted, then add the sugar syrup and stir it in well. When all is well combined, stir in the Grand Marnier.

Beat the eggs with the remaining ¼ cup sugar until they are thick and foamy. This will take 5 or 6 minutes in an electric mixer, a little longer by hand. Add about ⅓ of the beaten eggs to the chocolate mixture and, using a rubber spatula, fold them in gently but thoroughly; then add the chocolate mixture to the remaining eggs and fold the two together. Pour the batter into the prepared cake pan.

Put the cake pan into a larger roasting pan and add water to come a third of the way up the side of the cake pan. Bake for 1 hour. The cake is done when it feels springy to the touch and is just beginning to come away from the sides of the pan. Turn the cake out onto a cake plate and peel off the parchment. Serve warm with English Custard Sauce.

ENGLISH CUSTARD SAUCE

Makes 3 cups

2 cups milk
One half a vanilla bean
6 extra-large egg yolks
½ cup sugar
4 tablespoons Grand Marnier

Put the milk in a saucepan. Scrape the pulp from the vanilla bean, add it and the pod to the milk, and bring to a boil over medium heat. Stir occasionally to keep the milk from burning on the bottom. When it boils, turn off the heat, cover the pot, and let steep 15 minutes. Whisk the egg yolks with the sugar until the sugar is dissolved.

Set next to the stove a bowl into which you can strain the custard, a strainer, and a larger bowl of ice water into which you can set the bowl of custard sauce.

Reheat the milk over medium heat. When it returns to the boil, stir half the hot milk, little by little, into the yolk mixture; then, stirring constantly over medium heat, pour the egg mixture into the milk and cook and stir until the mixture is just beginning to thicken enough to coat the spoon. Remove from the heat and continue to stir for a minute or 2; then strain the mixture into a bowl and set it immediately in the ice water bath. Stir in the Grand Marnier. Let the sauce cool and refrigerate it, covered.

CHOCOLATE ANGEL FOOD CAKE WITH SOUR CHERRY ICE CREAM AND CHOCOLATE SAUCE

Angel food cake is a universal favorite. This chocolate version is wonderful with the unusual sour cherry ice cream.

Makes a 10-inch cake

Equipment: a 10-inch angel food cake pan

¾ cup flour
6 tablespoons unsweetened cocoa powder
1½ cups sugar
10 egg whites
¼ teaspoon salt
1½ teaspoons cream of tartar
1½ teaspoons vanilla extract
1 drop almond extract

Sour Cherry Ice Cream, page 281
Chocolate Sauce (recipe follows)

Preheat the oven to 350°F.

Sift the flour, cocoa, and ¾ cup of the sugar together 3 times.

Beat the egg whites with the salt and cream of tartar until soft peaks form. Sprinkle the remaining sugar over the whites 2 tablespoons at a time, beating after each addition. Beat until stiff peaks form. Fold in the vanilla and almond extracts. Gently but thoroughly fold in the dry ingredients, ⅓ at a time.

Pour the batter into an ungreased 10-inch angel food cake pan and bake until the cake has risen and a tester comes out dry, about 45 minutes. Don't worry if the top of the cake cracks a little.

Hang the pan upside down on a long-neck bottle to cool for about 1½ hours. Gently run a knife blade around the edges of the cake and turn it out onto a cake plate. Just before serving, fill the center of the cake with some of the ice cream and drizzle some chocolate sauce over all. Serve additional ice cream and sauce on the side.

CHOCOLATE SAUCE

Makes about 2 cups

½ pound bittersweet chocolate, Valrhona or a comparable brand, cut into small chunks
1 cup heavy cream
½ cup light corn syrup

Put the chocolate in a bowl. In a small saucepan, combine the cream and corn syrup and bring to a boil. Pour the hot mixture over the chocolate and stir until well combined.

SOUR CHERRY ICE CREAM

Makes 1 quart

1 cup pitted dried sour cherries
⅓ cup kirschwasser
1 quart good-quality vanilla ice cream

Put the cherries and kirsch in a small saucepan and bring to a boil. Turn off the heat, cover the pot, and let the cherries steep for 30 minutes.

Several hours before serving, take the ice cream out of the freezer, put it in a bowl, and leave it at room temperature until it begins to soften. When the ice cream is softened but not melted, add the reconstituted cherries to it and stir with a rubber spatula until the cherries are evenly distributed. Return the ice cream to the freezer for at least 1 hour before serving as directed above.

VINAIGRETTES, FLAVORED OILS,

&

OTHER KITCHEN STAPLES

KITCHEN STAPLES

The term "mise en place" ("put in place," or "set-up") is a French term used in professional kitchens to describe the materials a chef always has on hand. Of course this varies from kitchen to kitchen, but it usually includes at least such seasoning ingredients as chopped garlic, shallots, parsley, and other herbs; a good supply of sauces in constant use such as mayonnaise, vinaigrettes, and perhaps a butter sauce; an array of stocks; garnishes such as olives, nuts, or croutons. No home kitchen is likely to be similarly supplied, but both in using this book and in your daily life, cooking will be easier and more fun, faster, and more inventive if certain staples are maintained. Everyone knows about staples such as salt, pepper, oil, vinegar, and capers. The staples that follow are something else; they are homemade preparations that influence the style and help to develop the character of your cooking. With these staples on hand, you can enrich the flavors and appearance of the foods you cook, dress up the simplest preparations, or provide a dashing garnish at the last minute.

For example, if you made a batch of Tomato Compote, page 293, you could use two or three tablespoons of it to season a pot of rice, to fill several omelets, dress up a vinaigrette, or make a wonderful pasta sauce. Sprinkle Shallots Preserved in Red Wine, page 294, over steamed or broiled fish or grilled meat, serve a little mound of it with pâté or meat loaf, add it to a sauté of vegetables, or garnish a batch of buttered new potatoes.

I hope you will take these recipes, call them your own, and make them a foundation for creativity in your kitchen. Use them in new ways or as models for new staples you create. In order to make this a realistic possibility, you will have to depend on the freezer for storing. I encourage you to develop a reliable labeling system (masking tape and a fine-point permanent marker work perfectly) and freeze staples in small quantities.

VINAIGRETTES

U se these incredibly versatile mixtures not only as salad dressings, but also as sauces or marinades for grilled meats, fish, and seafood or hot or cold vegetables. In addition to basic oil and vinegar mixtures, vinaigrettes can contain vegetable juices, stocks, purees such as Tomato Compote, olive paste, and red pepper puree. And despite its name, vinaigrette need not contain vinegar; the acid can be contributed by wine, or lemon or orange juice. Other vinaigrettes in this book are Lemon Vinaigrette, page 55, Chervil Vinaigrette, page 64, and Herb Vinaigrette, page 129.

All the vinaigrettes keep 3 to 4 weeks in the refrigerator.

MUSTARD HERB VINAIGRETTE

Makes about 1 cup

1 tablespoon Dijon mustard
1 tablespoon minced shallot
1 teaspoon minced garlic
2 tablespoons white wine vinegar mixed with 2 tablespoons water
1 tablespoon chopped mixed fresh herbs: parsley, chervil, and chives
½ cup canola oil
¼ cup extra virgin olive oil
Coarse salt and freshly ground pepper

In a bowl, whisk together the mustard, the shallot, garlic, vinegar, and herbs. Continuing to whisk vigorously, add the oils in a thin stream until all the oil has been added and the sauce has emulsified. Season to taste with salt and freshly ground pepper.

CARROT VINAIGRETTE

Makes about ½ cup

1 cup carrot juice
1 tablespoon fresh lemon juice plus additional as needed
1 tablespoon white wine vinegar plus additional as needed
2 tablespoons olive oil
Salt and freshly ground pepper

In a small saucepan, boil the carrot juice over medium heat until it is reduced to ¼ cup. When the juice is cool, stir in the lemon juice and the vinegar. Whisk in the oil. The reduced carrot juice will be very sweet. Add enough additional lemon juice and/or vinegar to give it a sweet-tart flavor. Season with salt and freshly ground pepper.

RED PEPPER VINAIGRETTE

Makes about 1 cup

1 roasted red pepper
1 tablespoon Tomato Compote, page 293
Juice of ½ lemon
2 tablespoons white wine vinegar
½ cup olive oil
Coarse salt and freshly ground pepper

Peel the pepper, remove the seeds, and process it with the tomato compote to a fine puree in a food processor. Scrape the puree into a bowl and whisk in the lemon juice and vinegar. Continuing to whisk, add the oil in a thin stream. The sauce will not form an emulsion. Season to taste with salt and freshly ground pepper.

TOMATO VINAIGRETTE

Makes about 1 cup

3 tablespoons Tomato Compote, page 293
1 small clove garlic, minced
1 teaspoon minced shallot
2 tablespoons red wine vinegar
Coarse salt and plenty of freshly ground pepper
½ cup extra virgin olive oil
1 teaspoon chopped chervil or parsley

In a bowl, whisk together all the ingredients except the oil and the herbs. Continuing to whisk, gradually add the oil, incorporating it as much as possible. This dressing will not form a complete emulsion, so the oil will rise to the top after it sits for a while. Whisk in the herbs, taste, and adjust the seasoning. Whisk again before using.

FLAVORED OILS

Make small quantities of these flavorful oils to keep on hand in your refrigerator. You can use them to season virtually any plain poached, broiled, or baked fish. They're also great on grilled meat, chicken, and vegetables, and in place of butter on steamed vegetables. When making flavored oils, use a neutral-tasting oil such as canola, grapeseed, or safflower. The recipes that follow suggest proportions only; make more or less oil to suit your needs.

HERB OIL

Use one, two, or a combination of up to four herbs. Good combinations include: dill, chervil, and parsley; thyme and basil; chives, chopped shallot, and parsley; rosemary and chopped garlic; tarragon by itself.

Makes 1 cup

½ cup chopped fresh herbs
1 cup vegetable oil

Combine the herbs and oil in a small saucepan. Over low heat, warm them, then steep without allowing the oil to come to a boil for 15 minutes. Pour the mixture into a jar and allow it to steep overnight in the refrigerator. Strain the flavored oil into a jar or bottle. The oil will keep for 3 weeks in the refrigerator.

TOMATO OIL

¼ cup tomato paste
1 cup vegetable oil

Put the tomato paste in a small saucepan, add the oil, and whisk well. Over medium heat steep the mixture for 15 minutes. Whisk again and pour the mixture into a clear bottle or jar. Let steep in the refrigerator for 24 hours. The tomato paste will settle to the bottom. Decant the oil into a bottle or jar and store up to 3 weeks in the refrigerator.

FENNEL OIL

I small bulb fennel with tops—tops chopped coarse, bulb sliced thin
I shallot, chopped
I cup vegetable oil

In a little oil, sauté the sliced fennel bulb and the shallot for a few minutes without browning. Add the fennel tops and oil and steep over medium heat for 15 minutes. Allow to steep in the refrigerator overnight. Strain into a bottle or jar. The oil will keep for 3 weeks in the refrigerator.

CAPER OIL

I tablespoon minced shallot
I teaspoon minced garlic
I cup olive oil
3 tablespoons small capers, drained and mashed with a fork

In a small saucepan, sauté the shallot and garlic in a little of the olive oil over medium-low heat for a minute; add the capers. Pour in the olive oil, let it get hot, and steep it over low heat for 10 minutes. Pour the mixture into a jar, allow it to steep overnight in the refrigerator. Strain into a bottle or jar. The oil will keep for 3 to 4 weeks in the refrigerator.

HERB SACHET

Throughout this book you will find an herb sachet included in lists of ingredients. An herb sachet is a collection of herbs and spices tied in a cheesecloth bag. It is like a teabag; steep it in the liquid of soups, stews, and sauces to infuse them with the flavors it contains. The strength of these flavors can be controlled by adding or removing the sachet at any point in the cooking and it makes for easy removal of seasonings when a soup is pureed or a sauce is used without straining.

The basic herb sachet consists of black peppercorns, cloves, bay leaves, thyme, and parsley tied in a small cheesecloth pouch. Use a double layer of cheesecloth to prevent the spices from escaping and tie the pouch securely. Trim off excess cheesecloth at the top. The proportion of ingredients depends on what you're using it in, and many other ingredients such as garlic, juniper berries, and various herbs may be added.

TOMATO COMPOTE

A kitchen staple, this essence can be incorporated into many dishes or used on its own as a garnish. The more you have it around, the more uses you'll find for it. It works as well with fish and pasta as with meat and gives a lively accent to a sauce or a vinaigrette. Freeze the compote in small batches so you'll always have some on hand.

Makes about 2 cups

One 28-ounce can Italian plum tomatoes
2 shallots, diced
2 large cloves garlic, sliced
2 tablespoons extra virgin olive oil
herb sachet: 5 sprigs fresh basil
                 A 6-inch branch tarragon   } Tied together in a
                 3 or 4 fresh thyme sprigs   a double layer of cheesecloth
Coarse salt and freshly ground pepper

Using your fingers, remove the tomatoes from the can one by one and crush them, letting the juice and seeds run back into the can Put the tomatoes in a bowl and strain the juice over them.

In a 2-quart saucepan, lightly brown the shallots and garlic in the olive oil. Add the tomatoes and the sachet, bring to a boil, and reduce the mixture over medium heat until it is dry. Put the mixture through the fine blade of a food grinder or through a food mill. Season with salt and freshly ground pepper.

SHALLOTS PRESERVED IN RED WINE

This preparation is used in Foie Gras Terrine with Preserved Shallots, page 7, and Warm New Potato Salad with Preserved Shallots, page 197.

Makes about 2 cups

1 pound shallots, peeled and cut in ⅛-inch dice
3 cups dry red wine
3 tablespoons red wine vinegar
1 tablespoon olive oil
Lots of freshly ground pepper

Combine the shallots, wine, and vinegar in a saucepan and bring to a boil. Boil, uncovered, until all the liquid has evaporated, about 30 minutes. Watch carefully toward the end of the boiling time to be sure the shallots don't burn. Stir in the olive oil and season with plenty of freshly ground pepper. The shallots will keep, covered, for 4 weeks in the refrigerator.

GARLIC AND ONION JAM

Not to be outdone by California, the Hudson Valley has its own annual garlic festival in Saugerties, New York, and a couple of years ago it yielded a great discovery—rocambole garlic. Grown by Keith Stewart of Keith's Farm in Orange County, its flavor is intense yet mellow and it grows in uniformly large cloves with none of those tiny useless slivers usually found in the center of a head of garlic. It is especially delicious made into this jam, which offers an alternative to butter for bread and makes a splendid condiment for cold meat or fish.

Makes 1 cup jam

½ pound garlic, 3 or 4 large heads
1 pound onions, peeled
6 tablespoons extra virgin olive oil or clarified duck fat
Coarse salt and freshly ground pepper

Preheat the oven to 300°F.

Cut the heads of garlic in half crosswise and boil in salted water for 5 minutes. Drain.

Cut the onions into 6 wedges each and lay them in a 9-by-13-inch roasting pan. Scatter the blanched garlic on top, pour the oil over all, and season with salt and pepper. Roast the onions and garlic for 2 hours, until both are very soft.

Put the garlic and onions through a food mill and discard the skins. Using a whip, beat the puree until it emulsifies. Store the jam in a jar in the refrigerator, where it will keep, covered, for 1 week.

ROASTED GARLIC PUREE

This sweet, intense garlic puree is good in mashed potatoes, white bean or fava bean puree, with rack of lamb, or stirred into a vinaigrette.

Makes ½ cup

3 heads garlic
Salt
6 tablespoons extra virgin olive oil or clarified duck fat

Preheat the oven to 300°F.

Cut the heads of garlic in half crosswise and boil in salted water for 5 minutes. Drain.

Put the oil or fat in an 8-inch square roasting pan, add the garlic in 1 layer, and roast for 1 hour, until the garlic is soft.

Put the roasted garlic through a food mill and discard the skins. Save the garlic-flavored oil to use in cooking. Whip the garlic to emulsify it. Store the puree in the refrigerator, where it will keep, covered, for 10 days.

GARLIC CROUTONS

You should certainly make more than you need for the moment when you bake these crisp croutons because everyone loves to eat them as a snack. Serve them topped with a slice of fresh tomato, or with goat cheese as in Roasted Onion and Garlic Soup, page 50.

Makes about 30

One long, thin 8-ounce loaf French-style bread
2 small cloves garlic, peeled
6 tablespoons extra virgin olive oil
Coarse salt

Preheat the oven to 325°F.

   Slice the bread on the diagonal into ¼-inch slices. Puree the garlic or put it through a garlic press and mix it into the oil. Using a pastry brush, brush the oil sparingly over one side of the bread and place the slices, oiled side up, on baking sheets. Bake until crisp and just golden brown, about 15 minutes. Season lightly with salt.

BUTTER CROUTONS

Use these crisp croutons as a garnish in soups and salads or turn them into cinnamon croutons, page 43.

Makes 2 to 3 cups croutons

6 slices good-quality unsweetened white bread, crusts removed
4 tablespoons unsalted butter

Preheat the oven to 350°F.

Stack the slices of bread and cut them into ½-inch cubes. Melt the butter in a 9-by-13-inch baking pan and toss the bread to coat it all with butter. Toast the croutons in the oven, shaking the pan once or twice so they will brown evenly. The croutons will be crisp in about 20 minutes.

GARLIC ROASTED WALNUTS

Makes 2 cups

2 teaspoons finely chopped garlic
1 teaspoon coarse salt
½ pound walnut meats
1 teaspoon walnut oil

Preheat the oven to 350°F.

On a cutting board, combine the garlic and salt and chop as fine as possible, mashing it with the blade of a knife.

In a bowl, combine the nuts, chopped garlic, and walnut oil and toss them together thoroughly to be sure the seasonings are distributed evenly.

Spread the nuts in a single layer in a 9-by-13-inch roasting pan and bake 15 to 20 minutes. Check the nuts after 10 minutes and toss them to be sure they are browning evenly.

Let the nuts cool, put them in an airtight container, and store, refrigerated, up to 2 weeks.

CANDIED WALNUTS

Add I teaspoon cayenne pepper and I teaspoon salt to these nuts for a savory snack.

Makes 2 cups

2 cups walnut halves
½ cup brown sugar
I egg white
I tablespoon unsalted butter, melted
½ teaspoon cinnamon
½ teaspoon vanilla extract

Preheat the oven to 350°F.

   In a bowl, combine all the ingredients well, mixing with your fingers. Line a baking sheet with parchment, spread the nut mixture on it, and bake 10 minutes. Stir the nuts and bake 5 minutes more. Cool and store the nuts in an airtight container, refrigerated, up to 2 weeks.

HUDSON RIVER VALLEY SOURCES

DAIRY AND CHEESE

The Coach Dairy Goat Farm
R.R. #1, Box 445
Pine Plains, NY 12567
(518) 398-5325
Hand-ladled goat cheeses and yogurts
Visitors welcome

E.F.D. (Egg Farm Dairy)
2 John Walsh Boulevard
Peekskill, NY 10566
(914) 734-7343
Cultured butter, clabbered cream, and wild ripened cheeses
Visitors welcome

Hawthorne Valley
327 Route 21C
Harlemville, NY 12075
(518) 672-7500
Biodynamic farm, Alpine cheeses and yogurts
Visitors welcome

Little Rainbow Chevre
15 Doe Hill
Hillsdale, NY 12529
(518) 325-3351
Goat milk yogurt and Berkshire blue cheese

Old Chatham Farm Sheep Herding Company
155 Shaker Museum Road
Old Chatham, NY 12136
(914) 255-2494
Handmade sheep-milk cheeses
Visitors welcome

Ronnybrook Farm Dairy
Prospect Hill Road
Ancramdale, NY 12503
(800) 772-MILK
All-natural pasteurized milk, no additives

MEAT, GAME, AND FOIE GRAS

D'Artagnan (mail order)
280 Wilson Avenue
Newark, NJ 07105
(800) DARTAGN
Foie gras, game meats, game birds, rabbit, and buffalo

Hudson Valley Foie Gras & Duck Products
R.R. #1, Box 69
Brooks Road
Ferndale, NY 12734
(914) 292-2500

KNK Poultry Farms
R.D. #1, Box 128
Edmeston, NY 13335
(607) 847-8447
Poultry and rabbit

Millbrook Venison Products, Inc. (mail order)
R.R. #2, Box 133
Verbank Road
Millbrook, NY 12545
(914) 677-8457

Quattro's Game Farms (and retail store)
Route 44
Pleasant Valley, NY 12569
(914) 635-8202
Fresh game birds and poultry
Visitors welcome

FISH AND SEAFOOD

Eden Brook Trout Farms
R.D. #2, Box 425
Forestburgh, NY 12777
(914) 796-1749

Homarus Incorporated
76 Kisco Avenue
Mount Kisco, NY 10549
(800) 666-8992
Smoked fish and seafood
Visitors welcome on Saturdays

Fisher's Island Petite Oysters
Box 402
Fisher's Island, NY 06390
(516) 788-7889

PRODUCE, ORCHARDS, AND FARMSTANDS

American Family Farm
(518) 758-7213
Fax (518) 758-1899
Delivers fruits, vegetables, meat, and dairy from farmers direct to New York City in season

Apple Hill Farm
141 Rte. 32S
New Paltz, NY 12561
(914) 238-6190
Apples

Beth's Farm Kitchen
P.O. Box 113
Stuyvesant Falls, NY 12174
(518) 799-3414
Fruits, jams, and preserves

Breezy Hill Orchards
Centre Road
Staatsburg (Clinton Corners),
NY 12580
(914) 266-5967
Forty varieties of apples and
pears, berries and cider

Cabbage Hill Farm
115 Crow Hill Road
Mount Kisco, NY 10549
(914) 241-2658
Organically grown greens,
tilapia fish, cattle, sheep, and
ponies

Davenport's Farm Stand
Route 209
Stone Ridge, NY 12484
(914) 687-0051
Fruits, vegetables, pick your
own

Gill Corn Farms
Route 209
Hurley, NY 12443
(914) 338-0788
Corn

Green Chimneys Farm
Doansburn Lake Road
Brewster, NY 10509
(914) 279-2995
Produce and Education

Greig Farm
Pitcher Lane
Red Hook, NY 12571
(914) 758-1234
Farm market and pick-your-
own fruits, vegetables, and
flowers

Hawthorne Valley Farm
327 Route 21C
Harlemville, NY 12075
(518) 672-7500
Biodynamically grown
produce

Horn of Plenty
Route 28
Kingston, NY 12401
(914) 331-4318
Local farm produce, baked
goods

Hotalings Farm Market
Route 9H
Claverack, NY 12513
(518) 851-9864
Pick-your-own fruits,
vegetables, and pumpkins

**Hans Johansson's Mushrooms
and More (mail order)**
Box 532
Goldens Bridge, NY
10526-0532
(914) 232-2107
Fax (914) 232-2113
Fresh dried mushrooms,
truffles, berries, and exotic
produce

Kaatskill Cider Mill
4953 Route 32
Catskill, NY 12414
(518) 678-5529

Keith's Farm
Box 146
Westtown, NY 10998
(914) 856-4955
Organic vegetables, rocambole
garlic

Kohlmaier Farm
R.D. #5, Route 376, Box 61
Hopewell Junction, NY
12533
(914) 221-2383
Yellow-flesh potatoes,
Christmas trees

Locust Grove Fruit Farm
Box 244
Milton, NY 12547
(914) 795-5194
Forty varieties of apples,
peaches, and pears. All kinds
of fruit in season

Migliorelli Farm
46 Freeborn Lane
Tivoli, NY 12582
(914) 757-3276
Specialists in greens

Outhouse Orchards
Hardscrabble Road
Croton Falls, NY 10519
(914) 277-3188
Pick-your-own vegetables,
cider press

Ryder Farm
Road I, Starr Ridge Road
Brewster, NY 10509
(914) 279-3984
Organically grown vegetables
and berries

S&SO Produce Farms
234 Mount Eve Road
Goshen, NY 10924
(914) 651-4211
Black-dirt vegetables

Sauer Farm
640 Kings Highway
Saugerties, NY 12477
(914) 246-2725
Dairy, poultry, and vegetables

Stuart's Fruit Farm
Route 35
Granite Springs Road
P.O. Box B
Granite Springs, NY 10527
(914) 245-2784
Berries and apples

Terhune Orchards
North Avenue
Salt Point, NY 12578
(914) 266-5382
Apples and cider

Upstate Farms
Box 376
Red Hook, NY 12571
(800) 528-5125 or 5123
Fingerling potatoes

Windy Maples Farm, Inc.
276 Maples Road
Middletown, NY 10940
(914) 342-2648
Produce

COMMUNITY FARMERS' MARKETS

COLUMBIA COUNTY

Hudson Farmers' Market
6th & Columbia Streets
Hudson, NY 12534
(518) 828-9458

DUTCHESS COUNTY

Beacon Farmers' Market
Main Street
Beacon, NY 12508
(914) 897-2067

Main Market Place Farmers' Market
between Market & Garden
Street Main Mall
Poughkeepsie, NY 12601
(914) 486-4640

Millbrook Farmers' Market
Front Street off Franklin
Avenue
Millbrook, NY 12545
(914) 635-2281

GREENE COUNTY

Catskill Farmers' Market
County Parking Lot
CNR Bridge & Water Street
Catskill, NY 12414

ORANGE COUNTY

Goshen Farmers' Market
On the Village Square
South Church Street
Goshen, NY 10924
(914) 294-7741

Middletown Farmers' Market
Eerie Parking Lot
North & Depot Streets
Middletown, NY 10940
(914) 343-8075

Newburgh Farmers' Market
Marine Drive
Water Street & 4th Street
Newburgh Landing, NY
12550
(914) 569-7387

Port Jervis Farmers' Market
Municipal Parking Lot
Port Jervis, NY 12771
(914) 856-6694

ULSTER COUNTY

Boiceville Farmers' Market
Route 28
Boiceville, NY 12412
(914) 657-3328

WESTCHESTER COUNTY

Green Seasons Farmers' Market
Location TBA Downtown
New Rochelle, NY 10801
(914) 654-2186

Ossining Farmers' Market
Spring & Main Streets
Ossining, NY 10562
(914) 923-4837

Peekskill Farmers' Market
Bank Street
Peekskill, NY 10566
(914) 737-3600

Yonkers Farmers' Market
Getty Square
St. Johns Courtyard
Yonkers, NY 10701
(914) 963-3033

Cornell Cooperative Extension
Box 259
Millbrook, NY 12545
(914) 677-3488

Greenmarkets of New York City
For more information call
(212) 477-3220

Hudson River Foundation
40 W. 20th Street, 9th Floor
New York, NY 10011
(212) 924-8290
Festival and environmental information

WINES OF THE HUDSON RIVER VALLEY

Outstanding food is only part of the region's bounty. With its nineteen vineyards, the Hudson Valley is today a world-class wine region, producing wines that can compete with those of other world-class regions. Whereas in Europe and California wine making has always been considered part of food production and agriculture, serious wine production in New York State has seen its biggest growth during the last twenty years. It became increasingly clear that high quality wine to accompany fine food could never be made with the native Concord grapes. Because the state's climate is too harsh to allow known wine grapes to survive, New York State wine makers were inspired to develop hardy hybrids that would allow them to produce competitive wines. Today, through advances in growing techniques, producers such as Millbrook and Clinton Vineyards are growing *vitis vinifero*, the classic European wine grapes such as chardonnay, cabernet sauvignon, and cabernet franc, with great success.

WINERIES OF THE HUDSON RIVER VALLEY

WEST BANK

Adair Vineyards
52 Allhusen Road
New Paltz, NY 12561
(914) 255-1377

Baldwin Vineyards
Hardenburgh Estate
Pine Bush, NY 12566
(914) 744-2226

Benmarl Vineyards
Highland Avenue, Box 549
Marlborough, NY 12542
(914) 236-4265

Brimstone Hill Vineyard
61 Brimstone Hill Road
Pine Bush, NY 12566
(914) 744-2231

Brotherhood Winery
100 Brotherhood Plaza Drive
Washingtonville, NY 10992
(914) 496-3661

El Paso Winery
742 Broadway (Route 9W)
Ulster Park, NY 12487
(914) 331-8642

Johnston's Winery
5140 Bliss Road
Ballston Spa, NY 12020
(518) 882-6310

Larry's Vineyard
3001 Furbeck Road
Altamount, NY 12009
(518) 355-7365

Regent Champagne Cellars
200 Blue Point Road
Highland, NY 12528
(914) 691-7296

Rivendell Winery
714 Albany Post Road
New Paltz, NY 12561
(914) 794-9774

Royal Kedem Winery
1519 Route 9W
Marlborough, NY 12542
(914) 236-4281

West Park Wine Cellars
Rte. 9 W & Burroughs Drive
Box 280
West Park, NY 12493
(914) 384-6709

EAST BANK

Cascade Mountain Vineyards
Flint Hill Road
Amenia, NY 12501
(914) 373-9021

Clinton Vineyards
Schultzville Road
Clinton Corners, NY 12514
(914) 266-5372

The Meadery at Greenwich
8 Meader Road
Greenwich, NY 12834
(518) 692-9669

Millbrook Vineyards
R.R. #1, Box 167D
Millbrook, NY 12545
(800) 662-WINE

North Salem Vineyard
441 Hardscrabble Road
North Salem, NY 10560
(914) 669-5518

INDEX

Halibut Boiled in Milk and Bread
Sauce, 87
Ham, roast fresh, with red
cabbage and apples, 175–77
Harris, Doris, 274
Hazelnuts and aged goat cheese,
arugula and celery root salad
with, 56
Herb(s)
and cheese mashed potatoes, 188
mustard vinaigrette, 286
and radishes, potato salad with,
193–94
white wine and butter sauce
with, 70
Herb Oil, 290
Herb Sachet, 292
Herb Salad with Lemon
Vinaigrette, 55
Herb vinaigrette, chicken paillards
with, 129–30
Historical recipe, working with,
86
Historical recipes, revised
cedar-planked shad, 64
charlottes
apple, 246
onion, 20
halibut boiled in milk and
bread sauce, 87
onion-walnut muffins, 17
suppawn, 208
syllabub, 246–47
Home-Cured Venison Prosciutto,
121–23
Home-Style Roast Chicken with
Garlic and Fingerling
Potatoes, 133–34
Honey, buckwheat, carrots and
baby turnips caramelized in,
232
Horseradish
mashed potatoes, 188
and potatoes, boiled beef shank
salad with, 169–70

and red onion, potato salad
with, 195
Howard, Martin, 242, 276
Huckleberries, wild, roast saddle
of venison with, 115–17
Huckleberry custard pie, wild,
254–55
Hudson, Henry, xviii, 60
Hudson River
oysters, 18
shad, 66
trout, 73
Hudson River Club, 16
Hudson River School, painters
of, xviii, 86
Hudson River Valley,
characteristics and products
of, xvii–xx, 2, 16, 53, 94,
126, 140, 164, 186, 201,
207, 242–43
Hudson Valley Country Pâté,
22–24
Hudson Valley Marketing
Association, 243

Ice cream, sour cherry, 281
Ice wine jelly, foie gras terrine
with, 5–6
Indian Pudding with Butterscotch
Sauce, 270–71
Individual Deep-Dish Summer
Fruit Pies, 256–57

Jam, garlic and onion, 295
Jelly
ice wine, foie gras terrine with,
5–6
red wine, and watercress relish,
grilled venison rib chops with,
113–14

Kitchen staples, 283–300
Kumin, Albert, 242

Lamb, rack of, with white beans
and sweet roasted garlic puree,
180–81

Leeks
oyster stew with, 52
roasted oysters with, on the half
shell, 18–19
Lemon, prunes, and orange,
brandied, braised duck with,
138–39
Lemon vinaigrette, herb salad
with, 55
Little potatoes, 185–86
with caviar, 185
Little Rainbow Berkshire Blue
Cheese, in endive, apple, and
roasted walnut salad, 57
Little Rainbow ricotta, salsify
gratin with, 229–30
Lobster Gratin with Suppawn,
81–83
Lovage and parsley sauce, pan-
fried trout with, 73–74
Luman Reed Gallery, 86

Mallard Duck Breasts with Wild
Rice Custard, 96–98
Malouf, Jeannette, 145
Maple and walnut glaze, roast
chicken with, 131–32
Martin's Incredible Flourless
Chocolate Cake with English
Custard Sauce, 276–78
Mashed Potatoes with Variations,
187–88
Meats, 163–81. See also Beef
braised veal shanks with citrus
and sage, 173–74
curing of, 121
rack of lamb with white beans
and sweet roasted garlic puree,
180–81
roast fresh ham with red
cabbage and apples, 175–77
sliced buffalo steak with grilled
onions and garlic, 171–72
spiced loin of pork with baked
acorn squash, 178–79

Ryan, Elizabeth, 243

Sabayon, Tear of the Clouds,
    poached pears with, 266–67
Sacks, warm apple, with clabbered
    cream, 250–51
Sage
    and morels, sautéed sturgeon
        with, 79–80
    and mustard sauce, rabbit
        saddles with, 109–10
    braised veal shanks with citrus
        and, 173–74
Salad(s)
    arugula and celery root, with
        hazelnuts and aged goat
        cheese, 56
    boiled beef shank, with
        potatoes and horseradish,
        169–70
    green, basic, 54
    green, ingredients and
        preparation of, 53
    herb, with lemon vinaigrette, 55
    potato, 193–97
Salsa, summer, fresh corn custard
    with, 202–203
Salsify Gratin with Little
    Rainbow Ricotta, 229–30
Salt-Cured Foie Gras, 10
Sauce(s)
    butterscotch, Indian pudding,
        270–71
    chocolate, 281
    English custard, 278
    milk and bread, halibut boiled
        in, 87
    mustard and sage, rabbit saddles
        with, 109–10
    white wine and butter, 69
Sausage, Apple, and Pine Nut
    Stuffing, 156–57
Sautéed Foie Gras with
    Caramelized Pearl Onions and
    Fresh Currants, 13

Sautéed Foie Gras with Cider and
    Apples, 12
Sautéed Shad Roe with Bacon
    and Capers, 71–72
Sautéed Spinach with Garlic, 226
Sautéed Sturgeon with Morels
    and Spring Sage, 79–80
Sautéed Watercress, 226
Scallion and ginger custard,
    butternut squash consommé
    with, 45–47
Scalloped Yukon Gold Potatoes,
    192
Seafood mousse, poached trout
    filled with, 77–78
Shad
    boneless, layered with its roe,
        66
    cedar-planked, with chervil
        vinaigrette, 64–65
    characteristics of, 60
    fillets, baked, with sorrel sauce,
        63
    whole, baked in milk with
        potatoes and bacon, 62
    whole, baked in Millbrook
        Chardonnay, 61
Shad roe
    boneless shad layered with, 66–
        67
    poached, with caviar sauce, 68
    preparation of, 66
    sautéed, with bacon and capers,
        71–72
Shallots
    and bacon, warm potato salad
        with, 196
    and black pepper and garlic,
        braised beef with, 165–66
    broccoli rabe with, 224
    crisp fried, 239
    preserved, warm new potato
        salad with, 197
    preserved, with foie gras terrine,
        7

Shallots Preserved in Red Wine,
    292
Sherry syllabub, apple charlottes
    with, 246–47
Shortcake, berry, with white
    chocolate mousse, 252–53
Slaw, spicy fennel and cabbage,
    219
Sliced Buffalo Steak with Grilled
    Onions and Garlic, 171–72
Sorrel
    mashed potatoes, 188
    and potato soup, 37–38
Sorrel sauce, baked shad fillets
    with, 63
Soufflés, miniature pumpkin,
    268–69
Soup(s). See also Stock
    butternut squash, with ginger
        and scallion custard, 45
    chilled apple and potato, 42
    corn and codfish chowder, with
        tomato oil, 40–41
    oyster stew with leeks, 52
    potato and sorrel, with red
        pepper cream, 37–38
    pumpkin apple, with cinnamon
        croutons, 43–44
    roasted onion and garlic, with
        goat cheese croutons, 50–51
    three celery, 39
    wild mushroom broth, 48–49
Sour cherry
    ice cream, 281
    and wild rice salad, 158–61
Source list, 301–305
Spiced Loin of Pork with Baked
    Acorn Squash, 178–79
Spiced Pears, with roast goose,
    158–61
Spicy Fennel and Cabbage Slaw,
    219
Spinach, sautéed, with garlic,
    226
Spring menus, 66, 210